IDEOLOGIES AND INFRASTRUCTURES OF RELIGIOUS URBANIZATION IN AFRICA

Bloomsbury Studies in Religion, Space and Place

Series editors: Paul-François Tremlett, John Eade and Katy Soar

Religions, spiritualities and mysticisms are deeply implicated in processes of place-making. These include political and geopolitical spaces, local and national spaces, urban spaces, global and virtual spaces, contested spaces, spaces of performance, spaces of memory and spaces of confinement. At the leading edge of theoretical, methodological, and interdisciplinary innovation in the study of religion, Bloomsbury Studies in Religion, Space and Place brings together and gives shape to the study of such processes.

These places are not defined simply by the material or the physical but also by the sensual and the psychological, by the ways in which spaces are gendered, classified, stratified, moved through, seen, touched, heard, interpreted and occupied. Places are constituted through embodied practices that direct critical and analytical attention to the spatial production of insides, outsides, bodies, landscapes, cities, sovereignties, publics and interiorities.

Christianity in Brazil
Sílvia Fernandes

Global Trajectories of Brazilian Religion
Edited by Martijn Oosterbaan, Linda van de Kamp and Joana Bahia

Religion and the Global City
Edited by David Garbin and Anna Strhan

Religious Pluralism and the City
Edited by Helmuth Berking, Silke Steets and Jochen Schwenk

Singapore, Spirituality, and the Space of the State
Joanne Punzo Waghorne

Towards a New Theory of Religion and Social Change
Paul-François Tremlett

Urban Religious Events
Edited by Paul Bramadat, Mar Griera, Julia Martinez-Ariño and Marian Burchardt

IDEOLOGIES AND INFRASTRUCTURES OF RELIGIOUS URBANIZATION IN AFRICA

Remaking the City

David Garbin, Simon Coleman and Gareth Millington

BLOOMSBURY ACADEMIC
LONDON • NEW YORK • OXFORD • NEW DELHI • SYDNEY

BLOOMSBURY ACADEMIC
Bloomsbury Publishing Plc
50 Bedford Square, London, WC1B 3DP, UK
1385 Broadway, New York, NY 10018, USA
29 Earlsfort Terrace, Dublin 2, Ireland

BLOOMSBURY, BLOOMSBURY ACADEMIC and the Diana logo are trademarks of
Bloomsbury Publishing Plc

First published in Great Britain 2023
Paperback edition published 2024

Copyright © David Garbin, Simon Coleman and Gareth Millington, 2023

Marilyn Dunn has asserted her right under the Copyright, Designs and Patents Act, 1988,
to be identified as Author of this work.

For legal purposes the Acknowledgements on p. x constitute an extension
of this copyright page.

Cover image © Thomas M. Scheer / EyeEm / gettyimages.co.uk

All rights reserved. No part of this publication may be reproduced or transmitted
in any form or by any means, electronic or mechanical, including photocopying,
recording, or any information storage or retrieval system, without prior
permission in writing from the publishers.

Bloomsbury Publishing Plc does not have any control over, or responsibility for, any
third-party websites referred to or in this book. All internet addresses given in this
book were correct at the time of going to press. The author and publisher regret any
inconvenience caused if addresses have changed or sites have ceased to exist, but can
accept no responsibility for any such changes.

A catalogue record for this book is available from the British Library.

Library of Congress Control Number: 2022940081

ISBN: HB: 978-1-3501-5212-0
PB: 978-1-3503-4869-1
ePDF: 978-1-3501-5213-7
eBook: 978-1-3501-5260-1

Series: Bloomsbury Studies in Religion, Space and Place

Typeset by Newgen KnowledgeWorks Pvt. Ltd., Chennai, India

To find out more about our authors and books visit www.bloomsbury.com
and sign up for our newsletters

CONTENTS

List of figures — vii
List of tables — viii
List of contributors — ix
Acknowledgements — x

Chapter 1
INTRODUCTION: (RE)MAKING THE URBAN, (RE)MAPPING THE CITY
   David Garbin, Simon Coleman and Gareth Millington — 1

Part I
RELIGIOUS INFRASTRUCTURES OF 'DEVELOPMENT': VISIONS, DISCOURSES AND SCALES

Chapter 2
THICKENING AGENTS: MUSLIM COMMONS AND POPULAR URBANIZATION IN DAR ES SALAAM
   Benjamin Kirby — 19

Chapter 3
TERRITORIALIZED VISIONS OF DEVELOPMENT AND URBAN CHRISTIANITIES IN THE CONGO
   David Garbin and Aurélien Mokoko-Gampiot — 35

Chapter 4
THE ASPIRATION TO TRANSFORM: PENTECOSTALISM AND URBAN CITIZENSHIP IN CAPE TOWN
   Marian Burchardt — 55

Part II
TERRITORIALIZATION, URBAN CHANGE AND RELIGIOUS TIME-SPACES

Chapter 5
MOURIDE IMAGINARIES OF THE SACRED AND THE TIME-SPACES OF RELIGIOUS URBANIZATION IN TOUBA, SENEGAL
   Kate Kingsbury — 75

Chapter 6
BUILDING CHURCHES FOR THE CITY-TO-COME: PENTECOSTAL URBANIZATION AND ASPIRATIONAL PLACE-MAKING IN THE 'RURBAN' AREAS OF SOUTHWESTERN BENIN
    Carla Bertin   91

Chapter 7
THE TERRITORIAL TEMPORALITIES OF URBAN RELIGION: PENTECOSTALISM, NEIGHBOURHOOD CHANGE AND PLANNING CONTROL IN LAGOS, NIGERIA
    Taibat Lawanson and Gareth Millington   107

Part III
MORAL SUBJECTS, REMORALIZED SPACES AND THE POLITICS OF KNOWLEDGE

Chapter 8
THE DARK SIDE OF THE CITY: URBANIZATION, MODERNITY AND MORAL MAPPING IN ZAMBIA
    Johanneke Kroesbergen-Kamps   129

Chapter 9
RELIGIOUSLY MOTIVATED SCHOOLS AND UNIVERSITIES AS 'MORAL ENCLAVES': REFORMING URBAN YOUTHS IN TANZANIA AND NIGERIA
    Hansjörg Dilger and Marloes Janson   143

Chapter 10
MANAGING THE 'SENSIBLE SECULAR': DISCIPLINING THE URBAN IN A NIGERIAN CHRISTIAN UNIVERSITY
    Simon Coleman and Xavier Moyet   163

Chapter 11
NOTES ON AFRICAN RELIGIOUS EVERYDAY LIFE IN AN URBAN (POST-)PANDEMIC WORLD
    David Garbin, Simon Coleman and Gareth Millington   183

Chapter 12
AFTERWORD
    Caroline Knowles   187

Notes   191
References   201
Index   227

FIGURES

5.1	Diagram of circular reinforcement of resources for Mouride leaders	80
6.1	The villa and the church	99
6.2	The church of Pastor Claude	101
6.3	Collective prayer	102
6.4	Collective building	103
7.1	Satellite image of Onike neighbourhood	115
9.1	St Mary's International Primary School's courtyard with school-owned buses	149
9.2	Plaques on the AMA buildings	151
9.3	Redeemer's university's goals	155
9.4	FU's dried-up fountain	157

TABLES

7.1	Periods of Land and Property Acquisition by MFM in Onike Area	116
7.2	Showing Transition of Land Uses to MFM Owned/Leased Property in Onike	117
7.3	Mountain of Fire Planning Permit Applications at Yaba District Office of LASSPA (2010–18)	119

CONTRIBUTORS

Carla Bertin is a PhD candidate in Anthropology at Ecole des Hautes Etudes en Sciences Sociales (EHESS), Paris.

Marian Burchardt is Professor of Sociology at Leipzig University.

Simon Coleman is Chancellor Jackman Professor at the University of Toronto.

Hansjörg Dilger is Professor of Social and Cultural Anthropology at the Freie Universität Berlin.

David Garbin is Senior Lecturer in Sociology at the University of Kent.

Marloes Janson is Professor of West African Anthropology at the School of Oriental and African Studies (SOAS), University of London.

Kate Kingsbury is Adjunct Professor of Anthropology at the University of Alberta.

Benjamin Kirby is Junior Professor for the Study of Religion at the University of Bayreuth.

Caroline Knowles is Professor of Sociology at Goldsmiths, University of London.

Johanneke Kroesbergen-Kamps is Research Associate at the University of Pretoria.

Taibat Lawanson is Professor of Urban Management and Governance at the University of Lagos.

Gareth Millington is Reader in Sociology at the University of York.

Aurélien Mokoko-Gampiot is Senior Research Associate in Sociology at the University of York.

Xavier Moyet is Research Associate at the University of Kent and Visiting Fellow, Centre for Religion and Public Life at the University of Leeds.

ACKNOWLEDGEMENTS

Several of the chapters in this collection draw on papers presented at an international research symposium on the 'Moral economies of development in urban Africa' held in Canterbury, UK in June 2018 and hosted by the School of Social Policy, Sociology and Social Research (SSPSSR), University of Kent. The symposium received funds from the RUA project (Religious urbanization and infrastructural lives in African megacities https://rua-project.ac.uk/), one of the seventeen projects which are part of the Global Challenges Research Fund (GCRF)/British Academy *Cities and Infrastructures* Programme (led by Caroline Knowles). Alongside the authors in this volume, we would also like to thank John Eade and Paul-François Tremlett as well as Lily McMahon at Bloomsbury Academic for their help, enthusiasm and encouragement with producing this volume, and the anonymous reviewers for their helpful suggestions on the volume as a whole.

Chapter 1

INTRODUCTION: (RE)MAKING THE URBAN, (RE)MAPPING THE CITY

David Garbin, Simon Coleman and Gareth Millington

Bridging the megacity: An introductory vignette

In April 2018 the Commissioner for Energy of the Lagos State (Nigeria) inaugurated a flyover bridge in Gbagada, a densely populated downtown neighbourhood of Lagos. The Commissioner hailed the bridge as an 'epochal' project that would play a key role in the 'overall drive of the state government … towards the renewal of infrastructure projects all over Lagos in line with the megacity ambition of the state.'[1] Constructed with a view to reducing traffic congestion choking the decaying roads of an evergrowing metropolis, the bridge provided an excellent example of an 'aspirational' infrastructure embodying a key teleological promise of urban modernity: faith in the capacity of well-defined projects to produce measurable progress (Gupta 2018: 62). Channelling flows and creating affordances by enabling crossings and connections, bridges exercise significant metaphorical power as symbols of cooperation. Mirjam de Bruijn and Rijk van Dijk (2012a: 45) point out that 'a bridge connects but, it does much more, [i]t links different places and different people, and creates new opportunities for the building of relationships economically, socially, politically and culturally'; it exemplifies 'the social life of linkage' (ibid.) – contributing to a form of animation that de Bruijn and van Dijk see as central in many contemporary African cities, where the global is rapidly becoming ordinary (de Bruijn and van Dijk 2012b: 4).

Our focus must widen further, however, if we wish to fully comprehend the socio-spatial and political landscape within which the Gbagada flyover bridge was being embedded. This piece of civic infrastructure was entirely financed by the Pentecostal church Deeper Christian Life Ministry (commonly known as Deeper Life) as part of a larger development comprising a 600-place multilevel car park, road improvement and traffic lights, all adjacent to an imposing auditorium inaugurated a few months prior. The latter replaced a smaller structure that had proved unable to accommodate growing crowds of faithful supporters. With its 30,000-seat capacity (augmented by 7,500 seats for children in the basement), the monumental architecture of the new Deeper Life Gbagada auditorium signals the 'sensational appeal' (Meyer 2010) of Pentecostal Christianities that have for some decades been 'saturating' the urban landscape of the Nigerian megacity (Ukah 2016a).

On the day the bridge was inaugurated, the partnership between Lagos State and Deeper Life was commended as an example of a positive response to state 'infrastructural needs' by both the State Commissioner and the 'General Superintendent' of the Deeper Life Church, Pastor-Founder William F. Kumuyi. Pastor Kumuyi has led the global expansion of a church that started as a fifteen-member Bible study group on the campus of the University of Lagos in 1973 and is now said to include '500 churches in Lagos, 5,000 in the rest of Nigeria ... and 3,000 elsewhere' (church's website[2]). The pastor's assertion that such an infrastructural project 'should not be left to the government alone'[3] illustrates a wider Pentecostal drive for urban presence and intervention at multiple scales, which links the transformation of individual 'born-again' subjects to the planning, control and governance of entire environments carved out from what believers readily interpret as dysfunctional and immoral cityscapes (Burchardt 2017). In press reports, the new infrastructure of the bridge is said to have been donated for public use as part of 'the corporate social responsibility of the church to the community.'[4] Such claims are disputed in online commentaries that suggest that an apparently public-spirited donation to the city was actually a condition of being allowed to expand, imposed by the Governor of Lagos State himself.[5] In any case, it is clear that the bridge now plays both a symbolic and a logistical role in mitigating traffic congestion created by mass attendance at the church. In proposing to resolve the very problem it helped to create, the church has found a way to project itself materially and aesthetically into the daily life of the city.

Our story of the construction project goes further still, however. The building of the cathedral-like auditorium lasted thirteen years and involved the purchase of dozens of residential properties, impacting community life (and land/property prices), albeit with little official opposition or resistance. Instead, through the transformation of the neighbourhood into 'a Jerusalem of some sort' (as coined by the Guardian.ng),[6] the church is portrayed by both its leaders and state officials as a leading force of renewal, regeneration and development. The vision and aspiration behind such transformation are realized through the gradual remodelling and production of ambiguously 'public' spaces and collective infrastructures by religious actors.

Yet, while the portrayal of the bridge as a piece of significant urban infrastructure casts Pentecostal action into the civic sphere, other developments have resulted in the making of quasi-autonomous, urban enclaves. This volume contains extensive descriptions of the prayer camps constructed by religious groups in and around urban African contexts, including the one developed by the Deeper Life Church itself along the Lagos–Ibadan Expressway. The 'iconic' infrastructural feature of such enclaves is a wall rather than a bridge, visibly separating church life from external influences (though, as we shall see, still intended to have effects beyond its physical boundaries). Whatever shape they take, such material presences in and around cities like Lagos do not represent stubborn remnants of religious spatiality that have somehow resisted the 'advances' of commercial or state expansion. Rather, they work precisely within and through – adopting but also differentiating themselves from – 'secular', neoliberal processes of urbanization and place-making.

Religious agency in African cityscapes

We began with an example of a single bridge in one African city, but throughout this volume we explore a considerable range of practices and models of spatialization that are reliant on religious urban imaginaries – imaginaries that often (re)map African cityscapes as ambivalent sites of opportunity and progress but also of moral danger, uncertainty, temptation and vigilance. Africa is currently urbanizing faster than any other continent (Förster and Amman 2018: 3). In contemporary megacities such as Lagos, Cairo, Dar es Salaam or Kinshasa, religious groups are concerned by the immoralities of certain forms of urban living but they are not typically threatened by the urban per se; rather, they are playing influential roles in cities – not only by providing basic utilities, housing, health and educational facilities, but also through promoting their own ethical and moral motivations for urban activism. Many religious organizations share the Deeper Life Church's capacity to provide infrastructural resources for residents – both affiliated and non-affiliated – as they negotiate the unpredictability, informality and socio-economic uncertainties of African cities, against the common backdrop of a delegitimized and retreating state (Ferguson 2006; Olivier de Sardan 2014). In certain respects, as Burchardt (2015: 51) notes, these infrastructural interventions – exemplified by health and educational facilities run by Pentecostals – should be understood as self-consciously modern yet postcolonial incarnations of earlier forms of Christian missionary cultures, when 'conversion to Christianity and conversion to modernity were essentially collapsed together' (see also Comaroff and Comaroff 1997; van der Veer 1996). Throughout this volume we argue that, in African contexts, cities have become powerful venues for the creation and implementation of contemporary models of development that are playing an active part in remaking what it means to be urban. Alongside bridges and enclaves we will encounter numerous contexts inscribed by religious agency at multiple material and ideological scales: a dense market district (Kirby), a hospital (Garbin and Mokoko-Gampiot), FBOs (Faith-based development organizations – Burchardt), a cluster of villages that combine the rural and urban into the 'rurban' (Bertin), a quasi-gated neighbourhood (Lawanson and Millington), educational establishments (Dilger and Janson, Coleman and Moyet, Garbin and Mokoko-Gampiot) as well as whole cities demarcated as 'sacred' (Garbin and Mokoko-Gampiot, Kingsbury). Another chapter (Kroesbergen-Kamps) does not take as its object a single type of space but traces the ways narratives provide moral maps equipping believers to navigate their way through the perceived risks and dangers of urban life.

In examining the workings of these different cityscapes – projected, constructed, narrated – we highlight the need to explore how faith-based practices of urban development articulate moral subjectivities with individual and wider aspirations for modernization, change, deliverance and prosperity. Our argument is not that Africa provides uniquely different cases to secular models in operation elsewhere in the world; rather, our chapters demonstrate the importance of expanding our default understandings of the ethical, ideological and infrastructural impulses behind contemporary forms of the urban. Even given its specific characteristics, Africa can be an example quite as much as an exception.

Furthermore, while they have come to dominate the sensorial landscape and urban cultures of many African cities (De Boeck 2013; De Witte 2010; Pype 2012; Ukah 2016), Pentecostal churches like Deeper Life are not the only religious actors driving multi-scalar forms of urbanization. Among our case studies we provide various examples of Muslim shaping of city spaces – occasionally in mimetic competition with Pentecostals but more often organized around such institutions as markets, mosques and shrines. Although Catholicism does not play an especially prominent role in our contributions, the complexities of its position are brought out in Garbin and Mokoko-Gampiot's chapter on the Congo. They note that, at the most obvious level, the Kinois (Kinshasan) public sphere is indeed being Pentecostalized – the discipline and vaunting ambition of the born-agains combining with their opposition to a Catholicism that they associate with both moral laxity and past European occupation. In response, the older church retains a degree of prestige while displaying an impressive capacity for adaptation. In the post-colonial period, the Congolese Catholic Church faces the challenge of disentangling itself from associations with Belgian oppression while also being seen to promote post-Independence forms of Africanization. It finds 'secular' developmental action in the urban sphere an important means through which to achieve this balance.

In practice, our volume also shows that we should not view urban religious activities purely through the lenses of discrete world religions or specific denominations. Taking urban zones (neighbourhoods, districts, etc.) as units of observation encourages examination of interactions between ostensibly distinct religious groups. We are forced to ask when and where religious affiliation becomes salient, and when it is downplayed in favour of such factors as commerce and friendship (Dulin 2020). We must also examine what kinds of 'giving ground' are possible in the management of the politics of propinquity and distance across different parts of the city (Copjec and Sorkin 1999). Thus the 'super-dense' market district of Kariakoo, described by Benjamin Kirby in his piece on the Muslim commons in Dar es Salaam, becomes a 'thickened public' (De Boeck 2012) of urban experimentation that both permits and restricts overtly Christian presences within its bounds. In the process, it creates forms of urban living resistant to local planning regimes but increasingly linked to circuits of capital and knowledge in other parts of the world.

In line with the glocal character of Kariakoo, we argue that it would be reductive to locate urbanization only within the boundaries of a clearly defined 'city' (Brenner 2019: 27). Just as we explore varieties of civic infrastructure that range from bridges to enclaves, so we draw upon recent urban studies scholarship that follows Henri Lefebvre (2003) in stressing the need to consider the planetary reach of polymorphic, differentiated and multi-scalar processes of urbanization. Accordingly, 'planetary urbanization' as uneven spatial development can no longer adequately be captured by typological binaries such as centre/periphery, North/South or rural/urban. However, as will become evident, we suggest that 'the city' as a spatial and moral form still enjoys considerable resonance. Cities' ambivalent imaginaries and counter-imaginaries have not lost relevance in the context of what Lefebvre describes as the 'implosion-explosion'[7] (1996: 70–1) of twentieth- and twenty-first-century urbanization, a set of processes that have diminished historic city centres whilst simultaneously expanding the urban fabric to the extent where it is no longer a clearly identifiable non-urban elsewhere against which the city can be identified. Lefebvre himself pointed out that the city has survived beyond the generalized urbanization of society (*le tissu urbain*), with its 'image' creating affordances and its representations having 'real effects' (Millington 2016: 4, see also Wachsmuth 2014). Moreover, city images are oriented not only towards the past, but they can also project towards the future by striving to 'attain something not yet present' (Lefebvre, 2014: 582). In the section that follows we take this discussion further by examining the emergence of 'urban religion' as focus of both religious and urban scholars and the extent to which the interplay of religious and spatial processes can be understood through the prism of 'religious urbanization'.

Urban religion and religious urbanization

The cover of Steve Bruce's book *God is Dead, Secularization in the West* (2002) displays a church in the town of Armley (near Leeds, UK) that has been repurposed as a carpet shop. Similar stories can be told about hundreds of mainline churches across urban Europe that have lost their original purpose and been turned into commercial, leisure or residential spaces (see e.g. Mian 2008 or Velthuis and Spennemann 2007). These transformations may appear to represent ineluctable 'forces of secularity expressing themselves on the urban landscapes' (Hackworth and Gullikson 2013: 73) but they embody just one potential trajectory for the religio-spatial changes being articulated in contemporary cities. The 'reverse' conversion of secular buildings in Euro-American contexts – warehouses, offices, garages or cinemas – into places of worship is often driven by migrant groups (in particular Pentecostals or Muslims) (e.g. Garbin 2013; Krause 2008; Kuppinger 2014). Diasporic urban formations also link everyday habits, patterns of worship and ties of kinship across continents, as in the hybrid creation of 'London-Lagos' encompassed by Coleman and Maier's (2013) discussion of the transcontinental activities of members of the Nigerian Redeemed Christian Church of God (RCCG). The city in almost any part of the world can become a site where forces of secularization and desecularization converge in intense but uneven ways (see Eade 2012; Stevenson et al. 2010), a privileged terrain for those documenting the complex, 'infrasecular' reality of urban religion (della Dora 2016).

Stephan Lanz (2013: 21) is one of many scholars to document how modern urbanity has often been presented as the secular end product of the city's long spiritual decline. However, this general assumption was less the result of empirical analyses and more the product of two formative 'theoretical maneuvers' (Robinson 2006) in this field. The first has established, since the urban theories of Georg Simmel or Louis Wirth, a selective association between the city and modernity; the second, dubbed 'developmentalism' by Jennifer Robinson (2006: 4), conceptualizes cities outside the North as underdeveloped and deficient. Classic secularization theory more generally also focused on Euro-American contexts in positing modern industrial cities as spaces of pluralism and relativism, environments assumed to be conducive to rationalizing and *blasé* dispositions that would undermine both religious social control and the plausibility structure of any one religious tradition (McLeod 1996). However, recent attention to 'urban religion' is part of a wider move away from a tendency to construct secularization as a universal interpretive category of modernity, and towards a view that 'provincializes' European experiences of the secular (which, in any case, have been shown to be far from monolithic, see e.g. Kong 2010). The current interest in the ways religious and secular forces interact in city contexts also resonates with increased focus on the idea of 'lived' religion, which considers 'religious practice and imagination in ongoing, dynamic relation with the realities and structures of everyday life in particular time and places' as Robert Orsi writes in the 2002 introduction to his acclaimed study of faith and community life in Italian Harlem, *The Madonna of 115th Street* (first published in 1985). Significantly, the Virgin Mary as symbol may have lost some of her hold on the European migrants described by Orsi, but she has certainly found fresh devotees and new material forms among more recent Catholic settlers in American cities (e.g. Peña 2011).

Our interest in links between the religious and the urban goes beyond debates concerning the limitations of the secular and its analytical framings. There is a growing literature on urban religion and religious place-making that focuses on how religion 'makes place' and 'takes place' (Knott 2005: 43) through the active engagement of religious actors with city spaces in the form of moral 'mapping', ritualistic practices, public performance and so on.[8] Most scholarship on urban religion entails a dialogical ambition, which is to interpret the way in which cities' socio-spatial landscapes affect, transform, hinder or facilitate religious ethoses and practices, revealing how, in turn, religious actors refashion, adapt or reproduce particular modes or 'cultures' of urbanity. Subsequent studies have initiated questions around religious/ethnic plurality, the politics of visibility and invisibility (or aurality), conflict over places and the implication of what Engelke (2013) calls an urban 'ambient faith' rendering the boundary between secular and sacred in cities porous. While the 'spatial turn' in religious studies (Knott 2008) has shaped the study of urban religion with a strong emphasis on the material fabric, iconicity and 'texture' of religion, we argue that taking the production of religious urban space and religious urban imaginaries seriously also involves placing a particular emphasis on religious urbanization as a *process*. This point is particularly relevant in Africa, where social change, mobility, infrastructural disparities and growing inequalities, and informalization both shape and are shaped by new urbanizing realities.

In addressing these issues, we adopt a non-reductive view of religious urbanization. We understand it as (1) a process that is not reducible to the bounded socio-spatial lifeworld of 'the city', (2) involving multi-scalar changes in the fabric, materiality and infrastructure of everyday life and (3) reflecting the importance of a discursive reality (produced by or influencing a range of religious actors and leaders) related to the diffusion of urban cultures and identities, whether analysed as hybrid, complex forms or emically constructed as fixed categories connected to a range of dichotomies (e.g. 'village' vs 'city'). These categories may be socially significant in constructing a range of boundaries pertinent to religious imaginaries and aspirations, and thus central in the production of 'visions' for the city. They may inform a key dimension of many of our contributions, and one that is central to the making and remaking of the city: processes of planning – whether formal or informal, practical or impractical, realized or abandoned.

That said, we should not conflate categories with behaviour on the ground. In this volume, Carla Bertin traces the ways in which both urbanization and Pentecostalization can be traced far away from megacities, in rural Benin, and other work has pointed to the intellectual or ideological sleight of hand involved in asserting the city's isolation from other spaces. Thus Dilger et al. (2020b: 12) argue that networks of sites make cities always include places 'beyond', including both the 'rural' and the 'global', and that cities themselves are 'infrastructures of circulation that facilitate the movement of people, ideas and things between sites'[9]. Still wider forces prompting the transformation of material elements and structures ('the urban fabric') are reflected in processes of capitalist 'spatial fix' (Harvey 2001a) or splintering urbanism (Graham and Marvin 2001) occurring at a global scale, with both of these forces contributing to new ways in which to create inequalities among urban publics. Harvey's work in particular highlights capitalism's need to engage in geographical expansion and restructuring: in other words, its 'fix' implies not the creation of a steady state, but rather the chronic, restless search for short-term remedies to ongoing crises of economic, social and spatial reproduction.

To date, however, there has been limited scholarly interest in the connections between varieties of global urban restructuring and religious experiences of both space and spatial change. Baker (2015) in his preface to a recent volume on religious urbanism in South Asia, while addressing the secular blindspot of urban policy and critical urban theory, talks about 'the saturation of religion as a lived identity marker and embedded cultural and political reality *within* the very nation-states in which planetary urbanization is taking place' (Baker 2015: xvii, emphasis added). However, considering planetary urbanization as a *container* of religious realities brings the risk of minimizing religious actors' capacity to operate as (planetary) 'urbanizers', given how religious and urban dynamics reciprocally produce one another as 'urban-religious configurations' (Lanz 2013). In (mega)city environments, such actors are often key drivers of forms of socio-spatial change and urbanizing practices that could easily fit within the conceptual purview of planetary urbanization and splintering urbanism – including gated enclaving, property-led investments, polycentred suburbanization and so on (see for instance Becker, Klingan and Lanz, 2013).

We also need to acknowledge, however, the limitations in emphasizing the linkages between variegated and multidimensional forms of religious urbanization and processes of urban restructuring, understood in neo-Lefebvrian terms as concrete outcomes of the abstract logics of capitalist accumulation under neoliberalism. It has been increasingly argued that urbanization is unevenly shaped by neoliberalization, alongside other forces (see Parnell and Robinson 2012; Ong 2006), and although several studies have pointed to the blurring of religious and commercial space, it would be reductive to approach the contemporary production of religious urban space solely in terms of 'entrepreneurial religion' (Lanz and Oosterbaan 2016) or as products of a late-modern, neoliberal age. Historians like Rüpke (2020) who have recently explored the reality of 'urban religion' in the ancient Mediterranean world argue that while archaeological evidence shows that religion precedes urbanization, rituals and religious practices have had considerable impact in shaping the production of both shared and differentiated spaces, a key factor of the densification and growth of ancient cities. Rüpke describes a dialogical process linking the emergence of 'lived religious urbanity' to the fact that 'city-space engineered the major changes that revolutionised Mediterranean religions' (2020: 76; see also Urciuoli and Rüpke 2018).

Infrastructural lives

As indicated above, we understand religious urbanization as a multidimensional and socializing process (often requiring ritualized, collective labour or investment) which has been historically significant in the growth, organization and lived experience of urban life, and which is frequently now shaped by the complex interplay of secularization and desecularization. It involves the production and transformation of urban space, imaginaries and moral maps at multiple scales, while crystallizing collective and individual aspirations through the enactment of projections for the future. Although religious urbanization in its reach and resonance transcends the spatial universe of a bounded metropolis it often conjures powerful images, visions, symbols and metaphors of the city, or a city-to-come, as part of a changing repertoire of world views, beliefs or prophecies.

Our introductory vignette on the revitalizing role of global–local Pentecostal actors suggests to what extent these metaphors and discursive realities can rely on material transformation, themselves creating affordances and initiating linkages and connections. The Gbagada bridge constitutes, in that sense, more than an inert infrastructure providing the context of social and kinetic action. If 'cities are never complete totalizations of the urban' (Amin and Thrift 2002: 108), 'local' infrastructures like the Gbagada bridge which are meant 'to hold the urban together', to create fluid agglomeration and entanglement necessary for the city's continued functioning, are also part of a wider 'meshwork urbanism' (Amin and Thrift 2017: 160) of religious place-making at multiple scales. A dual process is at work here: cities are 'constellations of entwined infrastructures' (Amin and Thrift 2017: 106), making and remaking the urban, but infrastructures are also extending the reach of cities, materially, socially and economically, and they can become spatial symbols of new potential horizons and connections (see Coleman and Vásquez 2017, on the 'translocative' affordances of road networks among Nigerian Pentecostals).

In the last decade or so, there has been increased interest within urban studies in this question of infrastructural development and urban networks, often combined with a focus on the roles played by infrastructure in the globalization and uneven rescaling of the capitalist urban fabric (see Brenner 2019: 376–9). Much of this work has developed from an empirical and theoretical concern with cities in the Global South, with notions of 'lively infrastructure' and 'sociotechnical assemblages' promising 'an exciting anthropology of infrastructure that foregrounds the urban backstage to reveal the sociality of roads, pipes, cables, broadband, code and classification and the enrolments of the socio-technical systems that they are part of' (Amin 2014: 139). Some like Bennett (2010) have discussed the agency of materials invoked by the dynamic interplay between human and non-human actors. She reminds us that infrastructures are never inert, commonplace or neutral. Matter itself is neither dead nor passive; rather we occupy social worlds replete with 'enchanted materialities' and complexified by the 'vitality of things'. Recognition of infrastructural liveliness and vitality is an invitation to take these 'ordinary' forms seriously and it appears to offer scholars of religious urbanization a way of making sense of infrastructures that providers and users believe exist 'by faith of God', but these largely impressionistic accounts are lacking in historical detail. Graham and McFarlane (2015), on the other hand, advocate a more grounded approach by paying attention to 'infrastructural lives' based upon 'the engagements and perceptions through which infrastructures are lived and known' (ibid.: 12). It is a mixture of these approaches that guides the ways in which we conceive of the place of infrastructure in the wider process of religious urbanization.

Thus, we are here mindful of the dangers of celebratory accounts of 'lively' or 'enchanted' infrastructure, especially when empirical accounts often reveal how 'socio-technical infrastructures' are unevenly developed and create or perpetuate divisions and inequalities (Graham and Marvin 2001) and imbalanced citizenship rights (Lemanski 2019). In addition, Brenner, Madden and Wachsmuth (2011) argue that an enthusiasm for networks of material objects can resemble a 'naïve objectivism' that, while deeply immersed in the context of urban life, fails to consider the 'context of contexts' (ibid.: 233) in which urban spaces and locally embedded social forces are positioned. In other words, 'while the assemblage ontology focuses on the materials themselves, it is essential to consider the political–economic structures and institutions in which they are embedded' (ibid.). As such, we are mindful not to reduce urban infrastructures to either the material or affective. A non-reductive approach considers both the poetics and politics of infrastructures (Larkin 2013). Not only are nodes and connections in infrastructural networks important to apprehend, but also, in the context of religious urbanization, relations, affinities and ruptures between religion, state, economy and citizens. It is instructive we suggest, following Jensen and Morita

(2017), to view infrastructures produced, maintained and managed vis-à-vis religious urbanization as 'open-ended experimental systems' or 'emergent systems that produce novel configurations' of the city and urban life (ibid.: 618). The indeterminate temporality of the 'open-ended' and the 'emergent' is concomitant with our curiosity in the spatial scales and, indeed, limits of religious urbanization – in terms its planetary ambitions, certainly, but also its potential to reconfigure the totality that comprises the everyday infrastructural lives of urban dwellers.

For residents of African cities we are discussing in this volume (as elsewhere), the infrastructural world is bound up with the politics of everyday life, within an urban(ized) domain where freedom, domination, rhythm, routine, survival and opportunity are experienced by individuals at their 'closest' (see De Boeck and Baloji 2016). And yet, despite this permeation of the most minute details of existence, the quotidian has a myopic quality in that it is also where the totalizing, revolutionary tendencies of any society (and indeed, recognition of the scale, pace and direction of social change) evade comprehension and come to assume a 'natural' quality. As Highmore (2002: 1) puts it everyday life 'might be, precisely, the unnoticed, the inconspicuous, the unobtrusive'. Nonetheless, for Lefebvre (2000: 72) everyday life is always significant as 'the province of organization'. Everyday life is where individuals imagine themselves in relation to the myths and fictions of the dominant ideology of that society. Where the state and market are broadly aligned with religious ideas about the individual and the good life, such as the Pentecostal stress on the 'making and maintaining of borders that ... protect one's inner world from a chaotic outside one' (Robbins 2019: 188), people come to see themselves in these hybridized terms: all at once as citizen, consumer and as someone seeking, in conjunction with others, 'a kind of salvation that God will deliver only on an individual basis' (ibid.: 187). Infrastructural lives are configured within this nexus and a particular set of discursive realities but the everyday practice of these lives (re)makes the city in accordance with these emergent and novel relations.

Urbanizing 'development' and moral economies

It is apparent that through the provision of infrastructure including roads, bridges and electricity and services such as education and healthcare, urban-based religious actors such as The Deeper Life Church are actively engaged in (re) organizing the city and its collective and individual rhythms and routines, as well as its desires, subjectivities and aesthetic order. In Lagos, for instance, one does not have to be a member of a Pentecostal church to experience the transformative impact such churches are having on the city; from traffic jams, the reconfiguration of streets, the aural soundscapes of prayer to the ubiquitous logos of churches such as Mountain of Fire and Miracles Ministries (MFM) and Redeemed Christian Church of God (RCCG) which adorn buildings, billboards and vehicles throughout the city. As Brian Larkin (2018: 185) points out, the link between [religio-]politics and aesthetics 'is similar to what Raymond Williams referred to as structures of feeling – the particular quality of social experience that is produced by dynamics of historical change'.

Additionally, infrastructural opportunities provided by religious urbanization are also made legible through these everyday engagements and oftentimes they allow residents to experience and give legitimacy to particular visions for social/societal changes at various scales. For instance, to return once more to our introductory vignette, it is clear that the Gbagada bridge as an 'aspirational' infrastructure realizes and materializes the promises of an urban modernity embedded in a wider discourse of transformation and progress, which exists above and beyond a simple religious/secular dichotomy, as suggested by a growing literature on religion and development, in particular in African contexts (see Burchardt 2015; Deneulin 2009; Jones 2012; ter Haar 2009; ter Haar and Ellis 2006). Some of this literature begins to remedy development theory's 'blind spot' in relation to religion (ter Haar 2011: 5; see also Freeman 2012: 1). It points to the promotion and implementation of holistic religious models connecting individual remoralization and personal empowerment to wider notions of societal progress and well-being, and to interventions in the domains of education and health in urban contexts (see also Garbin and Mokoko-Gampiot, Dilger and Janson in this volume). Against the backdrop of the rolling back of the state and global diffusion of neoliberal governance agendas encouraging the involvement of 'third sector' actors and NGOs, there has been an increasing recognition of a legitimate developmental role for 'Faith-Based Organizations'. 'FBO-ization' and 'NGO-ization' are processes that often follow parallel or even overlapping trajectories. For instance, Burchardt (2015 and in this volume) in his ethnography of HIV/AIDS-related Christian activism in South Africa, observes that 'FBO-ization' was largely driven by the availability of international funding, which led religious groups to adopt the technocratic templates governing global development models. In Togo, Piot (2010) shows how religious discourses often mirror dominant development tropes by cultivating an ongoing state of crisis that calls for (radical) intervention and involves the idea of an active rupture with local ties and ancestrality. Contemporary religious vernaculars of 'development' can also be hybrid and not always necessarily aligned to dominant neoliberal ideologies of personal responsibility, entrepreneurship and risk-taking recurrent, for instance, in some Pentecostal circles (van Dijk 2012).

The underlying complexities of the relationships between contemporary forms of religious urbanization and discourses of both development and the neoliberal are brought out by long-standing debates over 'moral economy' (e.g. Scott 1976; Thompson 1971). The latter term poses the question of whether the religious and the moral must be seen as distinct from, and opposed to, 'purely' rational economic considerations. As Keane (2021: 6) has recently put it, the idea of a stark binary between these orientations becomes problematic if it suggests that modernity embodies ethically neutral stances, insisting for instance that the economic and the moral be kept apart while also suggesting that, over time, 'the former is corrosive of the latter.' An obvious counter to this position, notes Keane (ibid.), is that all economies contain moral value orientations, even as religious organizations tend to make such dimensions particularly explicit.

In light of such reflections, we must remain wary of linear models of disenchantment that assume bureaucratic and economic rationality, advanced technology and urbanization are mutually reinforcing elements of the inevitable triumph of the secular modern. Much more sociologically plausible, as authors show in this volume, are models that see religious groups as capable of adopting, adapting or indeed resisting models of rational economic calculation, even within the same movement or organization. It also becomes important to see how the urban offers a particular kind of medium for religious organizations to operate within modernity. Pentecostalism, for instance, is capable of both demonizing the city as den of iniquity and celebrating it as key sphere of opportunity; more subtly, city space provides believers with particular forms of physical affordances relating to scale, to visibility, and to the need to reconstitute religious agency not only through mass conversion or territorial warfare but also through infrastructural interventions in civic space, or indeed development projects.

Outline of the volume

The structure of this book both mirrors and rearranges the different components of religious urbanization discussed so far.

The first part of the volume is concerned with the interplay of infrastructural dynamics, visons of/for development and religious urbanization. Echoing our earlier discussion, infrastructure can be viewed here as not only channelling flows, generating affordances and coherence, realizing aspirations, but also providing the ecology of everyday life through the deployment of embodied cultural practices and modes of urbanity, as Kirby shows in his piece on Kariakoo, a multireligious inner district of Dar es Salam. From the perspective of urban governance Kariakoo may look 'chaotic'; but it is a complexly organized neighbourhood whose social openings and closures are strategic and adaptable. Mosques constitute significant forms of urban as well as religious infrastructure in the neighbourhood, but to characterize Kariakoo through tired tropes of the inherently 'enchanted' character of African life is to miss the point: rather, we must transform parochial models of the secular teleology of the city towards much more subtle understandings of how the affordances of the urban – variety of sensorial experience, highly managed self-presentation, potential for multiple group identification, and so on – are both medium and outcome of behaviours where the religious, the economic and the social cannot readily be teased apart. Drawing upon Simone's politics of urban intersection (2011) and recent works on 'popular urbanization' (Streule et al. 2020, see also Lawanson and Millington in this volume), Kirby shows how religious infrastructural dynamics create multi-scalar and ambivalent landscapes generating 'social thickenings' and 'repertoires of mutual recognition' while 'affording protective capacities' by foreclosing particular encounters and social relations.

In their chapter on 'urban Christianities' in Kinshasa, Democratic Republic of Congo, Garbin and Mokoko-Gampiot also discuss this relationship of religious plurality and urbanization, with case studies of infrastructures set up by Pentecostals, Catholics and Kimbanguists. They consider how the deployment of moralized and developmental imaginaries drives a moral economy of urban presence which increasingly involves the idea of remapping and (re)conquering 'frontier' territories such as post-industrial neighbourhoods or the ever-shifting peripheral 'bush' spaces of the sprawling Congolese megacity. They describe a religious social field operating at multiple scales and, discussing health and educational infrastructures as well as the making of a holy city (the Kimbanguist Nkamba-'New Jerusalem'), they suggest the extent to which religious urbanization is both 'aspirational and performative'. What is meant here is that religious urbanization endows space with moralizing affordances and redemptive potential, and the explicit ambition to construct alternatives to the dysfunctional, spiritually insecure and morally ambivalent megacity shows how religious urbanization (including infrastructure-making) is more than a simple by-product of individual transformations and reforms of the self, linked for instance to the idea of 'integral development', so prevalent among the Pentecostal groups they have studied.

In the chapter concluding the first section of the book, Burchardt also discusses aspirational dynamics and the 'vernacularization' (Levitt and Merry 2009) of dominant development idioms, drawing upon a case study of Pentecostal FBOs in post-Apartheid Cape Town. He shows how the transformative 'urban aspirations' of Pentecostal FBOs, in particular those involved in the fight against HIV/AIDS, crystallize various degrees of spiritual mapping and remoralization of everyday life. Here, no part of urban life is lacking in potential for being evaluated through ethical and spiritual lenses, and Burchardt sees this as a key component of religious urbanization. This engagement further entails the mobilization of globally circulating bureaucratic templates and development tropes, a process which is not immune from the sway of local patronage relationships, however. Consequently, the FBO actors Burchard describes become 'part of the ordinary business of development', of a kind of (unspectacular) 'ordinary urbanism' as they learn to seek economic but also social and moral resources and exert influence through conventional methods of governance and resource distribution. In doing so these actors have managed to 'stit[ch] the township streets, community centres and backyards together into a spiritual geography made up of places in need of services – and of redemption'.

In the second part of the volume, we ask what kinds of temporalities are deployed in processes of religious urbanization and FBO-led infrastructural and development? How do the categories of the past, present/everyday and the future relate to religious time-spaces of planning, transformation and aspiration? Each in their own way, the three chapters of this section address these important questions by exploring how the religious impulse to create and/or transform urban spaces connects to narratives of growth, conversion and regeneration. They suggest how religious time and urban time can overlap, diverge or recombine to compose the texture of everyday life or, like in the case of the Senegalese holy city of Touba discussed by Kingsbury, to anchor the sacred within a time-space of religious rhythms and rituals. Enabled by the collective labour and 'sacred remittances' of the members of this globally dispersed Sufi Mouride Brotherhood, the spectacular growth of Touba into a modern 'religious metropolis' reveals for Kingsbury the centrality of the 'spatial fixing' of both financial and symbolic capital in the context of an intense struggle for religious prestige and sacred charisma between competing Mouride spiritual leaders – Marabouts. Analysing the annual *Le Grand Magal* pilgrimage, Kingsbury's chapter shows the way a monumental sacred urbanity conceals a complex assemblage of formal and informal urban practices that connect the 'holy city' to a host of locales and publics situated beyond its confines. This sacred urbanity is contingent on the sacred heritage of a realized vision but is also linked to imaginaries of *projection* mapping urban expansionism onto a divine trajectory, providing a sense of futurity not dissimilar to the one mobilized by Congolese Kimbanguists and Nigerian Pentecostals engaged in building their own 'New Jerusalems'.

While also dealing with the politics and poetics of projection and temporality, Bertin's chapter draws on the study of religious urbanization of Benin's rural spaces to discuss a different kind of ontology of the (near) future, a linear – albeit uncertain and fragile – urbanizing temporality. Her chapter analyses the gradual religious 'rurbanization' of villages in Benin which operates through small-scale church planting spearheaded by Pentecostal actors who are bridging rural and urban worlds and mobilizing narratives of progress and modernity to gain local visibility and legitimacy. Pentecostal place-making is understood in this context as 'crystalliz[ing] a world of promises and future aspirations, both social and religious' but the slow and often interrupted process of church construction – shaped by the irregular availability of capital, resources, material and labour – shows the importance of theology of endurance and waithood, 'paradoxically self-fulfilling in its very non-fulfilment' (Reinhardt 2018: 114).

The chapter by Lawanson and Millington considers the temporality of religious urbanization in relation to planning regimes of 'megacity' Lagos, and like Bertin's piece, it highlights the significance of collective investment in development and construction and the local impact of Pentecostal territorialization. However, the Pentecostal actors described in the study – the MFM church in the densely populated inner neighbourhood of Onike – dispose of far more political and economic resources than the 'church planters' of 'rurban' Benin. MFM is known for its theology of 'spiritual warfare' and with its hundreds of branches across Africa and the African/Nigerian diaspora, it is one of the fastest-growing Nigerian Pentecostal megachurches. By acquiring and converting scores of residential properties in Onike over the last decade or so MFM has managed dramatically to impact the everyday life of a large number of residents, driving property inflation, imposing new urban rhythms and aesthetics as well as a multisensorial landscape leading some locals to move out of the area. The church has taken advantage of a 'bureaucratic gap' – the weakness of public planning systems – and gained local influence through patronage, while making claims, at the same time, about the infrastructural and moral regeneration of the locality, presented as rupture with a past of underdevelopment and spiritual insecurity. Discussing the challenges of applying conceptual templates such as 'gentrification' or 'popular urbanization' (Streule et al. 2020) to the reality of religious dynamics in African cities, Lawanson and Millington's chapter seeks to extend our understanding of how religious groups like MFM negotiate existing regimes of planning and urban governance – a topic scantily researched in both Global North and South contexts.

The third and final part of the book frames religious urbanization in the context of (re)moralization of space, with a strong focus on the socio-spatial implications of urban enclaving and related boundary-making processes. Beyond the 'bricks and mortar' of religious urbanization, another key thematic avenue of this section deals with the ways in which the 'city' is abstracted, objectified and mapped as part of a wider 'emplotment' and discursive reality addressing socio-economic changes, personal progress but also the pitfalls of modernity, as in Kroesbergen-Kamps' chapter. Her study of the circulation and impact of stories about the occult and Satanism in Zambia shows how images of life in the city and its material culture are evoked to generate a remapping of urban modernity – an urban modernity that is both seductive and threatening. The fear of the desires of the city expressed in Christian narratives of the occult reflects people's ambivalent relationship to 'expectations of development' in Zambia and the ubiquitous promises of modernity and urban consumption, in rapidly transforming cities such as Luzaka. Kroesbergen-Kamps suggests how these stories allow believers to navigate the contradictions of contemporary urban life. In addition, through their performative efficacy these narratives manage to conjure powerful evocative images of the city which are, she argues, central to the urban activism of Christian churches and more generally to a wider process of religious urbanization.

The second and third chapters of this section both explore the formation of 'moral enclaves' through the creation of educational infrastructures within differentiated and religiously plural (sub)urban landscapes. In their ethnographic study of Christian and Muslim educational institutions in Tanzania and Nigeria, Dilger and Janson discuss the emergence of religiously oriented schools and universities, and their 'walls of virtue' serving the wider purpose of delineating the contours of a moral geography through which a pluralized and ambivalent urbanity is made legible and experienced. Within these spaces, disciplinary mechanisms and moral discourses are produced to ensure the embodiment of religiously informed values aimed at creating a 'new generation of moral citizens striving for upward social mobility'. Moral enclaving does not necessarily mean a retreat to the confines of the local, however, as these educational infrastructures are embedded in translocal financial networks linking to the Middle East or North America; and mobilize a powerful sense of global imagined – Christian or Muslim – community.

Similarly, Coleman and Moyet adopt a non-reductive, 'delocalized', approach to our understanding of moral enclaves, and like Dilger and Janson they consider the porosity of secular/religious boundaries in religious quests to educate and (re)moralize urban youth. In a detailed analysis of the campus of Covenant University (CU), run by the Living Faith Church, they trace the numerous ways in which CU both erects and overcomes boundaries set up in relation to numerous scales of operation: it is both part of and partially separated from an adjoining prayer camp, from the city of Lagos, from a landscape of 'global' universities in which it wishes to place itself front and centre. Seen from one perspective, CU looks deeply enclaved, but to succeed on its own terms it must operate on numerous institutional, ethical and rhetorical registers at the same time. In doing so, it creates what Coleman and Moyet call a form of 'religiocity'– a proactive Pentecostal cosmopolitanism prepared to engage with, even to encompass, ideological practices apparently foreign to strict Christian devotion. The CU campus is fast becoming an attractive destination for many who are not denominational members, while as it cultivates a form of modern urbanity oriented to other cities and other parts of the globe.

This description of the multiple orientations of the CU campus may act as a suitable image for this book as a whole, and one that can sit alongside the flyover bridge in Gbagada with which we began this introduction. We do not claim in the following volume to have captured all possible configurations of the religious and the urban in contemporary Africa; and nor have we covered all the ways in which discourses of development are transformed through faith-based organizations. Nonetheless, we hope to have shown how the continuing power of religious ideologies and infrastructures are not to be viewed as 'puzzles' or 'oddities' in attempting to comprehend current trends in African urbanization and development. Equally, we have argued for the complex entanglement of African cities in multiple horizons of religious aspiration and scholarly analysis that must both encompass and go far beyond the experiences of any single continent.

Part I

RELIGIOUS INFRASTRUCTURES OF
'DEVELOPMENT': VISIONS, DISCOURSES AND SCALES

Chapter 2

THICKENING AGENTS: MUSLIM COMMONS AND
POPULAR URBANIZATION IN DAR ES SALAAM

Benjamin Kirby

Introduction

In recent years, researchers have drawn attention to the enduring, even *growing*, dynamism of cities as laboratories of religious 'experimentation' (Lanz and Oosterbaan 2016). In the African continent in particular, cities are increasingly saturated with innovative forms of public religious expression (Larkin 2016). This trend is notably pronounced in the case of Christian, Muslim and indigenous religious movements of renewal, with their widely observed embrace of mass media technologies, novel styles of public preaching and other creative practices of gaining audibility and visibility (Becker and Cabrita 2017; De Witte 2012; Hackett and Soares 2015; Meyer and Sounaye 2017). In this chapter, I am interested in how, by '[inscribing] themselves into urban life', religious groups in African cities are generating new possibilities for assembling and inhabiting cities (Becker, Klingan and Lanz 2013). Thinking with the case of Kariakoo, a super-dense market district in the city of Dar es Salaam (Tanzania), I propose that these everyday practices of religious experimentation may also constitute forms of 'popular urbanization' (Streule et al. 2020; see also Lawanson and Millington in this volume). This term denotes quotidian practices of city-making that are principally led by residents and their collective interests rather than centralized planning authorities, regeneration schemes or private developers.[1]

Recent interdisciplinary work on infrastructure proves highly suggestive for theorizing processes of religious urbanization, both 'popular' and otherwise.[2] In place of prevailing accounts of infrastructure conceptualized as 'a simple, inert, technical supporting structure', this literature instead approaches infrastructures as processual 'ecologies' constituted not only by material artefacts, technologies and resources, but also by embodied practices, cultural competencies, social meanings and organizational logics (Fredericks 2018: 15). As world-making formations, infrastructures do not only articulate relations between the elements that they circulate, but also reconfigure the environments through which these ensembles move (Jensen and Morita 2017; Larkin 2013; Tonkiss 2013). Through this lens, it becomes possible to conceptualize urban space itself as a composite outcome of multiple layers of infrastructural arrangement and operation (Larkin 2008). No less than paradigmatic urban infrastructures such as road networks and sewage systems, I propose that 'religious infrastructures'– enabling arrangements which are constituted by religiously coded components or which perform religiously coded operations – are deeply implicated in assembling cities (Kirby and Hölzchen, forthcoming). Through their participation in city-making processes, religious infrastructures become enmeshed with broader landscapes of socio-technical ordering, giving rise to what Stephan Lanz (2014: 30) calls 'urban-religious configurations'.

One fruitful line of enquiry has been to conceptualize urban-religious configurations with reference to globalizing processes of socio-spatial 'splintering' and 'fragmentation' associated with neoliberal urbanism (AlSayyad and Roy 2006; Lanz and Oosterbaan 2016). Speaking across Northern and Southern settings, this literature demonstrates how cities are increasingly being carved up into disarticulated citadels, enclaves and archipelagos, generating uneven patterns of urban development and infrastructural distribution (Angelo and Hentschel 2015; Graham and Marvin 2001; Graham and McFarlane 2015; McFarlane 2018). Along similar lines, Nezar AlSayyad and Ananya Roy (2006) devise the term 'medieval modernity' to spotlight the emergence of 'feudal' patterns of settlement, employment and citizenship in contemporary cities. In view of this work, the segregated 'religious enclave' has been identified as an emerging paradigm of urban development (Çavdar 2016; Lanz 2016; Ukah 2016a; see also Lawanson and Millington in this volume). One salient manifestation of this paradigm is a proliferation of gated residential estates governed by prescriptive regimes of 'religious rule', with residents financing autonomous security and utility infrastructures in order to facilitate their 'secession' from the wider city (AlSayyad and Roy 2006).

Elsewhere, this literature on religious enclaves is complemented by work on a very different form of urban-religious configuration, namely *multi-religious settings*. Speaking in particular to African cities, researchers have challenged accounts that conceptualize these spatial formations using 'one-dimensional' categories of 'cooperation' and 'conflict' between religious groups (Janson and Meyer 2016; Larkin 2016). They instead suggest we attend to the multiple forms of 'doing religion' and 'being religious' that residents variously contest, tolerate, ignore and borrow within these shared habitats. As Birgit Meyer (2013) demonstrates, these politico-aesthetic practices do not take place in a frictionless landscape; city dwellers must navigate sensorial 'regimes' which establish dominant aesthetic sensibilities, governing which forms of religious expression can assume an amplified public presence in a given habitat and which cannot. In this respect, individual districts and neighbourhoods, understood as socio-technical configurations, prove to be fruitful sites to think with (Bjarnesen 2015). In African cities in particular, individual districts, as AbdouMaliq Simone (2007: 68, 75) observes, increasingly appear to be 'more inclined to "go their own way"', 'disarticulating' themselves from one another and in some cases 'accentuating' their specific features. This then is suggestive of a different pattern of socio-spatial splintering from that of the segregated religious enclave: one that is not primarily constituted by perimeter walls and disciplinary regimes, but rather by concentrations of 'heavily exaggerated' urban styles with which new expressions of religious subjectivity and sociality are forged (Meyer 2013: 597; Simone 2004: 230–1; 2007: 75). In turn, these generate and govern access to what I call 'religious commons': collective goods – devices, infrastructures and resources – that are shared by religious publics and 'maintained and reproduced only through their use' (Elyachar 2011: 96). In contexts where religious commons are made available to those outside the originating group, as in the case that I present in this chapter, they can be thought of as *urban commons*.

I find the recent literature on urban religion and religious urbanism to be highly suggestive for theorizing African cities. However, there is a striking assumption across much of this work that these emerging trajectories of religious urbanization are principally animated by a desire to establish or anticipate conditions of governmental, spiritual and symbolic *control* over urban space (De Witte 2008: 691; Larkin 2016: 637–8; Ojo 2007; Stockmans and Büscher 2017; Trovolla 2015). These 'competing sovereignties' and practices of religious 'territorialization' are often taken to be scripted by 'fundamentalist' logics of ordering, particularly because of their association with renewalist movements (AlSayyad 2011; Lanz and Oosterbaan 2016). In this chapter, I use the case of Kariakoo to provide a very different account of what is at stake in some of these attempts to occupy and refashion African cities and districts. In addition to 'lived' and 'everyday' approaches to the study of Islam (Deeb 2015; Marsden and Retsikas 2013; Osella and Soares 2020; Schielke 2018), I take inspiration from AbdouMaliq Simone's early article on the 'worlding' of African cities. In this essay, Simone (2001: 25) advises that struggles over space and belonging in various African settings may not derive from a concern to 'bring territory under the control of a particular force', but could in fact constitute an attempt to create 'as many possibilities of linking that territory to a plurality of allegiances and opportunities' which extend the capacity of residents to come together and act at different scales. In what follows, I further develop this insight in conversation with my own analysis of religious urbanization in the Kariakoo district of Dar es Salaam.

In several respects, Kariakoo resembles a number of older, inner-city districts across the African continent that, in the wake of neoliberal economic restructuring and shrinking formal employment opportunities, have become lively sites of popular economic activity.[3] These are profoundly heterogenous spaces, both in terms of the demographic composition of those that live and work there, as well as the diverse activities that are staged in and through them. In this respect, it is notable that many such 'mixed districts' (Simone 2013) have become important sites of public religious expression. Kariakoo, for example, is home to a pronounced concentration of large and prestigious Friday mosques, some of which have, in recent decades, served as rallying points for protests against injustice in the city. It is precisely because of the 'thickenings of publics' (De Boeck 2012) that districts like Kariakoo afford, and indeed their capacity to evade and openly resist regulatory measures introduced by local authorities, that they have become such dynamic laboratories of urban experimentation.

As such, mixed districts serve as ideal sites from which to conceptualize popular expressions of religious urbanization in African cities. In this chapter, I examine quotidian city-making practices employed by Muslim residents in Kariakoo amid broader dynamics of socio-spatial disarticulation. More specifically, I investigate how they operationalize the 'thickening agency' of Muslim commons in ways that elicit alternative possibilities for making and inhabiting the city. The residents in question belong to a 'Muslim public' (Kresse 2018) that is not 'reformist' or 'renewalist' in orientation, being perhaps better characterized as what Stephan Lanz and Martijn Oosterbaan (2016) call a 'metropolitan religious mainstream' on account of both its dominant public presence and its heterogeneous composition.

This chapter falls into three parts. In the first, I provide a broad overview of the dynamics that have helped to engender Kariakoo's socio-spatial disarticulation within Dar es Salaam. In the second part, I use the example of Muslim dress practices to demonstrate how tacit and provisional practices of religious urbanization have contributed to these outcomes. Finally, I show how these somewhat ephemeral practices intersect with more programmatic forms of religious city-making, focusing specifically on the proliferation of large mosque complexes in Kariakoo. The analysis that emerges demonstrates how Kariakoo is enacted through coordinated ensembles of religious and urban practices, articulating a vernacular expression of urban(-religious) development characterized by built and social density; one that rearticulates the city as a shared platform for survival and resistance.

An off-centre city centre

First conceived in 1905 by the German colonial administration as an African residential area, Kariakoo was for much of the twentieth century the beating heart of Dar es Salaam's burgeoning associational life. In recent decades, Kariakoo has grown into one of the most important commercial districts in East Africa, attracting traders and real-estate developers from neighbouring countries, China and the Middle East. With a daytime population greater than any other neighbourhood in Dar es Salaam (Magina 2016: 114), Kariakoo has transformed from a residential suburb with a market at its centre to a *market district* populated by shopping arcades, wholesale stores and mobile street vendors.

Despite being positioned at the historic centre of Dar es Salaam, Kariakoo has become increasingly dislocated from the wider city, coming to resemble an 'island' sandwiched between the site of a former *cordon sanitaire* and the Jangwani valley floodplain (Moshi 2009: 130). While Kariakoo has little in common with 'highly structured and standardized spaces' of global economic circulation (Wiig and Silver 2019: 917), Kariakoo's disarticulation has, as I further elaborate below, enhanced its capacity to engage transnational flows of goods and capital. Indeed, the district has become a much livelier site of commercial and social activity than the city's designated Central Business District (De Blij 1963: 61; Mabin, Butcher and Bloch 2013). In addition to its specialized land use, Kariakoo embodies a distinctive form of urban development characterized by socio-spatial density. This is particularly evident in the case of its vertical building density, with local planning regulations encouraging the replacement of single-storey housing units with eight- and ten-storey blocks (Lupala and Bhayo 2014). Meanwhile, in the congested streets below, pedestrians jostle for space with wildly heterogeneous objects: carts, stalls, cars, lorries, bicycles and much more (Lupala 2002: 119–22).

Kariakoo occupies a curious position within vernacular development discourse in Dar es Salaam. On the one hand, the district has become a metonym for the various ills of 'under-development' that afflict the city; a site of infrastructural disrepair where experiences of socio-economic precarity and abjection converge, releasing a flood of unbridled entrepreneurial energies and frenzied construction projects. On the other hand, the staggering transformation that Kariakoo's built landscape has undergone in recent decades has become a subject of marvel and even pride. The district exhibits a form of urban development characterized by accelerating rates and expanding scales of urban densification; a truly 'home-grown' expression of urban modernity initiated not by any kind of regeneration scheme, but rather the accumulated efforts and aspirations of ordinary residents.

It is notable that the spectacular transformation of Kariakoo is to some extent felt to be an achievement shared by the 'urban majority' (Simone and Rao 2021). This partly derives from the fact that Kariakoo is perceived by many to be an *uswahilini* (unplanned or impoverished) neighbourhood. Ordinarily however, any claim to be affiliated with Kariakoo would exclusively belong to a distinctive public; one that is articulated in and through a specific set of urban styles and affective capacities. In this respect, Kariakoo is synonymous with the figure of the 'town boy', *mtoto wa mjini* ('child of the city'), or *mwenyeji* ('owner' or 'host'). These overlapping personas variously denote a privilege belonging to inner-city neighbourhoods, a claim to an established 'urban' identity and a 'street-smart' disposition (*ujanja*, lit. 'cunning'). As the reference to 'boys' suggests, these designations possess a gendered quality which reflects the demographic make-up of Kariakoo from its very beginnings (when it was home to a large population of male labour migrants from rural areas) up to the present day (where the public presence of young male business operators is more pronounced than that of their female counterparts) (Babere 2013: 135–7; Ivaska 2007: 214–17).

Far from being restricted to a uniform style or singular mode of bodily comportment however, Kariakoo presents residents with multiple opportunities to 'experimentally invest in a wide range of different roles and affiliations' to establish provisional collaborations with one another (Simone 2013: 1513). The proliferation of brightly coloured garments that display affiliations to associational football teams in Kariakoo prove particularly useful in this regard, most notably among men (Kirby 2020). In a materially and sensually congested environment, football colours operate as a succinct itinerary of one's moral and aesthetic 'co-ordinates', allowing residents to make themselves 'recognizable' to one another in a minimal and impersonal fashion. These stylistic practices provide a platform for generating and withdrawing moments of interaction with strangers without being bound to any sustained mutual obligations. They also provide a certain 'format' or 'script' for interaction which, in the case of football, can entail a staging of similarity (in the case of a shared team) or a staging of difference (in the case of rival teams) through expressions of playful antagonism (*utani*). These kinds of 'phatic labour' form part of a wider gestural commons to which Kariakoo's business operators, landlords and middlemen (*madalali*) have access, and that significantly enhances their livelihood strategies (Elyachar 2010).

This pronounced concentration of gestural and stylistic elements has further intensified Kariakoo's spatial disarticulation from neighbouring districts, conjuring an impression of a highly integrated public from which those that are uninitiated are excluded. As non-residents of Kariakoo often told me, alluding to the 'impersonal' familiarities that I have described, 'everyone in Kariakoo knows everyone'. For the many tens of thousands of consumers that pass through the district on a daily basis, these implicit associations and unspoken rules make it extremely difficult to determine whether you are truly being given something approximating a wholesale price (*bei jumla*), or how many levels of intermediary brokers are claiming a cut (*chajuu*) from your sale. The (often knowingly) exaggerated 'mythologies' about Kariakoo that circulate around Dar es Salaam lend it a certain notoriety that reinforces the impression that it is inscrutable and unpredictable (Hansen and Verkaaik 2009). This renders its social worlds further 'opaque' to local authorities and business competitors who might seek to interfere with their operations (Simone 2004: 4, 10; 2014:1515). In other words, these overlapping dynamics of social, spatial and stylistic disarticulation not only generate and consolidate particular modes of collectivity, but also afford Kariakoo a certain defensive capacity. In what follows, I demonstrate how different forms of religious ordering and expression contribute to these urbanizing processes, presenting two different examples: the first focusing on Muslim dress practices and the second on large mosque developments.

Outfitting the commons

Muslim residents assume a dominant public presence in Kariakoo, mobilizing various 'political-aesthetic' forms of religious ordering and expression to heighten their visibility and audibility (Meyer 2013).[4] The number and scale of mosque complexes; the volume of amplified *adhana* (calls to prayer); the prevalence of Muslim-coded dress practices, greetings and foodstuff; the incorporation of Islamic terms into building and shop names; the closing of streets for Islamic celebrations – each of these aesthetic practices contributes to an impression reproduced by residents and researchers alike that Kariakoo is in some sense a 'Muslim neighbourhood' (Ahmed 2018: 135; Becker 2008: 248; 2016: 35; 2018: 16; Olenmark and Westerberg 1973: 8).

In stark contrast, the public presence of Christians in Kariakoo is far more muted, despite there being such a large Christian population in Dar es Salaam that some now argue the city has no overall religious majority (Ndaluka 2012: 40). One reason that it is so difficult to make any straightforward judgements about religious demographics among Kariakoo's daytime population is that, unlike Muslim residents, Christians have limited access to immediately recognizable dress practices as a means of visibly performing their religious identities. In the cases of the five churches located in the district, none has the sort of public presence that mosques enjoy: each is located at a horizontal or vertical periphery of Kariakoo. Their relative 'invisibility' is particularly noteworthy given the proliferation of large church buildings in virtually every other neighbourhood in Dar es Salaam in recent years. Instead, Christian (and specifically Pentecostal) groups rely on more itinerant and ephemeral modes of public expression and proselytization: pastors occasionally preach on street corners, and small pickup trucks playing gospel music through loudspeakers intentionally lodge themselves in Kariakoo's traffic jams to sell CDs. As this suggests then, Kariakoo is governed by a prevailing sensorial regime which implicitly restricts the capacity of Christians to assume the kind of public presence maintained by Muslim residents.

Rather than taking this concentration of Muslim styles in Kariakoo to be indicative of a desire to control urban space *tout court*, I instead propose to explain it with reference to the wider dynamics of socio-spatial thickening that are taking place in the district. Here I draw attention to the considerable overlap between prevailing forms of Muslim self-presentation in Kariakoo and those that are associated with the aforementioned figure of the 'town boy'. Take for example the following conversation that I had with two of my primary interlocutors, Omary and Fundi Chomba, both of whom are young Muslim men who live and work in Kariakoo:

Omary: In Kariakoo people are town-dwellers. All of those that come to Dar es Salaam adopt this lifestyle. It doesn't matter where you come from, people are the same here; there is a general behaviour.

Fundi Chomba: Yes, newcomers here see a local tradition and want to be seen as a *mwenyeji* ['owner' of the city] so they take these on; they start gambling, or they take on the culture of insulting and abusing others [*utani*].

Omary: This is the behaviour of the cities [*tabia ya mjini*]. Everyone has to find something to be recognized in the city [in order] to cope. They buy certain clothes, a phone, get a new way of talking. There are certain values associated with cities. It's believed that to be in town, you have to be like X, Y and Z. The good side of city life is that sometimes when we fail, we turn to God. People come to the city and fail in everything, and then they start working with the Bible and Koran. Islam is the easiest way to live: you turn to God, and then your fellow Muslim can give you shelter and money.

Islam here features as a component within a wider style of inner-city 'behaviour' associated with Kariakoo, operating as an important source of 'shelter and money' for rural–urban migrants. The compulsion to find 'something to be recognized in the city [in order] to cope' speaks to the forms of self-presentation that Muslim socialities extend to residents, articulating a distinctive sense of religious urbanity which can itself be mobilized as a resource for navigating the city.

To further elaborate this point, I want to discuss the dress practices of residents in Kariakoo which are more discernibly 'Muslim' than any other neighbourhood in Dar es Salaam. Several of my interlocutors observed that where in the past young people would only wear Muslim dress at Friday prayer (*swala ya Ijumaa*) or at festivals (*sherehe*), these garments are increasingly worn on an everyday basis, with those who commute to Kariakoo from other suburbs making a conscious decision to do so. Again, rather than attributing this reassertion of visible Muslim identity to a renewed commitment towards 'controlling' space in any straightforward sense, I instead propose that it can be more convincingly explained with Omary as an impulse to 'find something to be recognized' through the adoption of a 'general behaviour'. As in the case of football colours, residents that present themselves as Muslim acquire a heightened legibility within the urban landscape. Through these performances of 'being Muslim', residents are ushered into certain kinds of encounters, with Muslim-coded garments, in the words of one of my interlocutors, quite literally '[attracting] greetings from others'. Muslim-specific greetings and honorific titles provide a reliable 'script' for interaction with not only strangers, but also long-standing acquaintances. Such phatic displays of mutual recognition 'make', in my friend Hassan's words, 'the brotherhood between Muslims stronger', further consolidating these networks of sociality (see also Kirby, Sibanda and Charway 2021: 304–5).

Together with other Muslim cultural forms in East Africa deriving from the Indian Ocean littoral, Muslim dress practices have long served to project an impression of respectability (*heshima*) (Becker 2018: 10; Glassman 1995: 61; Gooding 2017: 212; McDow 2018: 96). However, several of my Muslim interlocutors observed that in Kariakoo, Muslim-coded garments are poor indicators of whether a given individual is a 'good' Muslim or not. Along with those some deem to be 'bad' Muslims on account of their behaviour or lack of appetite for religious knowledge, I found that many Christian residents also elect to participate in Muslim dress practices. Here I am again interested in the dress practices of men who, as noted above, maintain a greater public visibility than women in Kariakoo. As one man emphasized:

> Most [men] who dress in a *kanzu* and *kofia* do so to identify as a Muslim leader or scholar, but inside [*ndani*] they have nothing. Anyone can enter a shop, buy a *kanzu*, and look like a *shaykh* when wearing one, but so many of those who do can't answer a single question about Islam.

Nevertheless, I found that such garments also exercise a moral claim on wearers, serving to restrict 'bad' behaviour. Another interlocutor helped me understand why:

> You can't wear a *kanzu* and ask a lady for a date. A *kanzu* brings respect to you. A certain type of person won't do these kinds of things at this time of day wearing this kind of clothing; won't talk to you with a swagger.

Similarly, a young Muslim man provided a rich account of how Muslim-coded garments bestow both prestige and extend a certain ethical claim over wearers:

> To wear a cassock or a full Islamic outfit can change you. Even me, I am only Abdallah, but if tomorrow I wear *kanzu* every day, they will call me Shaykh Abdallah. Those that wear a *kanzu* prohibit themselves from bad things. The *kanzu* is supposed to be accompanied by this habit and this other habit is prohibited.

What is fundamentally at stake here, as Fundi Chomba revealingly explained to me, is not 'what you have judged on your own', but rather that to 'enter a bar' or to 'swear in the street' while wearing a *kanzu* actually 'serves to put down the *kanzu* and not you'. In other words, there is a discernible sense of responsibility on the part of residents for ensuring that Muslim-coded garments are used 'appropriately' that has little to do with regulating individual behaviour, or indeed who is permitted to wear them. Accordingly, I understand this sartorial apparatus to constitute an urban common insofar as it is made available to both Muslim and non-Muslim residents in Kariakoo. In accordance with dominant sensory regimes, aesthetic sensibilities embroider Muslim garments with technologies of self-government (Meyer 2013). These administer the kind of behavioural repertoires that dress practitioners can incorporate into the Muslim social roles they co-produce with their attire. Clearly there remain misgivings in some quarters about the discrepancies between the different impressions that individuals stage as they move between social frames. Nonetheless, residents continue to demonstrate a 'regard' towards one another by respectfully cooperating in these performances and thereby maintaining the common, often because they themselves rely on its thickening agencies as a means of navigating the district (Goffman 1959: 45).

Attending to mosque matters

Thus far I have demonstrated how a 'thickening' of Muslim styles and socialities contributes to broader practices of self-aggregation and socio-spatial disarticulation in Kariakoo, rearticulating the district as a platform for residents to mutually align and expand their horizons of activity without external interference. I have also used the example of Muslim dress practices to show how dominant prescriptive and sensory regimes govern the use of these urban commons in ways that safeguard not only their ethnico-religious integrity, but also their aesthetic efficacy and recognizability. To complement this discussion, I now consider how these tacit and provisional forms of city-making intersect with more emphatic and programmatic efforts to calibrate Kariakoo's built and sensory landscape. To do so, I use the specific example of Kariakoo's mosque complexes, conceptualizing these as infrastructural elements that share and extend certain material, social and affective capacities.[5] As I go on to show, these buildings make an important contribution to wider efforts to reconfigure Kariakoo as a distinctive urban space.

Kariakoo is home to fourteen mosques (*misikiti*), a notably pronounced concentration for a district with a land area of only about 1.4 square kilometres (indicating an average density of one mosque per square 100 meters). These mosques are also impressive in terms of their scale, with several numbering among the largest and most esteemed in Tanzania. Several of my interlocutors who reside outside of Kariakoo regularly make a point of passing through the district to pray, even if this means contending with traffic jams. As this indicates, Kariakoo continues to form part of a larger relational and rhythmic 'topography' within the wider city and beyond, and its mosques extend the district's capacity to draw near different scales and spaces of operation (Amin 2013: 484; Simone 2004: 10). After prayer, the mosques' shaded verandas confer a certain solemnity and prestige on social encounters which increases their appeal. This is particularly true of multistorey complexes like Kwa Mtoro Mosque which is considered especially beautiful on account of its scale and ornate design, featuring stylistic references to global traditions of Islamic architecture. The pride and indirect prestige experienced by residents who pray there is further accentuated by the fact that its redevelopment was funded by Said Salim Bakhresa, a well-known business magnate with a claim to being an *mtoto wa Kariakoo* (child of Kariakoo). As much as the Mlimani City shopping mall and the new Kigamboni Bridge, mosques like Kwa Mtoro articulate visions of infrastructural modernity, operating as shared 'emblems of futurity' into which urban publics invest their desires and aspirations (Amin 2014: 137; Larkin 2013: 335). Simultaneously, Kwa Mtoro Mosque is not set apart from the district; it integrates itself into Kariakoo's rhythmic and stylistic landscape by articulating a density of built form and social interaction.

The spectacular sensory presence of Kariakoo's mosques is not restricted to their visual impression, but also their audibility: several non-Tanzanians that visited me in Kariakoo commented on the remarkable volume of the amplified *adhana* at individual mosques, together with the sonic polyphony that they collectively generate across the district. These sensory effects are particularly pronounced at the time of Friday prayer (*swala ya Ijumaa*) when the mosques are so full of Muslim worshippers that men spill out into adjacent streets, tessellating around abandoned lorries and across shop thresholds. When prayer begins, in marked contrast to the clamour which usually fills the streets, an intense silence descends on the district that is pierced only by the electronically amplified voice of the imam. The mosque presents the possibility of assembly, creating a temporary thickening of publics, but also imposes a certain immobility and quietude on other residents. When prayer concludes, men participate in 'shared repertoires of emotion' which generate a certain 'affective density' characterized by both tranquillity and jubilation, and they gradually disperse in a cloud of warm greetings and firm handshakes which resonate through the surrounding streets (Ross 2014: 2, 95).

The community of affect that is forged through the interplay between mosques and Muslim men is also known to produce very different repertoire of emotion and action. In recent decades, Friday prayer has periodically served as an assembly point for protest action in Kariakoo against the mistreatment of Muslims by the state. The coalescing bodies and affective intensities that thicken in Kariakoo's overflowing mosques present an unparalleled opportunity for generating feelings of collective indignation and a desire to mobilize (Kirby 2017a: 228-32). The irascible affects that these thickenings can elicit are particularly heightened in Kariakoo where experiences of precarity and collective struggles for livelihood congregate. In Dar es Salaam more generally, mosques are especially privileged sites of affective mobilization because of an incident in 1998 when, at a mosque in the nearby Mwembechai suburb where a demonstration was taking place, at least two people were shot and killed by state police. The memory of these events has become emblematic for many Tanzanians, and particularly those who feel politically disenfranchised (Kirby 2017a: 164-7). In Kariakoo, I observed that even the latent presence of this affective capacity possesses a discernible social productivity: many of the Christians that I spoke to in Dar es Salaam were keenly aware of the 'sensitivity' that accompanies Muslim cultural forms and particularly in the case of mosques where Muslim publics thicken. These impressions are no doubt partly informed by Islamophobic tropes which have been exacerbated by the political context of the War on Terror as it has unfolded in East Africa and beyond. However, some of my Muslim interlocutors confirmed that these associations are warranted, delineating how they actually confer certain protective affordances on Muslim publics. As Hassan explained to me, 'the police can't come to the mosque because they respect the place, and the government doesn't need problems with religion'. He added that 'both the government and society believe that the mosque is a good and safe place' where 'nothing bad can be done'. The way that Hassan oscillates here between alluding to a dynamic of respect(ability) and a latent threat of social disorder is highly revealing. Similarly, Omary told me that the police 'respect these people [Muslim worshippers] and these places [mosques], so they can't make a scene'. Because of this, Omary continued, 'the district policemen can't come here to the mosque to inspect the place, so those who are here are protected by the mosque'.

Notably, I found that Muslim dress practices afford a certain defensive capacity by means of a similar mechanism. 'To wear a *kanzu*', Fundi Chomba noted, 'is like a protection [*ulinzi*]'. This is no less true in the case of law enforcement agents, as another man explained:

> If a police patrol meets a man without a *kanzu*, they can be called and interrogated, yet if they do wear one the police will say, 'Oh, this is an *ustadh* [Muslim honorific title] so we won't take him in'.

As was seen above, those that wear the *kanzu* are compelled to display a certain social propriety consistent with the dignified kind of persona with which it is associated. The sight of an individual engaged in such a display of respectability being arrested would be widely perceived as gratuitous and even discriminatory, running the risk of arousing the irascible affects outlined above. When these stylistic practices are understood as a component within a wider infrastructural configuration, it becomes clear that the concentrated distribution of mosque complexes significantly augments the protective affordances of Muslim dress.

Consider, for example, how Fundi Chomba elaborated on the 'shield'-like operations of mosques:

> It is bad to sit on the steps of the mosque, but many who are day workers have to stay there so that if their phone rings, they can go from there. The new regional commissioner says that those that are found loitering on the street will be arrested, so the mosque is like a safe place for them to stay. If you are outside a house, for example, the police can go for you, whereas if you are at the mosque, you can say you are attending to mosque matters.

Several other residents shared the same observation, namely that mosques provide a credible pretext for inhabitants who are obliged to justify their presence in Kariakoo. Though routine crackdowns and forcible evictions of traders working in public spaces have a long historical precedent in Dar es Salaam (Burton 2005), recent decades have seen business operators face increased pressure from local authorities to be registered and licensed (Babere 2013; Bahendwa 2013; Brown and Lyons 2010; Malefakis 2019; Msoka and Ackson 2017; Steiler 2018). As a form of tacit resistance then, 'unlicensed' traders who participate in recognizably Muslim forms of self-presentation can, when compelled to explain what they are doing in Kariakoo, feasibly claim that they are in the district to observe devotional practices at a mosque.

Given the 'shield'-like operations of mosque spaces that have been described, and indeed given that mosque leaders already exert a degree of control over the stretches of street which are adjacent to the mosque entrances, it is no surprise that many mobile vendors cluster around them, selling refreshments and Muslim-coded goods, including garments, books, media products and medicinal items. Several of my interlocutors explicitly described Kariakoo's mosques as 'great commercial hubs'. To be sure, this way of speaking about the social lives of mosques did not correspond with more normative accounts of their purpose: some people insisted that 'the mosque is not a place to think about business', and that 'to think beyond *iman* [faith] about one's business while in prayer is unlawful'. One man told me that people are expected to 'immediately disperse' after prayer to 'look for one's livelihood'. However, several other interlocutors spoke at length about Kariakoo's mosques as important 'connectivity areas' that generate certain kinds of social encounters which may be advantageous for business operators. Hassan gave a detailed account of one way that this works:

> Some go to the mosque to meet rich people and ask for money. It is hard to meet them in their offices, to make appointments. In prayer, you shake hands and then get their business card or cash. People try to plan where [Said Salim] Bakhresa prays on a given day, and then when they ask for some money to pay for the fare from where they have come from, he will take them to the mosque welfare committee. So, people go to mosque for different reasons: first there is the real reason, then for the business appointment. This takes place even with Christians and churches, but the difference is that you will not be allowed to

sit next to a man like Bill Gates or the Prime Minister of the United Kingdom in church. When an MP or even the President of Tanzania enters a mosque, he leaves his bodyguards outside and you are free to meet and talk to him, to sit and pray beside him.

This dynamic relies on an emotional repertoire which obliges worshippers to adopt a 'neighbourly' disposition when interacting with fellow worshippers. Given that for most Muslims in Kariakoo there is no sense of 'membership' of a mosque in the way that there is of belonging to a church or welfare society, this condition of social 'promiscuity' is notably pronounced, especially in the case of Kariakoo where there are fourteen mosques in close proximity to one another. As in the case of the 'protective' capacities discussed above, this is another instance where the socio-technical composition of Kariakoo as an infrastructural assemblage is thrown into sharp relief: the district is iteratively enacted through provisional and programmatic forms of religious city-making that gather together disparate styles, built forms and affects. The thickenings generated by these practices not only afford residents new opportunities to mobilize against socio-economic precarity then, but also enhance their capacity to expand, consolidate and protect the channels through which they secure livelihoods.

Conclusion

I began this chapter by discussing a number of recent publications that draw attention to how religious groups in African cities are devising innovative practices to enhance their public presence. In doing so, they are reassembling the built, social and affective composition of urban habitats across the continent. In this chapter, I used the case of Kariakoo to demonstrate how these practices can be fruitfully conceptualized as forms of popular urbanization. My analysis has built on AbdouMaliq Simone's (2001: 25) suggestion that spatial politics in African cities might have less to do with securing territorial 'closure' than extending possibilities for residents to collaborate and act at different scales. While Simone (2004; 2007; 2014) has used this insight to shed light on religious entanglements with popular economic activities and transnational migration circuits, I have brought it into conversation with his observations elsewhere about the socio-spatial disarticulation of mixed districts. By examining emerging trajectories of popular urbanization in Kariakoo at the scale of the district, I have delineated how these dynamics may not only generate stylistic and social thickenings, but also contribute to related processes of urban splintering, affording protective capacities by *foreclosing* certain kinds of encounters with non-residents and police.

As I have shown, Kariakoo has been dislocated from other neighbourhoods from its very inception through a combination of colonial urban planning decisions and natural topographic barriers. However, in recent decades, new dynamics of economic, socio-spatial and stylistic thickening have reinforced Kariakoo's disarticulation, elaborating a distinctive expression of urban development chiefly characterized by density. This applies not only to Kariakoo's mutating built environment, but also the concentrated webs of sociality to which it gives rise, cultivating a gestural and stylistic commons that diverse residents mobilize to integrate and secure their livelihood strategies. These material forms of self-accentuation have been accompanied by a series of imaginative exaggerations that are reproduced by residents elsewhere in the city. On the one hand, Kariakoo is characterized as a site of underdevelopment and infrastructural disrepair. On the other, it is viewed as a spectacular expression of urban modernity in *uswahilini*, propelled by the unbridled entrepreneurial fervour and tight-knit cohesion of its residents. These imaginative associations render Kariakoo even more inscrutable and incalculable to those who do not belong to its public, further shielding its operations from interference on the part of local authorities and business competitors. Far from devitalizing the district, these dynamics of disarticulation and self-aggregation have considerably extended Kariakoo's capacity to engage transnational flows of goods and capital on its own, reticulated terms, thereby facilitating its emergence as a regional business hub where popular economic activity is concentrated.

These processes of urban thickening both generate and partly derive from a concentration of discernibly Muslim styles, socialities and sensory arrangements in Kariakoo. I have presented two different but intersecting practices of city-making; one more tacit and provisional, and the other more emphatic and programmatic. In the first case, I have shown how popular Muslim dress practices have been incorporated into Kariakoo's gestural and stylistic commons. Muslim garments grant residents a heightened 'legibility', steering them into particular social encounters and repertoires of mutual recognition which both extend and consolidate networks of sociality. I have also demonstrated how prescriptive and sensory regimes govern the use of Muslim forms of urban common, curating the production of 'respectable' Muslim social roles without disrupting their integration into popular forms of sociality, and thereby maintaining their performative efficacy. In the second case, I considered how large mosque developments in the district articulate a density of built form and social interaction, serving as emblematic manifestations of Kariakoo's distinctive expression of urban modernity which arouse a sense of pride among residents. I have conceptualized mosques as socio-technical configurations constituted by built forms, human bodies and cultural styles, emerging through coordinated ensembles of city-making practices, both provisional and programmatic. In Kariakoo, mosques harness the energies of residents and their individual experiences of precarity, forging communities of affect which enable them to feel and act together in new ways.

I have provided two examples of how mosques intersect with wider dynamics of socio-spatial thickening and disarticulation in Kariakoo. On the one hand, mosques generate socially 'promiscuous' spaces and shared repertoires of conviviality which further assist residents in expanding and consolidating their livelihood networks. They also provide legitimizing pretexts for 'unlicensed' business operators to elude the attentions of police, especially when combined with Muslim dress practices and the impressions of 'respectability' these can engender.

On the other hand, mosques serve as important rallying points for mobilization against social injustice. This latent capacity to arouse irascible affects induces among many a sense of mild apprehension in relation to Muslim cultural forms, particularly on the part of police and other non-residents, and thereby enhances their protective affordances. As each of these examples demonstrates then, Muslim commons not only operate as socio-spatial 'thickening agents', but also further augment the district's impenetrability and disarticulation. I have argued that these dynamics have facilitated Kariakoo's incorporation into transnational flows of goods and capital. Accordingly, such city-making practices serve to magnify the capacity of residents to operate across multiple scales (Simone 2001).

Because of their heightened exposure to processes of neoliberal restructuring, African cities have become global 'frontiers' of urban transformation (Comaroff and Comaroff 2012; Nuttall and Mbembe 2008; Pieterse 2008). Amid these dynamics, residents in cities across the continent are increasingly mobilizing religious commons – garments, gestures, affects, buildings, bodies and styles – as infrastructural devices for reassembling urban landscapes in ways that enhance their life-projects and collective strivings, holding together disparate lives and holding open new horizons of mutuality. Accordingly, if emerging trajectories of popular urbanization can offer more 'plausible' and 'inclusive' models of urban development than those initiated by centralized authorities and private developers (Streule et al. 2020), it is imperative that religious practices of city-making feature in such efforts to envision alternative urban futures.

Chapter 3

TERRITORIALIZED VISIONS OF DEVELOPMENT AND URBAN CHRISTIANITIES IN THE CONGO

David Garbin and Aurélien Mokoko-Gampiot

The devil is building his own city, in the invisible world. But the devil is lazy. He steals, he cheats. We had to stop making public the sums we collect during nsinsani, it was attracting witches, arousing their interest. Because the devil is not working, the devil steals and uses people. Us, we are working and we need to hurry to build the city of God.

– Kimbanguist 'Animateur', interviewed in Nkamba, Democratic Republic of Congo, DRC

Introduction

Nkamba, 150 kilometres south-west of Kinshasa, in the Democratic Republic of Congo (DRC), is the 'holy city' of the Kimbanguist church, which, according to Kimbanguist prophetic tradition is the 'city of God', a New Jerusalem 'where all nations will gather' (Isaiah 66). In the quote used as epigraph of this chapter the act of developing Nkamba is relocated within the domain of a spiritual battle, with evil forces both preventing the expansion of the holy city and contributing to the urbanization of the 'invisible world', by relying on stealing and cheating. As opposed to this evil – lazy and immoral – urbanization, the development of Nkamba crystallizes, for its part, a prophetic but also collective aspiration mediated by sacred 'work' (*misala*) taking the form of donations in kind, volunteered time and to a larger extent money collected during the ritual of *nsinsani*. The 'animateur' who, in the quote, links 'financial discretion' to a strategy to drive the witches away, plays a key role in this public and highly staged ritual, encouraging members to donate, by facilitating a festive atmosphere full of singing, teasing and laughter. *Nsinsani* rituals take place weekly in every individual Kimbanguist parish in the DRC and the Congolese diaspora, and the ones organized in Nkamba are quite sizeable, typically gathering thousands of pilgrims under the auspices of the Spiritual Leader. While a proportion of *nsinsani* donations is often kept by individual parishes to cover their running costs, large sums are earmarked for the construction of buildings and residences in Nkamba, to pay for the maintenance of infrastructures as well as to accommodate pilgrims. The Kimbanguist church, which started as a localized Kongo Christian messianic movement in the 1920s, has expanded transnationally, mostly through the migration of Congolese – and to a lesser extent Angolan – Kimbanguists to Europe (France, Belgium, UK, Portugal, Germany, etc.), North America (the United States, Canada) and African countries. In the Congolese context, and similarly to the Catholic church and a growing number of Pentecostal churches, Kimbanguists have, over the years, invested significant financial and social resources in what could be considered secular 'development' domains (education, health, micro-credit, agricultural cooperatives, etc.). Despite the centrality of Nkamba in the Kimbanguist prophetic theology, the church is also visibly present in the Congolese capital, one of the fastest growing cities in sub-Saharan Africa, a megacity where the great majority of urban residents have to deal with the everyday reality of economic informalization, social volatility and dysfunctional, 'syncopated' infrastructure (De Boeck and Baloji 2016).

This chapter draws upon data collected as part of the RUA project,[1] which explored the impact of religious urbanization in the postcolonial megacity environment of Lagos (Nigeria) and Kinshasa (DRC), complemented by long-standing research in the Congolese diaspora (Garbin 2014; Mokoko-Gampiot 2017). While we argue that the way religious actors understand and perform 'development' is differentiated as well as contextual and flexible, religious developmental dynamics often resonate with an idea and ideal of moral transformation and redemption at multiple scales. How are these promises of individual and collective (re)moralization articulated through particular 'urban aspirations' (Burchardt and Westendorp 2018)? How is the city imagined or reimagined, mapped or remapped through the process of religious urbanization? How are religious visions materialized and what kind of territorial, socialized and spiritual labour is involved in this process?

By focusing on the landscape of 'urban Christianities' in Kinshasa, we consider the importance of an urban ecology of interaction and differentiation while accounting for a range of shared dynamics, which include, as we shall see, connecting the making of (re)moralized subjects to collective aspirational quest for 'good governance', welfare and change, in particular in the realm of education and in a context of a perceived failure of the state to tackle corruption, rising insecurity and inequalities. As religious groups transform the city, they deploy their specific take on space and time, carving up, in turn, territories of lived experience and materializing projections for a (better) collective future, against the backdrop of an urbanity never devoid of meaning.

To address this multi-scalar moral economy of urban presence, we examine processes of religious urbanization among key actors of the religious field in urban Congo – Kimbanguists, Pentecostals and Catholics, with a particular focus on several specific case studies of 'urban-religious configurations' (Lanz 2014). These case studies include a school founded by the 'Maman Olangi church' (a transnational Pentecostal church well established in the Congo and the Congolese diaspora), a health infrastructure, the Miséricorde Hospital (set up by the Pentecostal New Jerusalem church), the Kimbanguist hospital in Kinshasa as well as the Kimbanguist holy city of Nkamba. The methodology used as part of the RUA research in the DRC context involves interviews with religious actors and staff, and participant observation in each site, including sustained periods of ethnography in Nkamba, in addition to focus group/workshop discussions with various stakeholders and church representatives. As mentioned above, we also draw, to a lesser extent, on complementary data collected among Congolese in France, the UK or United States – among Kimbanguists, Catholics and Pentecostals (Maman Olangi and New Jerusalem churches in particular).

While our case studies reflect diversified, often divergent theologies of time and space in the context of postcolonial, 'post-Mobutu' Congo (Pype 2012) they all form, in their own terms, 'assemblages of material, social, symbolic and sensuous spaces, processes and experiences where the religious and the urban are interwoven and reciprocally produce, influence and transform each other' (Lanz 2013: 30). Alongside religious investment in materiality, built environment and infrastructure, this chapter will thus explore how religious urbanization may also rely on acts of (re)imagining and envisioning both the *urban*, understood here as an evolving enmeshed system (see Amin and Thrift 2017), and the *city* as a morally ambivalent socio-spatial form – and as an idealized outcome of collective labour, especially in the case of Kimbanguists. In order to do so, we will first delineate the boundaries of the fragmented 'field' of urban Christianities in the Congolese/Kinshasa context before focusing on the mapping of Pentecostal educational environments as moral spaces of integral transformation and spiritual 'development', using as case study the school set up by the Maman Olangi church. The chapter will then proceed to explore the shared dynamics of what we call 'frontier development', illustrating to what extent the transformation and regeneration of urban and peri-urban space can be seen as part of both a wider quest for remoralization and infrastructural modernization, in particular with the example of the New Jerusalem 'Miséricorde hospital'. A section analysing the creation and activities of another health infrastructure, the Kimbanguist hospital, will follow, complemented by a focus on the Kimbanguist holy city and its place within a global geography of the sacred.

Religious landscape and the politics of boundaries

Like in many other African urban societies, Kinshasa's Christian landscape is highly differentiated and characterized by permanent competition, tension and contestation. It includes mainline churches (Catholic and Protestant), Pentecostals (forming a subfield itself extremely fragmented), Kimbanguists (divided into two branches), Prophetic churches (some claiming a Kimbanguist legacy) and other actors such as Jehovah's Witnesses, Branhamists[2] and so on. The diversity but also tensions and competing dynamics within this broader field and subfields have been reflected, among other things, by the emergence of a pluralized religious public sphere – in particular with regard to media and popular culture (see Pype 2012) – differentiated political positionalities (in times of elections for instance) as well as diverging interpretations of and attitudes towards notions of 'traditions', ancestrality and Africanity. While it is beyond the scope of the chapter to explore in detail these competing dynamics and their urban impact, it is necessary to say a few words about the ways in which boundaries are discursively drawn between the main actors of this field – particularly Kimbanguists, Catholics and Pentecostals – in relation to tropes of societal change, conceptions of moral/social order and 'development'.

Building on Bourdieu's conceptualization of social space as an economy of symbolic goods, Ukah (2016b) aptly shows how Pentecostal pastors in urban South Africa adopt powerful rhetorical strategies valorizing their 'authentic' missionary role and superior spiritual legitimacy while delegitimizing the relevance of established churches and other Christian actors, dismissed as charismatically powerless or 'bonded' to ancestral 'traditions' and 'superstitions'. In doing so, they deconstruct and reimagine the religious field in their own terms – without however radically changing the 'structuring structures' (Bourdieu 1990: 53) which have historically governed it. Similarly, in Kinshasa, Pentecostal actors have produced a wide range of claims constructing and legitimizing a moral and (more perhaps importantly) spiritual superiority. Within a fragmented and ever-changing religious field, Kinshasa's Pentecostals thus 'attempt to monopolize the definition of what is to be "a Christian"' (Pype 2012: 37).

Boundary-making work in relation to Catholics is particularly strategic here, especially given how the emergence of Charismatic activities within the Catholic church contributed to the early Pentecostal *réveil* ('awakening') in 1980s Kinshasa and also considering the prestige that Catholics still enjoy,[3] despite the influential 'Pentecostalization' of Kinshasa's public sphere. In this discursive regime of differentiation devaluing markers are incredibly wide-ranging: Catholics are dismissed for their supposed lax attitude towards alcohol consumption, their lack of Biblical knowledge, their downplaying of charismatic gifts and miracles, their 'aesthetic regime' (Butticci 2016) seen as promoting idolatry, their historical contribution to the colonial project, and so on. The idea of rupture so central in Pentecostal subjectivity often encompasses a cathartic, iconoclastic exclusion of a Catholic ritualistic and symbolic universe, in the midst of a post-colonial (and post-Mobutist) society in need of direction, purification, control and redemption. Similarly, while the figure of Kimbangu may be positively mobilized in post-colonial narratives of the nation, the legitimacy of the Kimbanguist church is dismissed because of its 'syncretic', 'unchristian' tendencies, its embracing of ancestrality and its 'false neutrality' (seen as support for the regime) during the Mobutu era. As Ruth Marshall (2009) argues in the context of Nigeria, Pentecostal discourses often question and challenge the *inherited* social, political and cultural forms they see as the historical grounds for the present (and permanent) crisis of governmentality, reflected by widespread instability, insecurity and corruption. Thus the 'born again' mode of governmentality – as a technique and practice of power – is seen as the only one able to offer the 'means of creating the ideal citizen, one who will provide a living incarnation of the *nomos* of a pacified and ordered political realm' (ibid.: 14).

Because of their growing influence, urban visibility/audibility, resonance, their performative colonization of public space (from streetscape, to public transports,[4] to social media) Pentecostals have become, in the context of Kinshasa, a sort of proximate 'master-Other' for non-Pentecostal urban actors. In the narratives of Kimbanguists and Catholics a key component of this differentiation is the perceived fragmented and disorganized structure of the Pentecostal field – with its thousands of churches and range of 'theological' orientations – a field seen as lacking coherence, consistency and stability. The Catholic organizational landscape is of course internally pluralized, with a multitude of religious orders (most of them transnationally organized) running parishes and associated institutions, which, in the case of schools for instance, can enjoy some degree of autonomy in terms of ethos, management styles or pedagogical approaches. Despite this pluralization, as well as the existence of tensions between the different orders and the socio-economic inequality between parishes, the organization of the Catholic network remains strongly centralized in its coordination and hierarchical structure (Titeca, De Herdt and Wagemakers 2013). This was seen as a clear marker of difference with Pentecostals, evidence of the legitimacy of the church for religious (but also social and political) governance by most of our Catholic interlocutors. To some extent, there was a comparable narrative among Kimbanguist followers who emphasized their organizational discipline based on a strictly centralized hierarchical structure and their wide-ranging network of institutions, mostly schools, established it is true, in a context of marginalization and exclusion of Kimbanguists from mainstream – Catholic and mainline Protestant schools – after independence (Mokoko-Gampiot 2017).

While Pentecostal pastors are the 'new cultural heroes' of the Congolese public sphere (Pype 2010: 130), questions of morality, charismatic power as well as suspected influence of the 'occult world' are central elements of differentiation in the religious field, and in particular they serve to draw boundaries between 'true pastors' and 'false pastors' in Pentecostal circles. Social media, and in particular Facebook, are used by Pentecostals to stage the struggle between Good and Evil, but, at the same time, material exposing the supposed immorality or excesses of Pentecostal pastors also circulates widely and has formed a genre in itself. These critical vignettes are extensively shared, 'liked' and commented, and have often transnational trajectories since they also feature for instance pastors from Nigerian or Ghanaian churches, and/or practices or rituals performed in these churches, such as spectacular/extreme exorcisms, 'bogus' miracles or prophecies.

In the Congolese context (including in the Congolese diaspora) some churches are more controversial than others. This is the case of, for instance, the Ministère Chrétien du Combat Spirituel ('Christian Ministry of Spiritual Warfare'), also known as 'Maman Olangi Church' following the name of the founder 'Maman' Elisabeth Olangi Wosho, who passed away in 2018. While the congregation is structured like most Pentecostal churches (with a central leadership and a division of roles clearly defined), its leaders often stress that, as a 'ministry' (*ministère*), it welcomes to its services believers from a wide range of churches, willing to reap the benefits of 'spiritual warfare'. Its main theology, familiar to most Kinois (inhabitants of Kinshasa), is heavily influenced by the master-trope of deliverance 'from ancestral bondage'. This process of deliverance is almost always synonymous with a radical, reflexive reassertion of extended kinship ties and a stress on individual spiritual empowerment against the pervasive ('second') world of witchcraft and occult spirits (Meiers 2013).

Maman Olangi's church, which has often been accused of 'dividing families', is very present in Kinshasa's cityscape and has appropriated several *parcelles* (plots) in the post-industrial neighbourhood of Limete, where its main praying ground is located. The church has also set up a small but growing network of schools and health centres and is developing another enclaved space at the periphery of Kinshasa, following, we were told by one of the members of the Olangi clan, the model of Nigerian churches such as the Redeemed Christian Church of God (RCCG) or MFM. These investments, particularly in the educational sector, reflect the increasing entanglement of religious, moral and business-driven aspirations, with religious groups and Faith-Based Organizations (FBOs) competing in the education marketplace against a backdrop of privatization and liberalization across the African continent (see Lauterbach 2016, Dilger and Janson in this volume).

However, many among our Catholics and Kimbanguist informants criticized Maman Olangi church for 'running health centres and schools solely as businesses', charging high fees which most Kinois cannot afford and excluding those not adhering to the Church's ethos. As part of the RUA research in Lagos, we encountered similar, recurrent perceptions of religious urbanization seen as exclusive or driving territorial segregations, in particular regarding the (large-scale) enclaved spatialization and expansionist visions of churches like RCCG or MFM. However, 'Olanguistes' we spoke to hailed their positive societal role and their 'duty' to fill the gaps left by a failed state ('*Etat démissionaire*') while, as we shall see in the next section, justified the need for a (re)moralization project operating at several scales and which, for instance in the case of education, echoes a wider vision for 'integral development'.

'Integral development' and moral citizenship

Given the intense struggle over charismatic authority/recognition and over the definition of the boundaries of a legitimate (Christian) symbolic order, the notion of field can be a useful analytical model to make sense of the dynamics operating within the landscape of 'urban Christianities' in Kinshasa. However, there are also potential limitations as Echtler and Ukah (2016) note when discussing, in the context of African religiosity, the relevance of Bourdieu's conceptualization of social space and his understanding of the social characteristics and functions of religious power, largely inspired by Weber's sociology of religion (Rey 2007).[5] Prioritizing an analysis of the 'field of forces imposed on actors as well as a field of struggles between actors' (Echtler and Ukah 2016: 16) and of the incessant competition over symbolic profit – despite the objectified disinterestedness of actors governing the field – risks overstressing the reality of congregational/ritualistic particularities legitimized as (de)valourizing differences, minimizing, in turn, the role of hybrid practices and the lived experiences of boundary-crossing (Janson 2021, McGuire 2008, Gez et al. 2021). Another issue is the supposed (ahistorical) 'autonomy' of the 'field' reflecting an unproblematic adoption of 'religion' as a clearly bounded category, inherited from Western conception of modernity and ideas of secular differentiation (Asad 1993).

Driving new forms of sovereignty and governmentality, the Pentecostal born-again movement has been described as a form of religious holism challenging rigid dichotomy between public and private and appropriating the codes of popular/media culture and modern, globalized consumerism. What Vásquez coined 'Pneumatic Christianity' has allowed a 're-enchantment of the material world' and 'the safe appropriation of all the commodities, from money to symbols, from bodies to culture, that now circulate at an unprecedented rate and have become charged with all manner of signification' (2009: 282). For Pentecostals, argues Comaroff (2009: 20), 'the life of the spirit extends ever more tangibly to profane realms beyond the space of the sanctuary and the time of worship, heralding a significant reorganization of the modernist social order as a whole'. Similarly, discussing the global emergence of the megachurch socio-spatial model, Coleman and Chattoo (2020) talk about the 'expansive enclaving' driven by churches like MFM in Lagos as a process reflecting the 'ability of the church to expand into and reform parts of the "unruly" city' (ibid.: 91). This encompassing form of territorialization operates without overt regulation, relying instead on contribution to order and security as well as the provision of 'morally approved entertainment', leisure goods and services (music school, bookshop, café, etc.) embedded very visibly within the local landscape (see also Lawanson and Millington in this volume), while attracting worshippers from all over Lagos. In the Congolese context it is also clear that Pentecostal urbanity involves a totalizing project linking individual born-again subjectivity to the (re)moralization of wider assemblages – such as the city or the nation – and, as Pype notes in her Kinshasa ethnography, a born-again Christian 'has the duty and the power to purify both private and public experience' (2012: 223).

In addition, and as hinted earlier, Pentecostal modes of governance draw upon holistic models of moral formation which are particularly relevant in spheres typically associated with charitable work and 'development', such as welfare, health or education. This was unambiguously evidenced by the discourses collected among staff at one of the schools established by the 'Maman Olangi' church in their Limete compound. The compound is a clear example of 'expansive enclaving' which comprises a large place of worship, a bookshop, a cooperative and various administrative buildings. With around 1,400 pupils across preschool, primary and secondary sections, the Limete school – 'Ecole Bérée'[6] – benefits from being centrally located, a stone's throw from strategic avenues connecting the local neighbourhood to the important urban communes of Lemba and Matete from where a significant number of the school's students come. At around $350–380 a year, the fees are indeed higher than most Kinshasa's schools and it caters mostly for children of middle- to high-income families. High-profile politicians, businessmen or army officers connected to the church are known to send their children to the school but school administrators and managers interviewed in Kinshasa were keen to paint a picture of class diversity and stressed the existence of a scheme for '*les cas sociaux*' providing assistance to poorer children and orphans.

Staff interviewed spoke at length about the notion of 'complete education' as being central to the ethos of the Bérée school, whose motto written very visibly on its outside wall and which reads '*informer, former, transformer*' ('to inform, train and transform'), is adapted from the church's slogan '*nous informons, nous formons et nous transformons*'. According to its director the school is a place where pupils benefit from '*un encadrement integral*', and where education targets 'body, soul and spirit (*corps, âme et esprit*)'. This ethical framework reflects the centrality of a Pentecostal moral habitus, produced and reproduced though a regime of intensive spiritual embodiment as this excerpt from an interview with a female teacher suggests:

> Here what we want for each child is that they have good morals [*des bonnes moeurs*]. We want them to be mature, complete and honest citizen, with integrity. This is why we are working hard, despite adolescence, despite difficulties, to educate, to educate and to educate more. In prayers, in wakes [*veillées*], in fasting sessions we exhort children to be role models, to be good citizens to reject unfruitful works [*oeuvres infructueuses*] like corruption, cheating [*la tricherie*], things like that. In Ecole Bérée we train children to be good citizens. To be serious in all things, in their lives. And to love God and to serve Him, so that when they are grown-ups, they remember.

From the outset the school was designed to be an extension of the Ministry, allowing parents to withdraw their children from educational environments deemed contradictory to the church's orientation or even seen as 'influenced by occultism and Free Masonry' as a parent (and church member) put it. Here again, the distinction with the Catholics was significant and the director accused some Catholic schools of using their connections with civil servants to obtain and pass on exam questions to their pupils. Bérée students, he commented, 'have been taught not to cheat and that cheating is an anti-value ("*anti-valeur*")'.[7] By contrast, the director stressed how, in Ecole Bérée, pupils could be educated 'according to the Word of God' in an environment prioritizing spiritual deliverance and transformation:

> This school has been created by our shepherds [*bergers*], Mama and Papa Olangi. They noticed that our children, the children of the Ministère when they were attending other schools they would see things that were contrary to the vision of the ministry. So they decided: 'No! we need to create our own school, we will see our children get deliverance, because there is not only science, there is also the spirit and the soul' … There are schools where they do the sign of the cross, where they adore statues. Whereas for us, this is contrary to the Bible. So we and the parents decided to create a school where children can be educated according to the vision of the Ministère du Combat Spirituel, according to the Word of God [*la parole de Dieu*].

The school, as an extension of the church, is thus where pupils can become autonomous and detach themselves from what is seen as a detrimental spiritual environment. This was, in essence, the message heard during one of the prayer services we observed and which was held at the back of the school building. In front of an assembly of fifty or so older children (12–15-year-olds), a Combat Spirituel pastor encouraged them to reject the 'negative judgements of family members' who are telling them that they 'will never succeed'. Instead, pupils were told to trust God and challenge the 'spoken curse' of their family by responding 'in the name of Jesus I will succeed', a counter-performative utterance of (individual) spiritual empowerment consistent with the overall theology of the Ministère. Since it is not really in the interest of the school to alienate parents, its environment is presented as one of spiritual transformation, empowerment and remoralization. Teachers talked about how the priority given to order and discipline was attractive to parents but above all how the cultivation of Christian principles was integral to upholding moral values among youth in the context of a 'sinful city' like Kinshasa. As one teacher stated, by inculcating in them 'the fear of God' pupils think twice about 'committing wrongdoings like stealing, cheating or being lustful and indecent'.

Through their educational experience – part of larger vision and mission of renewal and transformation – pupils were also relocated in a spiritual battle between good and evil forces, and as such were seen to be vulnerable to spiritual attacks and possession.[8] What was described as 'behavourial problems' – examples cited ranged from stealing, being rebellious or even rude to adult – and which 'cannot be explained' can thus be read through the prism of spiritual affliction and witchcraft (*kindoki*). This process both constructs and legitimizes the school as a space of moral disciplining but also, and above all, as a therapeutic space of intervention, where children can undergo deliverance involving intense praying session and fasting – '*cure d'âme*' or soul healing – with, as we were told, the approval of parents. The fact that witchcraft diagnostics on children are open to internal debate[9] does hardly change the controversial reputation of the Ministère and the Ecole Bérée in particular, among some sections of the Kinshasa population and in the diaspora. After the death of Maman Olangi, critical voices particularly intensified on social media accusing the Ministère and/or the Bérée school of estranging children from their families or using harsh discipline revolving around practices deemed extreme like repeated fasting. Because of the state's inability to properly regulate the religious field and thanks to the church's connections with Congolese politicians, the school is largely evading any external or state scrutiny regarding its pedagogical methods.

Religious urbanization and frontier development

Studies about social and economic change brought about by Pentecostal and Charismatic Christianity generally link idioms of transformation with personal moral reform and search for greater individual autonomy, expressed as a rupture with the past (Meyer 1998), or alternatively as 'realignments' (Engelke 2010) or acts of 'taking control' (van Dijk 2002; 2010) – especially in relation to the influence of kinship and ancestrality, like in Maman Olangi's spiritual warfare. Pentecostals are also said to operate within a this-wordly, 'new economy of affect', the born-again project of individual moralized transformation correlating 'with new forms of subject-formation under neoliberalism' (Kirby 2019: 16).

In her work on Pentecostalism and development in Ethiopia, Dena Freeman (2012) notes that this Pentecostal project of transformation 'start[s] with the self' before 'moving out to the social and material' (ibid.: 164). This idea of an ego-initiated, outward movement propelling collective change was indeed recurrent among most of our Pentecostal informants when discussing 'development' and societal transformation. To some extent, there was a similar discourse among Catholics and Kimbanguists in particular when it came to the sphere of education. Catholic actors and staff of Catholic educational institutions were for instance keen to stress the role of religious education in the constitution of a space through which particular values could be central to the making of exemplary 'moral citizens'. Here again the idea of a 'complete education' targeted at the individual was intimately connected to a need to uphold virtue and morality in the context of a 'corrupt society'. For Kimbanguists, the adoption of Christian values, both to remoralize society and to fight the influence of evil forces could not be separated from a recognition of the Prophetic power and legacy of Kimbangu, embodied by the current Spiritual Leader.

While for all actors of the religious field a holistic approach to spiritual power and transformation was central, it was Pentecostals who stressed more forcefully the role of an 'integral development' as a holistic yet person-centred approach that has the potential to drive the transformation of a wider 'environment', as this Maman Olangi youth leader stated:

> Something that differentiates us from NGOs: we put more emphasis on the person, the being [*l'être*]. The person is composed of body, soul and spirit and we focus on his or her integral development. We believe that development, as far as the person is concerned, does not begin with the environment. Just as in anthropology it is said that Man [*sic, 'l'Homme'*] conditions the environment and the environment makes the person what they become. Before the environment can influence Man, it is Man who first influences the environment. So the development starts with the being, the person, their interior and we focus on that.

However, at the same time it is also clear that, for Pentecostals, this production of an 'environment' by reformed individuals resonates with a quest for regenerating and remoralizing space, and the process of religious urbanization linked to the presence of the Maman Olangi's church in Limete can be seen as part of this wider logic. The Maman Olangi's church complex where the Bérée school is located was once a *friche industrielle,* an industrial wasteland, a place which was 'abandoned, dirty, where *sheges* [gangs of streetchildren] were roaming and prostitution was rife' as one church leader recalls. In fact, the deindustrialization of this large urban area of Kinshasa formerly known for its small workshops and food processing factories had been in great part caused by two waves of military-led looting sprees which took place across Kinshasa in 1991 and 1993 and destroyed most of its economic infrastructure. The gradual territorial takeover of the area by the Maman Olangi's church and dozen other Pentecostal churches can be seen as a part of a wider vision aimed at the conversion (and redemption) of a sinful, immoral society, with a territorial reconquest 'filling the gaps' of the post-Mobutu era – the frenzied looting incidents of the 1990s personifying the unpredictability of a chaotic and dysfunctional urbanity.

In that sense, religious urbanization does not operate here merely through the 'filling up' of neutral, empty spaces devoid of meaning, but rather through an active transformation and taming of an environment perceived to be already 'full' – of wilderness, crime, sins, disorder and so on – (Coleman and Vásquez 2017: 42). This is the case of the appropriation of post-industrial, declining urban spaces like the Limete neighbouroood but also of peripheral, peri-urban spaces, whose growth and densification has pushed outwards the external boundaries of many African metropolises, with sprawling megacities like Kinshasa or Lagos inexorably extending into their hinterlands (Gandy 2006; Simone and Pieterse 2017; Trefon 2009).

In Lagos, religious peri-urbanization often operates on a large – if not spectacular – scale. It is driven by churches like the RCCG which has built a self-sufficient and rapidly growing urban enclave – 'Redemption Camp' – surrounding 'bush' land where mass prayer gatherings often attract million-strong crowds (Osinulu 2014; Ukah 2016a; Coleman and Moyet in this volume). In addition to church auditoria and preaching grounds, these 'prayer cities' also often contain banks, shops, schools, hospitals and electricity and water infrastructure and are hailed as ordered, safe and crimeless. In fact, leaders of Maman Olangi church we met praised the RCCG's vision and its strategy of urbanization through the development of suburban enclaves, and have adopted the praying city model with the creation of 'Mahanaim City'[10] on the periphery of Kinshasa. While this compound is visibly more modest in terms of size and infrastructure compared to the surburban Nigerian 'prayer camps' it includes a school, cooperative, health centre and praying facilities. In addition, the project of building a university on the site also reflects the ambition of the church to emulate the holistic approach of the RCCG who has invested all levels of the educational marketplace. Maman Olangi's church, like most of its Nigerian counterparts (RCCG, MFM, Winner's Chapel, etc.) has, in last two decades or so, considerably extended its reach globally through transnational connections and migration. The availability of peri-urban spaces to be appropriated also allows the fulfilment of this expansionist aspiration, driven by an eschatological desire to create a boundless sacred city, defined in opposition (yet connected) to the adjacent megacity. In the case of the RCCG it is striking that this process draws on representations of a 'pagan land', echoing older references to the 'evil bush', central to nineteenth-century missionary (Coleman and Vásquez 2017).

Not all Pentecostal churches have the resources to acquire tracks of suburban land to enable mass prayer gatherings and realize their aspirations for expansion and autonomy through the creation of large 'moral enclaves' (Dilger and Janson in this volume). Yet peri-urban locations can crystallize the idea of what we could call *frontier development* for smaller churches lacking the capacity to embark on large-scale (sub)urbanization. It was the case, for instance, of the development of the Miséricorde hospital, another case study of our research. The hospital was built by the Congolese Pentecostal church New Jerusalem headquartered in Belgium but with branches in France, North America and in the Congo. It is located in a so-called *commune urbano-rurale,* a fringe area which lies both at the edge of Kinshasa and at the boundary of the rural hinterland (Trefon 2009). With the growing scarcity and inflation of land and housing within the city, these peri-urban spaces have attracted both Kinois leaving expensive and cramped city neighbourhoods and populations migrating from outlying, poorer rural areas. The availability of cheaper plots and the possibility of providing care to lower-income populations lacking affordable health facilities were, for church leaders, among the key reasons for 'planting' a religious hospital in this peripheral, remote area. In addition, church members and hospital staff were keen to point out how they had contributed to the general improvement and urbanization of area – 'the hospital brought development locally' to quote a hospital manager. This idea of 'pioneering' urbanization at the city frontier is reinforced by the fact that the road where the hospital is located took on the name of the leader of the church, who had the vision for the hospital in the first place.

The local impact of this religious urbanization can be perceived in several ways, for instance with the arrival of a small-scale informal economy – food and drink, stalls, mobile phone credit sellers – in the immediate vicinity of the hospital. It has also had some significant consequences in terms of local infrastructure. Since the area lacks access to piped water, the local hospital set up a borehole which some local residents are also using. To be connected to the electric grid the hospital had to spend thousands of dollars in equipment and material, including cables, circuit boxes, posts and so on, and even had to privately pay an engineer from the SNEL,[11] the national electricity company, to set up the connection. Soon, local residents started (most of them, illegally) to get electricity from this newly created connection entirely financed by the hospital, which in turn weakened the intensity of its own power supply. It has also left the hospital more exposed to *délestage*, 'load sharing', the irregular rotating supply of electricity across the urban region. As De Boeck and Baloji (2016: 99) note *délestage* is a perfect illustration of the 'syncopated' rhythms of infrastructures in Kinshasa and is metonymic of the volatility and unpredictability of urban life in the megacity. To respond to this infrastructural instability, the church – thanks to the financial contribution from its members in Belgium and the United States – purchased diesel generators and solar panels but with high running and maintenance costs whereas the hospital struggles to ensure that power is available during important medical procedures and operations. This infrastructural development needed for the functioning of the hospital revealed tensed relations with the state, its agents described as hostile and threatening as senior staff told us:

When there is a *mouvement associatif* [a 'charity group'] which wants to intervene in the social life of people that the state should be in charge of ... the state should help, giving them subsidies and exonerating them [of taxes], to encourage their work. But the state demands a lot of money from us, and yet we are helping the state to take care of its population. They are taxing us all the time, even to drill for the water, for the borehole. We even had to stop, we want to serve the population but they are threatening us with fines because we 'made do' [on s'est débrouillé, ie 'we did it by ourselves']. And the state doesn't have the capacity to bring drinkable water here because the water station pump doesn't have enough pressure to bring water up to here. So we chose the borehole option but the state is ... threatening us with fines and disconnections. Electricity same thing, we suffered so much, the state agents [*fonctionnaires*] coming and threatening us.

The construction of the Miséricorde hospital at the frontier of the city highlights a process of pioneering urbanization, bound up with a wider aspiration for territorial presence, remapping and legitimation. The plan to create a church parish on the land where the hospital stands is also part of the developmental vision spearheaded by the church in the Congo and its diaspora.

For the different actors of the field of urban Charismatic Christianities the idea of 'development' connects processes of transformation and redemption to various interrelated scales (from the individual to the family, the neighbourhood, the city, the nation and beyond). For Pentecostals, as Pype suggests (2012: 223), idioms of development and progress involve an essential unity between the individual and the social based on an 'engagement with the present and the future', enabled by the power of the holy city, harnessed to 'open up' and 'unblock' path to spiritual and material prosperity.

Within this developmental vision, religious urbanization is not merely a by-product of an ambition to refashion individual subjectivities, redeem (urban) society or even carve up protective spaces within it. Rather it shows to what extent religious experience – and in particular we mean here a range of practices, vision and aspiration for growth – is inherently spatial (Knott, 2005; Rüpke 2020), including for Kimbanguists and Catholics alike. Indeed, the latter also often pointed to the (frontier) urbanization and infrastructural modernization linked to religious missionization in the Congo:

Things that work today in Congo is thanks to the Catholic church and it has always been like that! I was born in a small village in Congo and I was able to reach the university in Kinshasa because there was this system of missionaries and I am grateful for the church ... If you go deep into the interior of Congo today, and there is electrical lighting, there is 90% chance that it is the parish that put it there. (Member of the London Congolese Catholic Chaplaincy, male, in his 60s)

It's thanks to religion and the Church that things are working back home (*chez nous*). If you go to the deep in the Bandundu, you'll find the mission Ngi, or another mission. You will find that there is lighting, there is everything you want to have. People leave distant villages to form new villages around missions. This means that the Church has always brought something new to the social life of the people. (Member of the London Congolese Catholic Chaplaincy, male, in his 50s)

Such accounts opposing the darkness of the bush, of the 'deep' Congo, and the 'light' brought about by Catholic developmental presence, echo colonial *mission civilisatrice* tropes, reflecting, perhaps, the idea brought forward by Perrazone (2019), building on Stoler (2008), that 'debris' of colonial mimesis (in this case, the fact that colonial power is resting, in part, on the internalization of its cultural and moral superiority by a Congolese elite of *évolués*[12]) have the potential to inform a politics of the present. However, many among our Catholic informants were also keen to disentangle the Congolese Catholic church from colonial Belgian oppression, or stress its increasing autonomy through a gradual 'Africanization' promoted by Cardinal Malula soon after Congo's independence. One Catholic interlocutor commented that 'if the church was on the side of the colonial power, it is not because it was the Catholic church, it was because it was the *Belgian* church (emphasis added)'.

The idea of autonomy was also central to Kimbanguists who developed their educational and health facilities as a result of historic marginalization and exclusion from state and religious (Catholics and mainline Protestant) institutions. This trope of self-reliance hinges around the collective memory of a 'golden age' of solidarity, the era of the *kintuadi* during the colonial repression, when Kimbanguists were forced to worship underground. While the moral economy and Kimbanguist ethos of development can be contrasted with the entrepreneurial aspirations of a large number of Pentecostal actors, there are comparable visions for urban presence and territorialization as we shall see in our final discussion of processes of place-making among Kimbanguists. We will focus more particularly on two Kimbanguist modes of urbanization and 'visions' of/for the city, the first ones linked to the presence of the church in Kinshasa and the second to the development of the town of Nkamba, as a 'New Jerusalem' for the Kimbanguists.

Urban visions of the Kimbanguist church (1): Kimbanseke hospital in Kinshasa

While Kimbanguist health and educational infrastructures are present across the Congo, it is in Kinshasa that they are mostly concentrated. There are twenty-one Kimbanguist parishes (*paroisses*) evenly distributed across the twenty-four municipalities (*communes*) of the Congolese capital and almost an equal number of schools (covering both primary and secondary levels). Over the years, Kimbanguists have built in Kinshasa a university, residences, conferences halls, offices, radio and television facilities as well as health infrastructure and clinics, including the Kimbanseke hospital. Opened in 1974, it was originally a smaller medical centre converted into a hospital in 1988 with the financial support of Israeli and American development agencies, and with some additional Belgian assistance. The institution is *conventioné*, that is, contractually a partner of the Congolese state, which supports the salaries and bonuses of the medical staff, and is integrated in the overall management structure of the DPS (Département Provincial de Santé, Provincial Health Zone). The electricity and water bills are also directly paid by the state but the institution does not benefit from any other public subsidies – for instance to purchase equipment, pharmaceuticals and other medical products or consumables, or, perhaps more importantly to improve/maintain the building.

The vision underlying the development of the hospital in Kimbanseke is akin to the one behind the creation of the Miséricorde hospital by the New Jerusalem church. Both hospitals relate directly to their immediate environments, provide health services to local lower-income populations and poorer communities and both are situated in remote, peri-urban areas of Kinshasa, in so-called *communes urbano-rurales*. Here it is important to historically contextualize the emergence of Kimbanguist urban infrastructures. Papa Diangienda, one of the three sons of the Prophet-founder Kimbangu, and the first leader of the church, invested a great deal in the expansion of Kimbanguist infrastructures in Kinshasa. This was part of a wider strategy of recognition and formalization, also connected to the belief that the church's presence in the 'sinful city' would herald a period of spiritual liberation and remoralization. Today many Kimbanguists see the Kimbanseke hospital as a testimony to Diangienda's vision for the church but also to his 'charitable philosophy', to quote one of the administrators of the hospital.

Kimbanguists see healthcare as part and parcel of an 'integral approach to development' (Cochrane 2011), contributing to a wider and collective aspirational quest for welfare and change (for Kimbanguists and non-Kimbanguists alike). This vision ties the betterment and advancement of the individual to the 'developmental' aim of impacting society as a whole, as suggested by one of the hospital's senior managers:

> We accept patients who are often insolvent, even for 1000 Congolese Francs [0.60 Dollars]! So our contribution is really significant. When we talk about development, you don't develop a nation if people are sick. Healthy people bring about development. So the Kimbanguist church contributes greatly to society and its development. Here people are destitute, the *commune* is semi-rural and you have a lot of unemployed people. If you are unemployed and you fall sick, it's a catastrophe.

The trope of work (*misala*), a key Kimbanguist precept (alongside mutual love – *bolingo* – and the obedience of divine laws, *mibeko*), is particularly significant here in the ways in which healthcare and the notion of development are articulated – 'a healthy individual is able to work and is productive for society' as one doctor stated.

While all types of patients are accepted, regardless of their economic status or religious affiliation, the Kimbanseke hospital remains a Kimbanguist institution above all. Kimbanguist patients are exempted from paying consultation fees since they are considered to have already contributed through their *nsinsani*, their church offerings. Religious membership and participation (mediated of course by offerings and donations) thus create affordances through an implicit system of redistribution and 'social security' outside other formal (public or private) structures (Leutloff-Grandits et al. 2009). Visually, the hospital is also recognizably Kimbanguist, with its walls painted in green and white – the church's distinctive colours. The Kimbanguist bodily regime is enforced within its space – for instance women wearing trousers or not covering their hair are denied access by the security staff guarding the entrance. There is a chaplaincy, a prayer room and a Kimbanguist religious service organized every morning, open to staff and patients. Kimbanguist prayer times, announced by a bell, are observed, pausing care and interventions for a few minutes, and patients throughout the day can request the assistance of a Kimbanguist pastor for spiritual support.

In the discourses of staff, while there was a widespread critique of patients who delayed urgent care 'to consult a Pentecostal pastor with the risk of worsening their condition' as one doctor put it, there was no rejection of the recourse to spiritual therapy or *tradipraticiens* (herbalists) in the name of biomedicine. That said, the use of fetishes or visits to *sorciers* and *féticheurs* (witch doctors) was disavowed outright as sinful and evil. The hospital also allows non-Kimbanguist pastors and cleric to assist patients should they request it. In that sense there is a recognition and acceptance that patients navigate a pluralized space of therapeutic possibilities. In fact, staff of both the Kimbanguist and Miséricorde hospitals stressed the necessary complementarity between spiritual and medical modes of intervention, both rejecting the therapeutic monopoly of pastors in some Pentecostal 'healing churches'.

The partnership between the state and the Kimbanguist hospital through the *convention* contract, while deemed crucial since it enables the day-to-day running of the hospital, is clearly not sufficient to address the chronic overall underinvestment in the infrastructure. The lack of state subsidies and the irregular payment of salaries to staff is made worse by the overall disengagement of the Kimbanguist church putting more emphasis and investment on the development of Nkamba, the holy city. While a particular Kimbanguist moral economy – the culture and history of self-reliance – explains the church's reluctance to solicit (at least officially and visibly to its members) external financial support and partnership, it is also clear that divisions and conflicts within the church, a history of financial malpractice as well as the existence of a rigid, centralized bureaucracy have had a negative impact on the church's attractiveness to potential donors and NGO/FBO partners (see Rich 2019). This explains for a large part why the initial support received from USAID and other government agencies, which reflected Papa Diangienda's effort to acquire legitimacy for a church undergoing formalization (and routinization), was not repeated. The Kimbanguist hospital has benefited and still benefits, however, from occasional support from the diaspora. For instance, in recent years, a London-based parish donated an ambulance, which was shipped to the DRC via container ship, and a Kimbanguist based in the United States was instrumental in obtaining medical supplies and second-hand equipment, including a CT scanner and an ultrasound machine. Despite the evident needs of the hospital for funds and equipment, the bulk of the 'sacred remittances' (Garbin 2018) – members' donations converted in development materiality – is directed to the expansion of Nkamba, reflecting the increasing importance of prophetic territorialization envisioned as an eschatology of spiritual regeneration and redemption.

Urban visions of the Kimbanguist church (2): Nkamba as holy city-yet-to-come

The urban role of Kimbanguists reflected by their iconic visibility (and audibility; see Garbin 2012) or, more importantly, perhaps, by their territorialized presence through educational or health infrastructures, cannot be separated from an aspiration to fulfil a charitable vision, but also to provide moral and spiritual solutions to acute 'developmental' challenges. In post-colonial times, Kimbanguists recast these developmental activities against the temporal backdrop of a 'community of suffering' (Werbner 2002), the horizon of an active, redeeming present, overcoming the anguishing invisibility and marginalization of the past. The trope of reversal, so central in Kimbanguist messianic theology, constructs a temporal universe of hope and prophetic expectation. This prophetic register is materialized by the collective effort to urbanize Nkamba, to turn a small rural town into a city of the future, with 'modern' and reliable water, energy and road infrastructure, with residential facilities able to accommodate pilgrims and guests in their thousands. This place-making relies on a dual mapping, firstly as a site of hierophany defined by an omnipresent telluric manifestation of the divine – finding its origin in the local birth of Kimbangu – and secondly as the divine, promised city. Nkamba is here envisioned as an ideal moral and social order, contrasted with the chaotic and sinful disorder of the earthly city – Kinshasa.

Furthermore, righteousness and exemplarity of behaviour is one of the ways through which 'conversion' to Kimbanguism is supposed to start, it is how people can be 'touched'. Similarly, the 'New Jerusalem,' now dwelling in Nkamba, is *exemplary*, crystallizing aspiration for sacredness, for a liberating future (built on an ancestral past), additionally an aspirational space for 'development' and modernization. The fact that development efforts are now concentrated on Nkamba expresses a shift of priority but not a total disengagement from Kinshasa, where Kimbanguist presence is still part of a wider socio-spatial claim, to maintain a legitimacy in terms of spiritual governance and urban citizenship. However, if Kimbanguists justify the 'recentring' of Nkamba by referring to its prophetic role, this process is also intimately connected to a major schism which occurred during the early 2000s and is driven by a conflict of leadership and succession. Access to the holy city as well as the act of contributing to its place-making through pilgrimage and work (*misala*) (including donations) have thus become the monopoly of the 'official' church, making sacred/ancestral territorialized legitimacy a crucial boundary between the latter and the 'dissident' church.

One of the most important aspects of this place-making in Nkamba is the tension between presence and absence. While this tension is to some extent related to what Engelke (2007) calls the 'problem of presence' – namely the problem of how to make an invisible God present (and thus how to materialize and make sensible the divine), it can be appropriately captured through the prism of temporality. At an experiential level, Nkamba's temporality is produced by the rhythms of daily prayers, rituals, annual festivals, pilgrimages and weekly religious services held there. This idea(l) of sacred and predictable temporality, is, again, frequently hailed as alternative to the uncertain, volatile and insecure temporality of Kinshasa – where the lives of residents unfold around truncated or absent infrastructures, anchored in an everlasting present removed from 'the teleological time-frames of the nation-state or the Pentecostal churches and the futures they propose' according to De Boeck (2013: 544). As a result, 'in these urban lives there is never a straight line between today and tomorrow, or between here and there, between possibility and the impossible, success and failure, life and death' (ibid.: 544).

For Kimbanguists, Nkamba is simultaneously present and absent, it is powerfully 'projected' to the community of believers (and ideally to the world) but still in the making, it is a sort of divine-city-yet-come. The current 'absence', that is, the non-completion, of the city is powerfully located within a wider poetics and politics of hope, integral to an aspirational mode of collective belonging. As Sarró (2015) argues, drawing upon Agamben (2005), messianism is not so much hinging on the idea of the future, rather it is the 'time that remains' that is so essential. Kimbanguists cultivate eschatological hope to endure a difficult present (in the Congo or as migrants in the diaspora) but the 'sacred waithood' linked to prophetic promises (*bilaka*) is not simply a passive act of wait-and-see *attentisme*. As Appadurai (2013: 127) points out, hope can be a 'force that converts the passive condition of "waiting for" to the active condition of "waiting to". While signs of the imminence of the realization of the prophetic promises of Kimbangu have abounded, what could be called prophetic milestones are often the product of collective work and mostly revolve around the development of the holy city built environment and infrastructure. However there are many 'blockages' in this overall development, and these are expressed by building projects getting delayed or abandoned (thus becoming 'ruins of the future', to borrow from Gupta 2018: 69), rivalries between churches/sections in charge of delivering particular projects, mismanagement of funds and so on. All these blockages are signs that evil forces are at work – and the spiritual struggle is also a race against the 'Devil who is also building his own city in the invisible world' as stated in the quote used as epigraph for this chapter. In a way, the case study of Nkamba illustrates a specific form of religious urbanization hinging on hierophanic conception of space and contrasting with Pentecostal strategies of urban appropriation and enclaving, but which also operates in great part by 'fixing' the collective labour and flows of materiality and capital. For Kimbanguist the work of urbanizing Nkamba is essential in defining and maintaining the boundaries of a moral community deployed transnationally and longing for a stable and powerful centre. The production of space to build the city of God on earth is a deeply socializing and ritualized process, which sees the space-time of the unfinished city-yet-to-come, the 'suspended city', becoming a prophetic chronotope of hope and anticipation.

Conclusion

This chapter examined how, in the context of urban Congo, religious urbanization operates as a multidimensional process occurring at different scales simultaneously, linking local (often embodied) dynamics of territorialization to aspirations for global reach. This scalar perspective encourages us to think about the wide of range of ways religion 'takes place' and 'makes place' (Knott 2005: 43), revealing how the production of religious space (or the production of space by religiously driven actors) is not solely the reflection or the iconic expression of collective beliefs and ethos. While the emergence of a new religious subject is key to tropes of reform and renewal, in particular among Pentecostals, the process of religious urbanization is more than just an 'expansion outward' of individual transformations, produced through the ripple effect of an increasingly encompassing force spreading across society. Socio-spatial scales, in this perspective, do not merely 'contain' each other – like Russian dolls – nor should they be viewed through the prism of a fixed territorial hierarchization. Scales are interdependent, often complementary, as well as dynamic and changing.

Trying to eschew a homogenizing portrayal of 'urban Christianity', the chapter discussed the existence of both a differentiated field and a range of shared dynamics. We saw in particular the ways in which ideals of moral transformation and redemption can connect individual subject-formation to wider aspirations for development and welfare. In that sense, religious urbanization is both aspirational and performative: by carving up or transforming spaces, endowing them with moralizing affordances and redemptive potential, religious actors' ambition # is to construct an alternative to the disorderly, chaotic, dysfunctional and sinful megacity. There are variations however among religious urban infrastructures (such as health or educational facilities) in particular in their degree of inclusivity, whether they engage with their immediate environments as part of a charitable/developmental mission or operate as more selective 'expansive enclaving' centres across larger urban horizons.

Moreover while these spaces, as 'alter-cities', reimagine themselves as models of social and moral order, as implicit critiques of the 'fallen city' and its pervasive 'spiritual insecurity' (De Boeck 2013), they often reproduce or connect to, each in their own way, an outside social and/or urban world whose dynamics they oppose. For instance, Nkamba while often construed as detached from its disorganized, immoral and dangerous outside is also experienced as a place of patronage and *intrigues politiques*, where intense conflicts for leadership are played out, but also where the fear of evil forces is expressed through anxiety over spiritual permeability and porosity. Nkamba, in fact, connects horizontally with a host of other places, not least to Kinshasa, but also to Kimbanguist diasporic peripheries increasingly influential within a wider sacred geography. Such disjuncture between the politics/experience of religious socio-spatiality and the 'poetics' of normative/theological accounts of territorial sacrality have been documented elsewhere, for instance by Kingsbury (2018, and in this volume) in her study of Touba, the holy city of the Murid Brotherhood, or by Osinulu (2014) in his work on the RCCG's 'Redemption Camp' which, according to him, constitutes 'a refraction of the existing social order from the nearby city (and Nigerian society more broadly) into Pentecostal Space' (ibid.: 132). In many cases, while religious urbanization and religious infrastructural developments promise to address the insecurity and syncopation of the post-colonial present, the programmatic project of renewal and hope does not constitute a challenge to entrenched uneven power-geometries (Marshall 2009).

Moreover, we want to suggest that religious actors – as 'urbanizers' – tend to put a strong emphasis on autonomy and self-sufficiency, in a context where dysfunctional/unpredictable connections to (public) infrastructural systems are part-and-parcel of everyday life in megacities like Kinshasa. Investment in alternative sources of water and power supply, for instance, is seen as a prerequisite for the production and management of enclaved religious space but also for the functioning of educational and above all health facilities to compensate for the irregular energy and water provision from the 'syncopated' and incomplete 'grid'. In fact, if they may incarnate (or aim to incarnate) the biopolitical power of a centralized authority (e.g. the state), infrastructural systems can produce hybrid assemblages of improvisations, diversions and innovations (Amin and Thrift 2017: 122), creative alternative logics of governance.

Additionally, when discussing the example of the Miséricorde hospital we noted how the question of infrastructural access and provision was linked to tension and constant friction with state agents and *fonctionnaires*. Discourses collected among urban religious actors often conjure images of the state seen as a threatening, predatory force, failing in its mission of welfare and care for populations. However, we want to suggest that even if collective practices of city-making posit moral blueprint for ideal/perfect societies – the intention here is not simply to 'replace' the state. Despite its institutional weakness and apparent 'collapse' (Reno 2006) and the fact that urban governance can appear to be socially administered through hybrid 'informal' assemblages, the state is still a powerful performative and 'referential system' in the Congolese context (Perazzone 2018). In order to locate the place and role of religious actors within a wider system of urban (micro)governance there is thus a need to recognize that religious forms of urbanization can exist 'as well as' or 'through' secular, state/public or commercially driven urban forms, even if on the ground, these distinctions are often blurred.

Chapter 4

THE ASPIRATION TO TRANSFORM: PENTECOSTALISM AND URBAN CITIZENSHIP IN CAPE TOWN

Marian Burchardt

Introduction

In this chapter, I explore how Pentecostal Christians seek to transform urban spaces in the South African city of Cape Town by engaging with what they consider social evils and ills. In particular, I examine Pentecostal efforts in fostering new forms of urban citizenship through the founding of faith-based organizations (FBOs) dedicated to the struggle against HIV and AIDS. Especially in the context of the donor-driven promotion of religious involvements in HIV/AIDS programmes, South Africa has witnessed the emergence of this new kind of FBO: a voluntary non-profit organization, based on the principles of a particular religious tradition, working towards collective goods, embedded in civil society and modelled along the lines of its secular sibling, the NGO.[1] This is the cultural meaning the acronym 'FBO' came to acquire in local civil society discourse and that I refer to when using the notion of FBOs in this chapter.

Like other parts of Africa, and in fact most parts of the world with a long-standing presence of Christianity, South Africa has a long history of Christian charitable activity in fields such as education and health. These activities were institutionalized through mission schools and hospitals and were central components of early missionary Christianity and its efforts in evangelization and the cultivation of modern, 'civilized' subjects (Comaroff and Comaroff 1997). In recent history, the intricate intertwinements of charitable practice and evangelizing crusades have made a forceful return in the area of Pentecostal and Charismatic Christianity.[2] It is particularly here that links between charitable practice and evangelism were conjoined with concepts of formal organization and institutionalized through the notion of FBOs.

Initially, however, the majority of FBOs operating in the townships of South Africa's urban agglomerations grew out of mainline churches such as the Anglican, Methodist, Presbyterian and Roman Catholic Churches.[3] As a consequence of their long-standing charitable traditions, they already had comparatively complex institutional infrastructures that could serve as vantage points for the formation of

FBOs. What was rather surprising were the ways in which Pentecostal Christianity made its appearance in the lives and in the cultural imagination of diverse social groups as a provider of social services and agent of development. Most of these Pentecostal FBOs that have risen in number in the past twenty years are dedicated to issues of development, service delivery and humanitarian assistance and engage in activities such as assistance for orphans, health education, income-generating projects and especially programmes related to HIV/AIDS.

This begs important questions as to how Pentecostals imagine urban spaces and seek to transform them in line with their religious visions. Thus far, most research on Pentecostalism and urban transformation has focused on the ways in which Pentecostals construe urban spaces as terrains with particular spiritual valences (Marshall 2009; Meyer 1999). As such, urban spaces harbour evil forces that manifest in social ills such as violence, crime and poverty but also the promise of leading a 'good life' even as urban environments appear as precarious and tension-laden. In fact, Pentecostal notions of 'good life' seem to constantly run up against a range of adversities that are part of the urban worlds they inhabit. Perceiving urban worlds as terrains in which evil forces and spirits bring disarray into social relationships and keep residents entrapped in states of spiritual darkness and illness, Pentecostals are driven by the impulse to transform urban spaces; an impulse directly corresponds to their missionary zeal to 'save souls' (see Dilger, Burchardt and van Dijk 2010) and augment the presence of the Holy Spirit.

What has been explored to a much lesser extent is how Pentecostals have begun to enter the cultural worlds of urban civil society in a twin effort to pursue their theological goals and create new forms of urban citizenship. If by citizenship we mean the bundle of claims to participation people make in a given polity as well as their capacities to enforce such claims, then Pentecostals have indeed become central to urban citizenship in post-apartheid South Africa. The notion of urban religious aspirations (Burchardt and Westendorp 2018; van der Veer 2013) appears as particularly apt to capture the ideational elements and practices on which such claims to urban citizenship are founded.

As I show in this chapter, cultivating such aspirations by engaging with notions of social support, development and urban transformation, FBOs have moved beyond the established confines of congregational life. My argument is the following: Pentecostal engagements in development engender complex connections between two distinct processes. On the one hand, they offer to Pentecostal communities new social spaces for expressing their faith and for promoting their moral agendas. On the other hand, development work urges Pentecostal communities to recast their activities in the logic of formal organization and accountability (proposals-grants-projects). On the ground, however, these logics are subverted as beneficiaries construe FBOs as *patrons* and deploy Pentecostal identities and practices for mediating access to FBOs and the resources they command. As a result, Pentecostal transformations of the city are grafted on relationships of power that characterize NGO-driven patronage. At the same time, Pentecostal belonging becomes a new idiom through which these power relationships are articulated.

Furthermore, critical scholarship has shown how the 'NGOization' of development has been an effect of neoliberalism that has often served to depoliticize concerns over social inequalities and global social and economic disparities by transforming them into questions of a technical fix (Choudry and Kapoor 2013; Ferguson 1990). The focus on Pentecostals offers a fresh perspective in this regard as it points towards the ways in which NGOization not only depoliticizes development but also turns it into a question of morality.

Taking these dynamics into account, the chapter examines how Pentecostal urban aspirations play out in the field of engagements with health and illness, in particular HIV and AIDS. It also shows how in contemporary Cape Town the incursions of Pentecostals into urban civil society drive processes of religious urbanization in which religious belonging and membership facilitates access to resources and configures urban hierarchies and forms of stratification. Before addressing these moral economies of urban religious citizenship, I will first describe how the concept of urban religious aspirations can be useful for analyzing the dynamics around FBOs and urban transformations.

Urban aspirations in the segregated city: Transforming urban spaces in Cape Town

Few other cities in the world appear as polarized as Cape Town whose urban spaces continue to be fundamentally marked by the legacies of colonial rule and the racist segregation policies of the apartheid system. Even as apartheid legally came to an end in 1994, people in the formerly white suburbs and residents of the non-white townships and informal settlements live worlds apart (Besteman 2008; Geyer and Mohammed 2016). At the same time, they are integrated into a hierarchically structured urban economy in which different racial and ethnic groups interact on a routine, usually daily basis but where extremely unequal social positions mark most social encounters.

Wealth, capital, employment opportunities and tourism are concentrated in the affluent suburbs and the city bowl, and only townships' residents with jobs in these parts of the city have reason to go there while for the unemployed majority these urban spaces remain distant and elusive.

By contrast, for most residents, life in the townships is marked by poverty, lack of basic infrastructure and some of the highest crime levels in the world. In a context of sluggish economic, typically jobless most residents depend – directly, or indirectly through kin relations – on welfare grants whose implementation has paralleled the neoliberal restructuring of South Africa's economy since the late 1990s (Ferguson 2015) or make a living out of petty jobs in retail or other parts of the informal economy. If historically apartheid laws, especially the so-called Group Areas Act passed in 1951, were confined to the non-whites in these 'territories of relegation' (Wacquant 2016), it is now poverty that entraps them in the townships.

Importantly, the lifting of the apartheid pass laws, which restricted the mobility of non-whites inside South Africa to labour considered necessary to sustain white urban economies, in the mid-1980s propelled massive migration movements from impoverished provinces, especially the Eastern Cape and former homeland of Transkei, into Cape Town. These movements came along with new forms of urban sprawl and the establishment of informal settlements. Made up of shacks, typically built of corrugated iron, wood and plastic, these are essentially unplanned zones of auto-construction (Caldeira 2017; Holston 1991). While, given the lack of basic infrastructure such as water and electricity provision as well as roads, informal settlements are zones of far-reaching urban exclusion, they also gesture towards migrants' creativity and ingenuity in the making of urban lives and spaces (Simone 2004). This duality of urban experience, oscillating as it does between anger over one's entrapment and hopefulness, is epitomized in perceptions of street life: while, as a site of crime, violence and drug trade, the street is a zone of concentrated urban risks, it is also the sphere of sociality, leisure, pleasure and erotic encounter (Burchardt 2013).

Khayelitsha, where I carried out most of my field research, is growing very dynamically and has an estimated population of more than 2.4 million residents.[4] Roughly 75 per cent of the residents live in informal settlements and 24 per cent have no access to electricity. Unemployment is officially at 47 per cent, though it even reaches 70 per cent in some neighbourhoods and 19 per cent of households are registered as having no income at all (Burchardt 2015: 1–2). Because of the close associations of HIV risk and poverty, it is not surprising that Khayelitsha still is the district with the highest HIV infection rate in the Western Cape province[5] and a place where material resources to confront the disease were especially scarce. Significantly, the spatial restrictions that have come with the Covid-19 pandemic have compounded the problems of poor township dwellers.

Since around 2000, residents of informal settlements and township have begun to mobilize against the multiple forms of infrastructural exclusion to which they are subjected. Popularly known as 'service delivery protests', these mobilizations have centred on the lack of running water and toilets, resulting in Cape Town's 'poo wars' (Robins 2014), and rejected the introduction of water meters and neoliberal pre-payment systems (von Schnitzler 2008). Some of these protests were driven by competitive party politics, while others were spontaneous grassroots actions. To a fair degree, however, they were also nourished by a lively landscape of NGOs and other civil society organizations that had started to address social problems and issues of local development during the same period. Significantly, many of these social movement organizations and NGOs had emerged as spearheads of the fight against HIV and AIDS. Ranging from small groups of mutual support to donor-driven NGOs, these organizations have politicized infrastructural exclusion, fashioned collective claims on urban citizenship and developed new imaginations of urban space and urban transformation.

While Christian mission churches played some role in these mobilizations, Pentecostals were, for a long time, seen as peripheral to them. This marginality is owed to the fact that while Pentecostals converged with secular groups on the diagnosis of the social ills (crime, poverty and disease) befalling Cape Town's townships, they often identified different causes and proposed different remedies. Chiefly, in line with their Manichean world view, Pentecostals perceive urban spaces in dualistic terms of evil versus saved spaces (Marshall-Fratini 1998: 309). In this context, evil emerges through practices of witchcraft, in other words, illicit ways of marshalling malignant forces in an effort to cause misfortune. Through place-protective practices such as prayer and blessings, Pentecostals counter such efforts and craft moral geographies made up of 'good' and 'saved' places, as networks of places with particular, spiritually anchored phenomenological qualities.

While engagement with the spiritual forces is certainly a dominant way in which Pentecostals perceive and imagine to transform urban spaces, it has rarely been noticed how they have become part of urban civil society, especially in the context of the struggle against HIV and AIDS. Such practices matter because they tie residents into networks of affective sociality. As Pieterse (2011: 18) highlighted 'the importance of reading the affective functions of popular practices, because it is only through the redeployment of such registers that one can begin to fathom what is going on in the real city'. Importantly, the practices that give rise to FBOs entwine the immaterial with the material. Drawing on anthropologists Arjun Appadurai (2004) and Peter van der Veer (2015), I construe these immaterial dimensions in the notion of 'urban religious aspirations', by which I mean the multiple ideational sources – including values, motivations, imaginings and spiritualities – that underpin people's religious investments in urban life.

Urban religious aspirations are not necessarily part of, or inspired by, a politics of (ethno-) religious belonging or identity. Rather, they engage with valued goals and express the desire to become a certain kind of religious subject crystallizing around an ethics of personhood (Hirschkind 2006; Mahmood 2011). Furthermore, urban religious aspirations are not fixed to particular urban spaces or, by definition, territorially circumscribed, though the practices they inspire can be localized. Instead, they engage with urban spaces as elements that make it possible to achieve certain goals. Neither are urban religious aspirations material, though the practices they animate certainly co-produce urban materialities; this, in turn, shapes them, in a recursive pattern.

Peter van der Veer (2015: 4) sees the usefulness of the notion of urban aspirations in its ability 'to get away from the static connotations of the concept of "identity" that tends to fix people to what and where they are rather than to what and where they aspire to be'. Following Arjun Appadurai (2004: 68), I regard these aspirations as cultural capacities, oriented towards the future, related to wants, preferences, choices and calculations. In line with these suggestions, I employ the idea of urban aspirations to explore Pentecostal efforts to create new organizational practices at the interface of civil society and religious belief and belonging. While the debate on aspirations has thus focused on economic aspects, little is known about how urban aspirations are fuelled by religious sources and values. I now trace the emergence of Pentecostal faith-based organizations as well as the kinds of urban aspirations and popular practices that gave rise to them.

The emergence of Pentecostal FBOs: Engaging organizational templates

Within the narratives of leading members of Pentecostal FBOs, the emergence of these organizations is often framed through a foundational myth. Mobilizing specific Pentecostal idioms, these myths centre on the creation of awareness of the needs of poor communities. In order to illustrate this issue, I begin with the case of the organization 'Living Hope Community Centre' (LHCC). The organization was founded in 2000, has more than a hundred employees, is multidenominational and strongly Pentecostal in its ideological orientation. It mainly operates in Cape Town's southern suburbs and townships such as Ocean View and Masiphumelele while their clients also comprise destitute whites. The organization offers healthcare services, provides education and training, runs food gardens and various other livelihood-sustaining programmes and has even made its way into public schools where LHCC's educators take over life-skills courses, which are part of official curricula. Institutional capacities expanded tremendously when LHCC managed to attract funds from the American President's Emergency Plan for AIDS Relief (PEPFAR) initiative for the implementation of HIV prevention programmes in 2005. In an interview, Doris, a white woman of Zimbabwean origin and one of the programme managers, explained:

> It was back in 2000 that we started working with HIV. At the time, I was working in a Christian radio station. But it was like God said to me, 'Doris, how can you be part of a radio station telling people about Jesus and what are you doing with the homeless people you see everyday?' And so I started a soup kitchen.[6]

Most of the other employees and volunteers of LHCC, and in fact of many other Pentecostal FBOs I worked with, provided remarkably similar narratives when talking about the founding of their organizations and their motivation to work for them. What was typical for Pentecostals, and strongly distinguished their accounts from those of FBO workers affiliated to the mainline churches I studied, was the conviction that working for 'the poor and the needy' offered a supreme way for sharing the gospel.[7] 'Telling them about Jesus' was often presented as overriding any concern with social problems, poverty and disease reflecting the fact that for them spiritual salvation precedes material salvation. In the eyes of Pentecostal FBO workers and in an astonishing contradistinction to the discursive logic of the prosperity gospel (Marshall 2009), health and material salvation were derivative to and only enabled by, but not coextensive with, spiritual salvation.

While these accounts help to shed light on the aspirations of people to found FBOs and to start working for them (Bornstein 2002), they have little to offer when it comes to explaining how FBO operations are put on a more sustained basis and become stabilized. In order to address this question it is helpful to remember how HIV/AIDS interventions have been spread across vast institutional fields comprising highly diverse sorts of organizations and to explore how the idea of Pentecostal FBOs has been diffused in such processes. With regard to organizational diffusion, De Waal (2003: 254) has argued that:

There is an un-theorized consensus on what an HIV/AIDS program should look like: it should be founded on voluntary counselling and testing, education (preferably by peers), provision of condoms, efforts to overcome denial, stigma and discrimination, and care and treatment for people living with HIV and AIDS ... Even when undertaken by a government ministry, army or private company, it is essentially an NGO model of public action.

The power this 'un-theorized consensus' has clearly extended into the Pentecostal domain while the institutional mechanism through which it unfolds is remarkably standardized. Outside of already existing FBOs, responses to HIV/AIDS by church congregations often depend on the enthusiasm of pioneering individuals who mobilize others. As church-based projects grow in size and demand for their services increases, there is a need to mobilize resources exceeding what is locally available. In order to improve the management of their operations and to qualify for funding from donors, church-based projects invariably assume a formalized structure, step by step morphing into FBOs. In the process, FBOs get involved in the highly standardized procedures of proposal writing, grant application, project management and financial reporting. These organizational changes are paralleled by the adoption of the rhetoric and buzzwords of secular development discourses.

The development of LHCC is a striking example of this. Already during the 1990s Pastor John, the founder of the centre, began to mobilize local communities around HIV/AIDS and other social problems through 'social ministries' and organized a group of permanent volunteers. Importantly, this activism was linked to the emergence of Masiphumelele, first as a squatter camp, and later a township, far removed from black residential areas. Pentecostal social ministries added an element of religious urbanization to this process. In 2000, LHCC was founded as a formal entity since, as they acknowledge in a report, 'as their efforts grew, the need for a centre, separate from the church, became urgent'.[8] During the same year, they purchased a piece of land for the centre and vegetable gardens with the help of a generous donation from an American coreligionist. With regard to taxation, both ownership of the plot and the management of activities could have been organized through the church or an FBO. But after all, with a view towards future growth they opted for the FBO strategy and founded the 'Fishhoek Baptist Church Community Trust'. As donations and funding grew, one ministry after the other was added ('Living Grace' for food support, 'Living Care' for women's health, 'Living Right' for HIV prevention and Christian lifestyle and 'Living Way' for income generation), while the PEPFAR funds granted in 2005 marked a sea change in organizational growth.

This organizational expansion came along with new forms of Pentecostals' spatial presence in the city. Creating offices, participating in municipal civil society councils, engaging in door-to-door campaigns or providing counselling and other social services in the premises of other organizations, Pentecostals reinvented themselves as urban actors outside a purely religious domain. At the same time, when reflecting on their activities even volunteers from very small and strictly local Pentecostal neighbourhood initiatives spoke the language of 'capacity building', 'social capital formation' and 'community outreach' as activists were highly aware that the public use of these categories provides for maximum match with those high on the agendas of possible donors.[9]

This process of diffusion is not limited to organizational models and the discourses surrounding them but extends itself into the areas of activities Pentecostal FBOs are engaged in. In all of the organizations I studied HIV/AIDS projects were highly 'canonised'. This would typically include self-help or support groups, anti-stigma and education campaigns, psychological counselling for HIV-positive people, home-based care schemes and sometimes the construction of HIV-testing facilities but also soup kitchens, other feeding schemes, income-generating activities such as bead-making and even training for 'destitute parents' on how to raise their children.[10] Clearly, many HIV-positive people are also poor and readily positioned as 'in need' of any kind of assistance. At the same time, such categorizations point towards the rise of a particular urban bureaucratic assemblage; an assemblage that donor-driven bureaucratic languages with material infrastructures of support which Pentecostals turned into project leaders and clients. And yet, this somehow peculiar assemblage of activities raises an intriguing question: what is the logic that leads FBO workers to understand soup kitchens and so on as HIV/AIDS projects?

The logic of projects

In general, it is clear that the availability and the massive increase of funds for the fight against HIV/AIDS have provided huge incentives for FBOs to frame all sorts of charitable activities as HIV/AIDS projects. As donors put maximum emphasis on reaching certain programme targets, collaborating with particularly motivated communities is extremely important for them in terms of expected project performance. As a consequence, in order to improve their terms of eligibility for funding, FBOs need to show that their communities are mobilized, volunteers motivated and basic urban infrastructures established (Swidler and Watkins 2009). FBOs are thus not only urged to consider and present their activities as related to HIV/AIDS but also to conceive of and fashion whatever they have already been doing before in the area of charity, as *projects*. As the 'project' is the fundamental unit of operations within the institutional field of development, every activity that can be translated into a project is likely to enhance to the image of an FBO in the eyes of donors as particularly professional and as a valuable partner.

Another example further serves to illustrate this point: in 2006, a drama group made up of church youth of a US-American evangelical congregation visited Cape Town to perform a play around issues of HIV/AIDS in schools and various churches. The group had been invited by LHCC while the contact to the group's home congregation had been established during one of the many fundraising trips of LHCC leaders to the United States. The underlying idea was that youth groups in the communities in which LHCC operates should be inspired to form drama groups themselves and to adapt the plot so as to fit their own social and cultural context. It was clear that for this to materialize further funding would be necessary, and LHCC came to provide the institutional umbrella within which the HIV/AIDS drama groups could be organized – *as another project*. The driving force behind this process was that LHCC had the organizational structure, knowledge and networks that allowed it to transform an evangelically inspired HIV/AIDS drama into a sustained activity that would be eligible for funding. To this end, however, it had to be on HIV/AIDS, it had to be a project and it had to be organized through an FBO.[11]

What is often much less obvious is that the vast array of activities that FBOs clamp together in the category of 'HIV/AIDS projects' also serves to provide greater space to manoeuvre between the funding priorities of donors and what FBOs construe as 'people's needs', for themselves and in front of local audiences. In this context, the following remark made by Doris from LHCC is instructive:

> Within the first four months [after the founding of the soup kitchen], four of the people that were homeless and live in the streets, died. And I was starting to learn about HIV. I realised that three of them were probably HIV-positive. And so I was sort of flung straight into having to face HIV face to face. And so that has resulted in this centre, working together with the homeless and the unemployed because they are a high-risk group for HIV.

LHCC employees knew of course through their day-to-day experiences that, most of all, the homeless needed homes and the jobless jobs while what they could offer were HIV/AIDS projects. Stories like this, however, and the way they attach different meanings to projects make it possible for FBOs to justify assistance for the homeless as HIV interventions (even though the homeless may only figure in the reports submitted to the PEPFAR head offices in Pretoria as 'people reached' or 'people trained').[12]

Similarly, there was a series of different meanings attached to the youth drama groups and their incorporation into LHCC's operations. While for some of LHCC's members it was really about supporting creative approaches towards HIV prevention, combining, as it did, drama with messages about sexual abstinence and 'Christian lifestyles', the message spread amongst parents was sometimes that drama keeps youth away from mischief and involvement in crime and gang activities. There was a clear recognition that fear of crime was of much greater concern for many people in the community than HIV/AIDS. For others, in turn, the drama group was most of all an important opportunity to proselytize amongst the participants and to bind them more closely to the organization.

These alternative meanings, however, such as manifest in the quote above also open pathways for FBOs to establish contacts and work with clients who may not be interested in participating in HIV/AIDS projects at all – and vice versa. FBO workers are generally aware of the fact that in Cape Town, which has been virtually flooded with HIV/AIDS projects during the past decade, many people are not particularly interested or even turn their backs when they are targeted as participants in HIV/AIDS campaigns. The consequences of this dynamic were particularly salient for the educators of Think Twice, a small FBO that offers life skills courses organized around issues of HIV prevention and sexual responsibility to students in public schools and so-called personal growth groups. These groups are made up of teenagers, where they discuss similar issues in greater depth.[13] Think Twice has seven employees and close organizational ties to the 'Jubilee' Pentecostal Church, which is globally active.[14] Donations to the programmes mainly come from the UK. The head offices are in Lower Wynberg and employees and volunteers work by visiting schools in different townships but also the city bowl. Educators told me that because of this oversaturation effect they rarely address issues of HIV/AIDS head-on (see also Levine and Ross 2002). They rather talk about 'the gift of love and sexuality', about responsible relationships and the value of limiting sexuality to the confines of monogamous heterosexual marriage. Again, what was an 'HIV/AIDS project' in the administrative record had entirely different meanings for Pentecostal FBO workers and project participants.

Possible clients may thus shy away when being targeted as participants of HIV/AIDS campaigns – unless their participation helps them to establish some sort of relationship of reciprocity within which FBOs work as *patrons*; in other words: they may use their relationships to FBOs in order to mobilize affective ties and to deploy their personal dependence with a view to achieving some external goal. No example is better suited to elucidate this process than the notorious training workshops (see Smith 2003; Swidler and Watkins 2009). In summer 2006, I participated in a 'health and nutrition workshop' that was organized in an LHCC community hall. About thirty visibly poor people from the local neighbourhood had gathered when Thembisa, an HIV-positive woman and community worker for LHCC, began her talk. The workshop lasted for about an hour and covered topics such as prevention of tuberculosis and HIV, personal hygiene and issues regarding the nutritional values of food products, cooking, the importance of regularity in eating habits and so on. Importantly, it was framed through collective prayers at the beginning and the end. In order to introduce participatory elements Thembisa tried to stimulate a discussion but the only people who asked questions were LHCC volunteers that were present. Other participants showed few signs of interest in the topic and some actually slept. After all, it was clear that many had come because of the sandwiches that were offered after the workshop had finished. During subsequent conversations I also learnt that many of the participants were 'clients' who regularly participate in LHCC projects of all kinds. The important point is therefore not that clients came to 'feed their bellies' but rather that the workshop served to reproduce 'ties of dependence' through relationships of patronage. This in turn raises a broader set of questions as to the diverse benefits of participating in FBO programmes and to the dynamic network of social positions in which they are generated, and how access to these benefits is entangled with the specificities of Pentecostal Christianity.

The above observations convey a powerful sense of the ways in which Pentecostal FBOs have adapted themselves to the technocratic and official templates governing development work across the world. Local Pentecostal organizations are moulded into the models of action promoted by the dominant discourse on civil society and its main protagonist, the NGO. Simultaneously, they incorporate the same mechanisms of patronage into their operations that link people, opportunities and resources in NGOs. These structural dynamics alone, however, are insufficient to explain the operations of Pentecostal FBOs since they fail to take into account how the specificities of Pentecostal discourse and identity shape the meanings, discourses, images and practices around which Pentecostal FBO work is organized.

Pentecostal identity and discourse affect the organizational dynamics of Pentecostal FBOs in two distinct ways: first by shaping the *self-understanding* of FBO workers and their cultural constructions of work; and second by shaping their *practices*, internally as well as in relationships to their clients and beneficiaries. In the following section, I show how both the construction of self-understanding and practices are interlocked processes but also how the connections between the two are mediated through the nature of their field of intervention, in the given case: HIV/AIDS.

Pentecostal idioms at work

One way in which Pentecostal discourse shapes FBO operations is by providing scripted idioms whereby FBO work acquires specific meanings for employees and volunteers. At once these idioms are the forms in which these meanings can be expressed. An important element here is the notion of a *personal dialogue with God*. Pentecostals often spoke about all kinds of solutions for problems they encounter in their day-to-day work practices in terms of God's advices on how to handle certain situations and especially on how to spread the word so that they may help others. In conversations with colleagues and interviews, some FBO workers openly addressed the difficulties they faced, for example, when working with prostitutes or criminals. Dialoguing with God was the specific linguistic form through which thinking about these problems was expressed.

Often these dialogues took shape through *prayers*. Prayers are of course a fundamental and ubiquitous element in religious life. But the way the *efficacy* of prayers is understood in Pentecostal FBO work is very different from that in mainline Christianity. Consider the case of Sarah, for instance, a forty-three-year-old woman who volunteers as a lay counsellor for Izandla Zethemba.[15] This FBO is based in the township of Gugulethu and linked to the Pentecostal church Khanyisa (literally meaning *church* in Xhosa), which is itself a product of Jubilee's efforts of 'church-planting'. In one meeting she recounted how she visited a bedridden AIDS patient to assist and feed him:

> I went there and I gave him his plate and I said 'you must eat!' and it was so amazing that he ate. Before, he couldn't eat ... Then I watched him eating and he ate all the plate and I was so joyful. I went to my colleagues and said, 'he ate a whole plate!' I am so glad, God answered my prayers!

Just after this remark I asked whether this patient was on treatment and she confirmed that he had just begun his antiretroviral (ARV) therapy. Importantly, Sarah did not view biomedicine and prayers as mutually exclusive therapeutic strategies. In general, Pentecostals closely associated the success of their daily work with the transformative power of the prayers, which invariably preceded all activities.[16]

A second important element within Pentecostal discourse is a certain way of reconstructing their activities and motivations in the notion of 'calling'. This is true for both employees and volunteers and was typically expressed in phrases such as 'God had a special plan for me' or 'God needed me'. Again the case of Sarah from Izandla Zethemba is instructive in this regard. In a biographical interview I conducted with her she explained that before beginning to work as a counsellor her life was marked by all sorts of failures and frustrations. She remembered that initially because she was 'shy and couldn't speak' she had been scared of being a counsellor:

> I said I can't speak. First I was like Moses, when God wanted to use Moses and Moses said 'I'm slow with speech, take my brother Aaron' … So I told them I was like Moses. But God said 'Go! I'm going to put words into your mouth!' I couldn't speak. But with God's grace and God's work I can do it. I am doing it!

Here, the idea of a calling is constructed through a direct analogy between her sudden personal faculties and a biblical sequence. While FBO workers deploy the notions of calling usually in an individualized manner as a way of accounting for their motivations and engagements, in other cases such as manifest in the above quote by Doris from LHCC the calling is even taken to interpret the existence of the organization itself.

Both *calling* and *personal dialogue with God* are closely associated with a third concept, that of *God's plan*. For FBO workers, hearing and following God's call means to help to fulfil his plan for them, namely to serve the people by spreading his word. In connection to the calling, again this plan is understood in a highly personalized and individualized manner. In the context of the interpretation of FBO work, however, the notion of God's plan acquires a much broader meaning in that the Pentecostals equate their efforts in working with clients with making *their lives* cohere with that plan as well. The personal dialogue with God, asking questions and receiving answers, then, is important as a way of knowing and constantly proving that what they do really conforms to that plan.

In some cases, the calling coincides with the beginning of the conversion to Pentecostal Christianity. That is, the moment of hearing and following the call initiates a process whereby people convert to Pentecostalism and *simultaneously* to FBO work. In these cases, FBO work and its multifarious mixtures of practical assistance and evangelism are rendered the primary field in which followers enact their newly acquired faith in an often dramatic and highly committed fashion. In other cases, people have already been Pentecostals without having received the call to FBO work. Dialogues with God, prayers and testimonies of callings enable

Pentecostals, as Engelke (2007: 178) put it, to inhabit a Christian language that would bind speakers and listeners in shared hermeneutic webs. Importantly, these webs in turn facilitate the workings of Pentecostal FBOs *as organizations*.

All this implies, of course, that being a Pentecostal is intimately associated with one's position in the concentric structures of FBOs involving leadership, employees, volunteers, clients and other beneficiaries. In order to become an employee of a Pentecostal FBO one is generally expected to be a Pentecostal. Pentecostal belonging though is constituted and socially recognized in complex ways. Being a Pentecostal involves having accepted Jesus Christ as a personal saviour through an individual religious experience and having undergone a process of conversion and concomitant personal transformation in which this acceptance is understood to be embedded. As with Pentecostals elsewhere in the world (Robbins 2004), the entirety of these experiences and ritualized constructions are brought together and discursively represented in the notion of 'being born again'. In general, Pentecostal FBO workers were able to give rhetorically elaborated and emotionally charged accounts of their own experiences of becoming a Pentecostal. Often such accounts were narrated in public testimonies, that is, staged performances of authenticity in which biographical storytelling is used to intensify collective religious experiences. In some sense, these accounts were themselves important discursive elements in Pentecostal FBO culture in that they helped to remind people who they were – first and foremost – and to reproduce the sense of calling that shapes 'Pentecostalism at work'.

Pentecostal discourse and identity, however, not only affect organizational dynamics by providing the cultural meanings that sustain self-understanding and FBO culture; they also shape FBO *practices* in two important ways: first, in relation to internal dynamics; and second with regard to work practices at the interface with clients.

The concentric hierarchical networks through which FBO work is organized are closely linked to the ways of being Pentecostal and the maturity one is perceived to have acquired in religious terms. In the organization Think Twice, for instance, it was clear that all employees were Pentecostals. What is more, all of the educators I interviewed had completed a full year of volunteering in a Pentecostal Church with Jubilee. This voluntary work included assistance with maintaining the church premises, charitable activities as well as participation in evangelistic crusades. It seemed evident that only after completing this voluntary engagement they would be eligible as Think Twice employees even though this was not stated in straightforward terms. We may say with some confidence, however, that in FBO work Pentecostal faith operates by mediating the entire set of relationships, interactions, practices and expectations that structures the field of Pentecostal development. In other words, it is less belief than *Pentecostal belonging* that links people and opportunities in collective action.

Conversely, some volunteers also explained that sustained contact with these organizations provided the contexts in which later conversions took place. Both volunteers and employees in turn often showed great satisfaction if clients or beneficiaries converted and joined affiliated churches such as Khanyisa or Jubilee as a result of their relationships to FBOs such as Izandla Zethemba. Therefore, membership in a Pentecostal church and the display of Pentecostal identity through certain forms of speech and religious practice are extremely important when it comes to explaining organizational dynamics and the ways in which patronage works in the Pentecostal domain.

The possibility of converting people is of course central to the ways Pentecostal discourse shapes FBO operations at the interface with clients and beneficiaries. Pentecostals are very much driven by evangelistic zeal and the desire to promote their faith. In fact, through FBO operations Pentecostals' religious urbanization draws together two distinct urban imaginaries: urban civil society that makes claims on service delivery in the name of citizenship, and urban Pentecostalism that advances claims on territories of salvation in the name of Jesus. Evangelizing through offering mundane social services, Pentecostal FBOs stitched the township streets, community centres and backyards together into a spiritual geography made up of places in need of services – and of redemption.

Yet this evangelism works often less on the surface level of proselytizing than through the specific symbolic concepts they deploy. In conversations with groups of clients, regardless of whether they were HIV-positive people, drug-users or people with a criminal record, Pentecostals typically described people's life circumstances in terms of 'individual choices' and 'decisions'. Betty, one of LHCC's counsellors for instance, remarked: 'I always tell them [her clients], you can choose to get into mischief or drug or you can choose to have a good life!' Similarly, Jenny who works as a life skills educator for Think Twice mentioned when talking about her work experiences with high school students: 'I tell them "Think about what I said but in the end your life is in your hands. It is your choices and your decisions. It's you!"' While the rhetoric of responsible choices has diverse genealogies in behavioural pedagogy, in Evangelical theology it acquires a very distinct meaning in Pentecostal FBO work. Here, it serves to incite people to reconsider and scrutinize their lives on the same dramatic and emotionally charged terms that are also understood to animate people to make a choice for God (see also Maxwell 2006). In other words: conversations with clients are largely understood in structural *analogy* to the notion of conversion. The Pentecostal idea of 'breaking with the past' (Meyer 1999) is thus transposed into the registers of earthly social existence and personal progress.

Likewise, the improvements in life that are envisioned to result from FBO interventions are construed as effects of conversions to a life according to God's plan. Pentecostal FBO workers thus consider themselves as *missionaries*; they see development work as a frontier project, the township as the shifting terrain to be conquered and its inhabitants as the souls to be saved. Pentecostal FBO workers and pastors often pride themselves to be amongst the first to serve new informal settlements that have emerged through multiple waves of migration from impoverished rural areas and the continuous urban sprawl they have spawned across the Cape Flats. And they routinely describe their mission in these areas as demanded by the Holy Spirit who had called them to these urban frontier zones to fight against poverty and evil spirits, and to thereby empower the new residents.

Religious urbanization thus extends along the pathways of urban marginality in ways that turn these urban margins into centres of evangelism.

If in this sense Pentecostal FBO work can be regarded as conversionism writ large this does certainly not imply that beneficiaries readily perceive it on the same terms. It appears problematic to me to argue, as Bornstein (2005) does, that in faith-based development religious faith works through 'lifestyle evangelism' as such arguments largely ignore whether these activities have religious impact on beneficiaries or not. It rather seems that the main effect of Pentecostal discourse is to enjoin upon their beneficiaries certain vocabularies of behavioural change; vocabularies whose deployment mimics the dramatic enactments of Pentecostal faith but in the first place signifies 'conversions to personal progress'. Contrary to Bornstein, I also contend that the concrete field of work does make a difference to the ways Pentecostal discourse may shape it.[17] It was, for instance, very obvious that despite many difficulties Pentecostal FBO workers appreciated engaging with HIV prevention since sexuality was high on their moral agenda. Furthermore, Pentecostal FBOs were particularly eager to do counselling as it was through counselling that they could build the kind of personal relationships in which the Pentecostal psychologizing rhetoric of 'personal change' was expected to bear fruits.

The clear distinction between the impact of Pentecostal discourse on internal processes and on relationships with beneficiaries breaks down in the moment one acknowledges the multiple ways in which clients may become volunteers, volunteers turn into employees and begin professional careers in the field of FBOs. The best illustrations of Pentecostal patronage in FBO work are the cases of HIV-positive people becoming full-time employees of FBOs on the basis of a personal conversion.

Importantly, from the point of view of clients, dividing Pentecostal patronage into material and authentically religious motivations and resources may constitute an artificial dichotomy. Thembisa, for instance, the LHCC worker mentioned above, came in contact with the organization in the context of a Pentecostal 'crusade' a year after being diagnosed HIV-positive during the antenatal exams that were related to her second pregnancy. At the time, she was already enrolled in an HIV/AIDS support group and had some income through her work as social worker in an orphanage. However, later she was laid off and through the crusade became a client of LHCC programmes where the staff quickly saw her commitment to personal improvement. In an act of radically breaking with the past, she converted to Pentecostalism, left her partner, quit her biomedical treatment and was 'born again', in her view, without HIV:

> Doctors are not God, they just give you result of scientific exam but that's a lie. They tell you, you are gonna die. But you are still alive. They are not God. So why should I bother? They just use their machines. You never know, today CD4-count is low, maybe tomorrow it is up again. I was well treated but it is my understanding. You don't know what God is doing overnight. HIV doesn't exist in my blood that is what I believe.

Importantly this is *not* to suggest that such conversions were purely instrumental or opportunistic but rather that Pentecostal development work constitutes the assemblage of spiritual and material opportunities in the context of which they 'made sense'. For clients such as Thembisa, material and spiritual resources converge in an overall idea conversion to personal progress and autonomy. For her, this even implies that she should be able to live without ARVs.

Thembisa's trajectory is certainly a typical one but must be contrasted with that of many clients who do not have the cultural, religious and material resources to engage with LHCC on the same terms. These clients certainly welcomed LHCC programmes but the Pentecostal discourse on self-activation and self-improvement remained opaque to them. They demonstrated the kind of religious commitment to LHCC Christian principles but mainly with a view towards securing continued admittance. Alcoholics and substance users, for instance, would refrain from drug consumption at the premises of the centre but continue outside. Likewise, clients would live as unmarried couples outside the premises but not show their intimate relationships while participating in programmes. They would participate in prayers in earnest but rarely initiate spontaneous prayers themselves. In conversations outside the premises, they also sometimes voiced misgivings about the 'holiness' of LHCC workers.

In an important article, Richey (2012: 829) has demonstrated how participation in ARV treatment programmes in South Africa in practice often hinges on the fulfilment of certain requirements by clients. Richey writes: 'Clientship implies the exchange of political rights for social benefits, and while it involves bargaining, and thus some degree of autonomy between the parties, its distinctive meaning derives from unequal constraints on that autonomy.' In a similar way, in both LHCC and the FBOs linked to Jubilee, clientship implies the exchange between religious commitment and social benefits. While membership and participation in FBOs are organized in concentric circles (leadership – permanent employees – temporary fulltime employees – part-time employees – interns – volunteers – clients) the social benefits accruing from involvement are vertically correlated to these circles.

In the organizations I studied, status promotions from client to volunteer or volunteer to employee were always framed as, and made dependent upon, 'having matured in the faith' (see van Dijk 2001) while the degree of maturing was seen as a matter of Pentecostal habitus. When accompanying professional Think Twice educators to life skills trainings they would invariably initiate prayers asking God to help them open the hearts of their clients, a practice I rarely saw when interacting with volunteers. The Pentecostal habitus was expressed in the naturalized and taken-for-granted deployment of certain idioms of which the personal dialogue with God and the belief in callings, and God's plan, were most salient.

It is also because of these differences in attachment to 'faith' amongst FBO workers and beneficiaries that more than belief it is *religious belonging* that binds them. Since in FBO work, Pentecostalism operates by mediating connections between resource flows and religious identities in terms of unequal reciprocity and, as Richey put it, 'unequal constraints on autonomy' I suggest that Pentecostal involvements in the HIV/AIDS world foster clientship rather than citizenship. In addition, Pentecostalism shapes organizational dynamics by prioritizing religiously based transnational networks (mainly with US partners) and selecting activities that lend themselves to be linked to Pentecostal ideologies of self-improvement and activation.

Conclusion

Pentecostal efforts to engage with what they perceive as the city's social ills can usefully be captured in the notion of urban aspirations. Aspirations to transform urban spaces do not only play out through the desire to plant churches at close proximity to one another (Knibbe 2009), evangelize in the streets and amplify the voice of the Holy Spirit but also through the moral economies of development and service delivery. All of these practices draw on particular spatial formats and material forms (Burchardt 2020). Taking place in churches but also urban parks, community halls and residential backyards, they draw on particular urban geographies which they invest with spiritual meaning. I suggest that the case of Pentecostal FBOs in Cape Town provides some broader lessons on the intricate links between urban aspirations and religious urbanization.

Firstly, while being religiously inspired, Pentecostals' urban aspirations are enmeshed with a landscape of urban governance structures. As I sought to show, Pentecostal aspirations are refracted as they engage with the bureaucratic languages and categories of civil society-driven development on the one hand, and with the mechanisms and favouritism inhering in patronage relationships. And it is through these refractions that Pentecostal claims on urban citizenship become acts of urban clientship in practice.

Secondly, Pentecostals' urban aspirations are driven by urbanization just as they give the process of urbanization a particular shape and direction. The ongoing proliferation of new neighbourhoods through urban sprawl or inner densification, the rise of new urban margins and material cleavages and the emergence of new urban inequalities, infrastructural exclusions and bodily needs provide the lines around which Pentecostal activities cluster. Urbanization produces the spaces which Pentecostals seek to transform in particular ways, turning urbanization into a process with religious characteristics.

Finally, I suggest that the story of Pentecostal FBOs also tells us something about the very limits of urban aspirations as it speaks to debates about urban diversity. By virtue of Pentecostals' desire to hand the city over to the Holy Spirit and to create spaces for its reign, their urban aspirations often gesture towards radical ruptures. However, as Pentecostals become part of the ordinary business of development, and of 'ordinary urbanism' as it were, to some extent they also become ordinary actors of urbanization. They respond to financial incentives, seek funding and submit to governance mechanisms. Existing forms of urban governance may thus constrain Pentecostals' aspirations to transform. Interestingly, this also has consequences for urban religious diversity or 'superdiversity', which many scholars found to be a hallmark of contemporary cities. While religious innovations and heterodoxies continue to engender new spiritualities and religious commitments, this diversity is flattened once it hits the machine of urban governance. Religious urbanization is thus nothing extraordinary or eccentric when measured by the yardstick of dominant models of urban studies but part of the 'ordinary city' (Robinson 2006).

Part II

TERRITORIALIZATION, URBAN CHANGE AND RELIGIOUS TIME-SPACES

Chapter 5

MOURIDE IMAGINARIES OF THE SACRED AND THE TIME-SPACES OF RELIGIOUS URBANIZATION IN TOUBA, SENEGAL

Kate Kingsbury

Introduction

According to hagiography, in the late 1800s, a Senegalese Sufi saint, *Cheikh Amadou Bamba*, sought respite in the shade of a lone tree while wandering across the wilderness on a mystical retreat. He had a vision that one day the spot would comprise an immense sacred centre, Touba, which he established in 1887. The city was later built by disciples to honour Bamba as the founder of the Mouride faith. Mourides now number in the millions, residing not only in Senegal but also globally across the Senegalese diaspora, whether in Europe, North America or in countries as far-flung from Senegal as China, from where they send 'sacred remittances' (Garbin 2018) to contribute to the city's growth and development.

Touba is the example *par excellence* of a religious space that has undergone spectacular urbanization. At the time Bamba erected the village, Touba constituted a tiny outpost with a handful of inhabitants in the inhospitable Western Sahel. In 1952, the city of two thousand people had obtained water adduction thanks to a piped network of local boreholes. By 1964, the city housed around five thousand inhabitants. By the 1980s, its marketplace had flourished thanks to trade links with innumerable cities around the world, from Paris to New York. By 2010 the population of Touba was estimated at close to a million (Foley and Babou 2010) and the sacred city was fully urbanized replete with electricity, roads, a hospital, schools and its own TV station, 'Touba TV', broadcasting religious messages daily to national and global audiences through live internet streaming.

Aside from a considerable increase in population, Touba today contains one of the largest mosques in West Africa and a vast market, which during the annual pilgrimage, the *Grand Magal*, boasts tens of thousands of stalls. The word *Magal* means to celebrate and give homage. Disciples known as *talibés* flock to the city to celebrate their founder and his vision. Many travel from the Senegalese diaspora. The religious festival impels a further influx of at least four million devotees into the city. This event is an important driver for trade, and for the construction of amenities to support the masses of devotees, whether it be the erection of temporary tents or permanent improvements in sanitation systems. *Le Grand Magal* has a significant economic impact not only on Senegal, but also worldwide. Thus, a religious vision as well as the related festivities have shaped the socio-spatial geography of Touba – and the economy of the wider region – transforming it from a desert village into a booming city that boasts a unique form of religious urbanity which melds both mass consumption with sacred ethos and spatiality.

For Mouride disciples, Touba is a holy city. *De jure* it comprises a rural autonomous community within the state of Senegal. *De facto* it is an independent territory, a globalized emerging megacity, governed by Mouride leaders, *marabouts*, who are the founder's direct consanguineal descendants. Between 2007 and 2009, I visited *Le Grand Magal* in Touba as part of a larger ethnography of the Mouride movement (Kingsbury 2014). I also attended 'mini *Magals*', which are smaller festivities organized to celebrate an individual *marabout* and regularly visited Touba outside of pilgrimage season. I conducted participant observation, as well as engaging in formal and informal interviews with Mourides both in Touba and in Dakar.

Touba features in most of the narratives I have collected as a critique of the secular, materialist, modern world, a city lauded as an alternative to other urban spaces, such as Dakar, and implicitly Western modernity. For instance, one of my informants, Momar,[1] told me: 'Touba is a place for communion with God, far from the troubles of Dakar, where you forget greed and envy.' Another disciple, Mbaye,[2] described: 'You will feel it, when you arrive, it is the realm of God'. *Talibés* talked about Touba to me in these terms, narrating the holy city as an ideal sacred place cut off from the secular, profane and material world – 'a paradise' as many put it.

Eliade (1959) states that a religious locale does not connect to other places horizontally as an urban city does, but rather connects vertically to heavenly realms. Replicating this argument, Touba, and in particular the mosque's minaret, has been depicted by Ross (1995) as an *axis mundi* for believers. The author's geographic analysis seeks to map urban Sufi design in the city as evidence of eschatological power manifested upon space. While Mouride narratives described Touba as distant from the immoral metropolises of the outside world, they also present the city as a timeless space. However, one of my key arguments in this chapter is that the city cannot be reduced to solely a sacred site, a transcendental time-space disconnected from its surroundings nor can it be perceived of as purely a globalized urban metropolis running on abstract time. Studies of Mourides and Touba (Bava 2003, Riccio 2003; Sow, Oumar and Gomis 2020) suggest that the continuous growth of the city is due to its ever-increasing global connectedness, in particular through remittances sent by Mouride migrants and transnational trade activities. Yet it must be acknowledged that this urbanization is impelled by a religious vision that continues to motivate Mourides and as such the city eludes binaries: in Touba there are always myriad notions of time and space at work.

This chapter thus explores the tensions between the way in which the city is imagined and portrayed by disciples, and the production of urban realities driving the growth of a 'religious metropolis'. I underline how the relation between religion and materiality should never be 'conceived in antagonistic terms' (Houtman and Meyer 2012:1), and how there is a need to recognize the role religion has in catalysing urbanization and the expansion of urban economies. I build here on the recent scholarship on 'urban religion' which explores 'the dynamic engagement of religious traditions ... with specific features of the industrial and post-industrial cityscapes and with the social conditions of city life' (Orsi 1999: 42–3).

Numerous works have explored contemporary religion and cities in Europe and the Americas (Allievi and Nielsen 2003; Eiesland 2000; Vásquez and Marquardt 2003). However, urban studies on contemporary Africa have been uneven, sometimes reifying ideas that 'urban modern is necessarily secular' or consists of a 'site of progress' versus the idea that religion embodies the inverse: the 'traditional', 'the failure of modernity' and 'is external, incidental or peripheral to ... urban modernity' (Hancock and Srinivas 2008: 620; see also Dussel 2002; Uberoi 2002; van der Veer 2001). Instead of persevering in approaches that owe much to secularist presumptions, it is necessary to analyse the 'shifting' and often overlapping 'geographic and social boundaries' between what is 'religious' and what is 'secular' time and space (Hancock and Srinivas 2008: 620–1). The study of urban religion as 'lived religion'(Orsi 1999) urges us to understand how faith may not only create religious urban spaces and territories but also mediate experiences of these through ritual practices and performative means (De Vries 2001:1–6). Furthermore, scholarship by urban researchers of post-colonial religious spaces has demonstrated that urban temporalities may be multiple, creating 'senses of time' in the religious imagination, rather than operating according to 'abstract time' (Crang 2005: 510). Through acts of memory, specific time-spaces are constructed (Till 2012), allowing the religious community to forge collective narratives that link them to urban spaces through joint faith, as it is the case in Touba.

The chapter proceeds as follows. I start by describing how the process of religious urbanization in Touba has been historically connected to struggles over charismatic authority and prestige before exploring how Mourides navigate and perceive the urban space as 'holy' and the ways in which they link their experience to an active and continuous production of the sacred. These 'sacred socio-spatialities' are forged through discursive, material, acoustic and embodied mediations by Mourides, producing, in turn, a powerful *imaginaire* of the 'holy city', in particular during events such as *Le Grand Magal*. I also discuss the many time-spaces that exist in Touba, drawing attention to the fact that multiple temporalities and non-binary understandings of space are necessary to capture the socio-urban 'thickness' of the city (see Kirby, this volume).

Religious urbanization and the politics of the sacred

A large proportion of the financial capital behind Touba's spectacular religious urbanization (including the building of *La Grande Mosquée*) was collected over the years from Mouride disciples, not only in Senegal, but also globally, within the wider Senegalese diaspora (Foley and Babou 2010). The profits accrued from disciples' free labour also played a key role in this development, in particular the labour from Mourides cultivating peanuts on their *marabouts'* farms, a form of worship that Bamba initially invented for those who could not read, and had no inclination for studying the Qu'ran. As Buggenhagen (2012: 88) has noted, Mourides readily divest of money to obtain salvation as constructing the holy city is seen not only eschatologically as a guarantee of entry into paradise in the afterlife, but also as 'building heaven on earth' since it is understood as a fulfilment of Bamba's vision. Disciples' funds are therefore converted into sacred capital through the creation of an urban environment perceived as fixed in time forever through its association with the divine.

When asked about how Touba developed, Mouride disciples I have talked to usually recount that it was 'through the grace of Allah' and resulted from Bamba's immeasurable religious power. While they perceive the city as a symbol of unified Mouride faith, more critical historical accounts of the city's inception (see for instance Guèye 2002) reveal that it grew out of internal power struggles. Although the city is largely autonomous from the state, and this is a source of great pride for Mourides, the symbolic confrontation between non-Mouride state politicians and *marabouts* camouflages a 'reality of partial accommodation' (Cruise O'Brien 2003: 3). As will be detailed, Mouride leaders have indeed called on the state for aid to ensure basic needs are met.

Bamba had four brothers, who had many spouses and children. Bamba married twenty-nine wives with whom he had numerous children. Since his death, his children, his siblings and their children have vied for control over Touba and the symbolic, human and financial capital that is part and parcel of land ownership. According to Sufi tradition, a disciple cannot access the divine nor communicate with God without going through a holy intermediary graced with arcane knowledge and mystical power, that is, a *marabout*, who acts as a spiritual teacher and guide. *Cheikhs* are also believed to emanate *baraka*, spiritual blessings, which flow into those around them. Bamba was the superlative source of *baraka*. Mourides surmise that all his consanguineous kin inherited his celestial potency. The only way for disciples to acquire *baraka* is through their *marabout* (Diop 1981: 90; Kingsbury 2018). In return for their auspices *talibés* offer their *marabouts hadiyya*, usually in the form of cash money but sometimes gift victuals, houses, cars or administrative favours.

Talibés usually choose their *marabouts* according to their prestige and power, or they may be bonded to them through long-standing family affiliations. *Marabouts* depend upon disciples for their reputation and riches. All *talibés* revere the *Khalifa General*, the leader of all Mourides. Additionally, each *talibé* generally swears allegiance to an individual *marabout*, in an act called *njebbel*. The disciple will provide his *marabout* with oblations and seek spiritual guidance from him thereon out in. Cruise O'Brien describes it as an exclusive, voluntary 'engagement of total personal obedience', although if dissatisfied with his *marabout* the disciple 'can break the relationship' (1971: 88–90). *Marabouts* contend with one another for followers and may clash with one another as they seek to win the favour of the *Khalifa General*. He is supremely powerful, extending resources as well as capital to those under his aegis.

The Mouride order has long experienced tendencies towards dissolution. It divided upon Bamba's death in 1927. Disciples and *marabouts* bickered over who would succeed Bamba and become the first *Khalifa General*. According to Wolof tradition, inheritance passes to the oldest living brother, in this case denoting *Cheikh* Anta. Notwithstanding, it was common knowledge that Bamba bequeathed the role to his eldest son Mouhamadou Moustapha Mbacké. The two *marabouts* argued behind closed doors. In Touba and Dakar violent confrontations took place between their *talibés*. The very first *Grand Magal* was organized not only to commemorate Bamba but to unite divided factions and cool tensions.

Touba rapidly became akin to a chess board, religious leaders calculating their moves to ensure their dominance over disciples and resources. *Serigne* Mouhamadou realized that owning prime land parcels entailed visibility and power. He struggled to obtain Darou Khodoss, a large plot of land with a strategic position opposite the mosque, before his rival, Anta, who also sought to buy it (Guèye 2002: 159). *Serigne* Mouhamadou leveraged his political affiliations and raised substantial financial capital from family and *talibés* to make the purchase. The new *Khalifa* commanded disciples to move to his plot by *ndiggel*, religious order.

In the 1930s Mouhamadou mobilized disciples and affines to commence construction upon *La Grande Mosquée* before any other *marabout* could do so. This action caused discord. Anta sought to halt him but failed. *Serigne* Mouhamadou guaranteed his lineage significant financial, social and symbolic capital which it still leverages today. In reaction to Mouhamadou's realty investments, other *marabouts* rushed to acquire and erect their own *quartier*. *Serigne* Bara, Mouhamoudou's brother, rapidly purchased Gouye Mbind, another well-appointed piece of land. He likewise called upon his disciples and kin to populate the neighbourhood.

When I asked *talibés* about how settlement initially transpired in Touba, I received responses similar to Lamine's[3] who told me how '*marabouts* and disciples were moved by the hand of God and the grace of Bamba and felt for spiritual reasons they must move to the territory'. Although there may have been instances where this was the case it seems apparent that in-fighting between *marabouts* who sought to establish themselves, their families and their disciples, in order to legitimate and maintain their power as well as amass resources, comprised much of the impetus for the construction of Touba, the mosque and initial settlement (O'Brien 2003: 43; Guèye 2002: 150–80).

Since the inception of Touba as a sacred space, Mouride leaders have thus sought to acquire land as an external manifestation of their *baraka*, extending their religious authority. The successful erection of impressive edifices and the development of well-populated, urbanized neighbourhoods in turn meant a capacity to attract more disciples which in turn created more wealth. Disciples' *hadiyya* (donations to their *marabouts*) were converted into further material wealth used to finance more construction in Touba, thus creating a cyclical process allowing leaders to make their sacred mark through fixed spatialities, leading to an increasingly urbanized environment.

Marabouts pledged important titles to their entourage to encourage their move to Touba, thereby further bolstering their position. After all, Touba was a village in

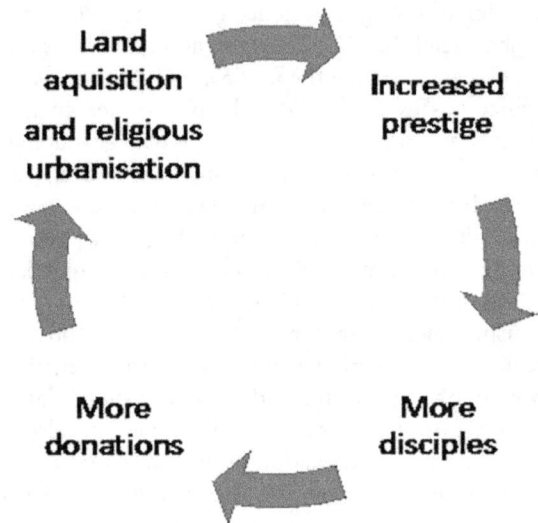

Figure 5.1. Diagram of circular reinforcement of resources for Mouride leaders.

the wilderness at this point, therefore not necessarily an attractive prospect (Guèye 2002: 160–9). *Marabouts* continue today to vouchsafe prime pieces of land to members of their family, their entourage and influential disciples, ensuring these persons grant them favours and services as well as strengthen their position and maintain their patronage.

In 1946, following Mouhamadou Moustapha's death, a new rivalry erupted. *Serigne* Falilou, son of Bamba, was named *Khalifa General* much to Mouhamadou Moustapha's eldest son, *Serigne* Cheikh's, disgust. The two adversaries aligned themselves with different political leaders – *Serigne* Cheikh with the mayor of Dakar and leader of the Senegalese Party of Socialist Action; Lamine Guèye, and *Serigne* Falilou with Leopold Senghor, the president-elect. Once again tensions escalated and in 1952, numerous *talibés* were injured in a violent fracas (Guèye 2002: 160–2). Nonetheless, *Serigne* Cheikh maintained his social standing. He had inherited one of the most important pieces of land. He rapidly expanded his demesne beyond Touba's confines to include vast tracts of arable land, ensuring that disciples could provide free labour for him on his peanut farms, thereby further augmenting his financial capital as well as spatial and symbolic prestige via urbanization.

In order to thwart his rival's territorial and pecuniary predominance, the new *Khalifa General*, supported by his uncles, built the district known as Touba-Mosquée. This process of religious urbanization was clearly linked here to the enactment of charisma, authority and power. In a move aimed at undermining his predecessor's actions, Falilou also changed the date of *Le Grand Magal*. Under the previous *Khalifa*, the *Magal* was celebrated on the date of Bamba's death. Falilou altered it to the date of Bamba's exile from Senegal at the hands of the French colonialists.

The second *Khalifa* summoned his disciples to work on *La Grande Mosquée*. Falilou decreed that until the mosque was complete, no other large edifices could be erected. Much like his predecessor, through shrewd manoeuvres Falilou hewed an indelible mystique for himself by controlling the use of, and expanding, urban space. His *pièce de résistance* was the completion of *La Grande Mosquée* in 1963 which materially and mythologically fixed his status in the city as sacred leader in the minds of all Mourides.

Since *La Grande Mosquée's* completion subsequent *marabouts* have added extensions, improvements and lavish embellishments, rendering it into the opulent fane it is today. Guèye argues that the mosque is 'the symbol of the power of Bamba's predictions' (Guèye 2002: 86 my translation). In the eyes of Mourides this may be so. But the mosque is not merely an edifice that honours the memory of the founder of Mouridiyya. It is also a testament to the will of each Mouride *marabout* to manifest their power and prestige upon the landscape. Mourides themselves recognize this. For example, when touring the mosque, disciples who reside in Touba tend to point out to guests how different aspects of the structure were built by different *marabouts*, detailing their achievements and life stories.

Furthermore, in these politics of religious urbanization, the role of *dahiras* is also important to consider. *Dahiras* are voluntary social organizations consisting of disciples who assemble around projects or missions. Different *dahiras* constantly jostle for prestige and the recognition of the *Khalifa General* and from Mourides as a whole. They enact their power struggles upon the urban space of Touba and thus urbanization in Touba is the result, in part, of their collective mobilization. Situations of tension arise when one is favoured over another. For example, under *Serigne* Saliou, the fifth *Khalifa General*, the *dahira* known as *Hizbut Tarqiyyah* consisting of well-educated and affluent students managed to obtain power and funding in the early to late 2000s. Under the Khalifa's aegis they were put in contact with influential figures, allotted significant funds and conferred the honour of organizing *Le Grand Magal*. Other *dahiras* were affronted by this decision. This led to confrontations between members of the *dahiras* that spread as far as Dakar but often played out, quite literally in concrete terms, on the urban landscape of Touba.

Foley and Babou (2010) have described how a *dahira* known as *Matlaboul Fawzaini*, whose members live primarily in North America and Western Europe, spearheaded a project to build a much needed local hospital. The disciples raised $10 million in funds and accruing symbolic capital and realizing Bamba's vision, the *dahira* rose substantially in status after the building's completion. Babou and Foley assert that millions of dollars were invested in this hospital project, which, after a Ministry of Health visit in 2004, was deemed not to have followed construction standards. As a result, approximately 80 per cent of the total space had to be torn down and reconstructed. The final structure still had many shortcomings. Years later these issues perdure and the hospital has endless financial challenges, relying on the state for many of its needs, entailing a 'fragile balance of responsibility' for operating costs between Mouride authorities, hospital administrators and the Ministry of Health (ibid.: 89). Given that *dahiras* in Touba vie for prestige and power, the symbolic capital *Matlaboul Fawzaini* accrued upon the hospital's completion outweighed any of its material shortcomings. The *dahira's* hospital project demonstrates how urbanization in Touba as much as it is impelled by salient infrastructural needs, is as much, if not more so, the product of religiously embedded plans, dreams, visions and ideals projected onto space (see also Gregory 1994).

Both *marabouts*, and collectives of disciples have thus engaged at a frenetic pace in the urbanization of Touba in a context of competition for charismatic capital. Mourides have built ever-multiplying neighbourhoods, institutions ranging from health clinics to universities, a television station, vast libraries and even fitness centres. The city is also surrounded by innumerable farms belonging to many *marabouts* which have a vital impact on the national economy. The largest, *Khelcom*, belongs to the *Khalifa General*. For *marabouts*, urbanization entails the externalization of their *baraka* on the land and for this reason leaders have often competed in construction in a bid to demonstrate their prepotency via urban space. For disciples, construction converts into sacred capital both in this life and especially in the afterlife. Despite clashes between disciples, *marabouts* and *dahiras*, as I will now demonstrate through the medium of religious rites during *Le Grand Magal*, Mourides coalesce, unified as they imagine a common vision of the city and an ideal of the order itself.

Geographies and performances of religious imaginaire

The Mourides, like many religious communities, present themselves as homogeneous and conjoined via an *imaginaire*. Bayart (2005), drawing upon Anderson (2006), uses the term *imaginaire* to describe how states and social groups are imagined and imagine themselves as unfluctuating and stable with fixed immutable identities, despite being 'infinite and ungovernable', and consisting of 'heterogeneous, constantly changing figures' (Bayart 2005: 233). This concept of the *imaginaire* is useful for looking at the Mouride order, which, like the nation-state as Bayart describes, is a mutable group, whose leaders, and disciples, are constantly changing over time. For example, since the death of Bamba, the order has been headed by eight different *Khalifa Généraux*. Bayart acknowledges that identities (whether religious and/or political) are cultural, ideological and historical constructs, and urges us to look at performances of identities – revealing the importance of multiplicity and hybridity.

Performance is crucial to consider to understand the role that *La Grande Mosquée* plays in Touba as it binds a particular religious discourse, an *imaginaire*, to an urbanized and ritualized sacred geography. *La Grande Mosquée* stands right in the centre of the city, completed after many years of unpaid labour by devoted disciples using funds raised from *talibés*' purses. Oriented towards Mecca, its central minaret dominates the city's skyline at 87 metres high. A vespertine illuminated star at its apex ensures it is discernible over 20 kilometres away on a clear night. Like other vertical objects, such as church towers or obelisks, the minaret symbolizes the *axis mundi* (Mekking 2009: 23–49) and the *qutb al-âlam*

(Ross 1995: 227). Mourides perceive it as connecting the heavens with the earthly plane. As Coleman and Elsner expound, notwithstanding incompatible interpretations that appear to contest the sacred, the sites in themselves 'constitute the sacred in the eyes of ... believers, precisely by absorbing (even casting a discreet veil over) discrepant religious discourses' (Coleman and Elsner 1995: 208).

Within the stage of the mosque's walls, the cemetery and in the *musallâ* (the open-air prayer ground that is situated in front of the mosque) *Talibés* engage in rites that take the form of a drama that draws from the imagined story of their founder's life. The mosque, cemetery and prayer-ground are efficacious as symbols not so much because they communicate meaning, although they do this as well. Rather, their primary effectiveness is revealed in and through performances which take place in a social space whereby 'participants are engaged with the symbols in the interactional creation of ... reality, rather than being merely informed by them as knowers' (Schieffelin 2013: 107) thereby reifying and inscribing sacred meaning on these spaces. These performances, consist of discursive, narrative, acoustic and embodied actions which mediate the perception of space (see De Vries 2001: 1–6).

The mosque and other symbols are construed as and create an imagined Mouride past. This is preserved in hagiographic texts and myths that describe a Mouride identity and a vision of the past, the present and the future. For instance, accounts of Bamba's exile by the French to Gabon feature improbable events which are frequently related as Mourides circumambulate monuments during *le Magal* and particular monuments are associated with particular stories, inscribing the space with sacredness through the performance of narrative.[4] These narrative performances, such as storytelling during the visitation of sacred spaces, continually infuse the imagined past in the present, 'inventing tradition' (Hobsbawm and Ranger 1983), defining people, places and actions as sacrosanct in the present day, through their connections to Bamba. This discourse reappropriates and reifies dichotomies used by the colonizers, such as those of modernity and tradition. The Mourides have adopted and adapted these paradigms to create a clear historical and metaphysical distance between themselves and the colonizers, casting Bamba as a figure who strived to preserve traditional Wolof identity and culture and fought against the French, whilst also suffusing urban space with sacrality.

Nevertheless, an examination of Senegalese history reveals that Bamba, willingly or unwillingly, became an important colonial ally. Bamba was exiled by the French for numerous years, which has indelibly cast Bamba as a spiritual hero in the eyes of all Mourides. Yet disciples barely, if ever, mention that Bamba, and in particular his entourage, eventually colluded with the French, providing them with favours in an *échange de services* that has been well documented (Cruise O'Brien 2003). The French authorities recognized the Mouride potential to aid both economic growth and the colonial project of conquest. Since the French needed income from peanut cultivation they eventually sanctioned the Mouride movement's agricultural cultivation, allowing the order to spread over much of the country in return for the latter's pacifist acceptance of French rule. This increased the wealth of Mouride leaders. The *tariqas*, once perceived as a security threat, proved to be highly productive entities in the colony, constituting not only spiritual milieux but also farms for the cultivation of peanuts. The Mouride leaders agreed to serve as an initially reluctant but eventually reliable intermediary between colonial state and colonial citizens to disseminate messages and ensure the subjects' cooperation in the colonial venture (Robinson 1999).

Hastrup has remarked: 'The story of the past is a selective account of the actual sequence of events but it is no random selection' (Hastrup 1992: 9). This *échange de services* which gave them access to resources and space allowed them to establish the Mouride presence on the land via peanut farms and religious schools.

Religious spaces are produced and governed in Touba by different modes of enacting and embodying the sacred. Every day disciples can be seen static as statues as they kneel, before the mausoleum, barefooted and freshly washed in their *boubous* on the cool marble tiles. In the sepulchre silence and motionlessness are imposed, whilst in the prayer-ground piety is produced through *techniques du corps* (Mauss 1934) which involve movement and sound, such as chanting and specific corporeal motions. Heads bowed, disciples lower themselves onto their knees, then bow their heads to the ground, after which they raise them again. These visceral, visual, tactile and aural experiences are integral to the performance of piety and anchor the *corps vécu*, or lived body, within the phenomenal field (Merleau-Ponty 2002: 113), producing the sacred in space.

Immersed in this symbolic construction of the sacred, disciples collectively enact their affirmed allegiance to Mourdiyya and its founding father, reifying their religious ontology through rites that involve ad hoc corporeal techniques. The 'mental self-models' that are the 'little red arrows' (Metzinger 2003: 331) that allow disciples to phenomenologically navigate their map of reality, are now restructured, whilst the map – which as Baudrillard noted 'precedes the territory' (Baudrillard 1981: 1) – is itself redrawn afresh. Coumba[5] told me that after a visit to Touba's mosque: 'I see the world around me more clearly, I understand why Allah has made it so.'

Le Grand Magal has been lauded by Mourides as the example of superlative Mouride organization. Yet during my various trips to Touba to attend the pilgrimage, there were issues with security, lack of sanitation, electricity supply, distribution of water and other logistical quandaries which could not, after numerous years of such predicaments, be dismissed as teething problems. The Mourides have relied upon the state aid to guarantee safety, water and electricity supply in Touba but due to frequent fracas, and even murders, the government has had to send in police and military aid to maintain order. While the city is imagined as a 'purely' autonomous space differentiated from the nation-state, in reality Mourides rely upon the government's aid for the successful organization of *Le Grand Magal*, as well as the resources that derive from Dakar and further afield. When Mourides assemble to celebrate Bamba's exile, they enact a drama that rewrites another reality, one in which religion is defined in opposition to the state, when in fact it is integral to the state (Cruise O'Brien 2003: 129). Many Mourides assert that the modern state is an alien institution with little legitimacy, unlike the Mouride order whose authority over Touba is divinely ordained. Symbolic confrontations with the Senegalese State and government orchestrated by Mouride leaders mask the truth of intimate ties between government and religious leaders (Cruise O'Brien 2003: 27) and the dependence that Touba has on the state to supply resources and services when its own are not sufficient.

Time-spaces of Touba: le Grand Magal and the urbanized economies of the sacred

We have seen how the spatial enactment and performance of the sacred was both relying on and further reinforcing a powerful *imaginaire* of Touba as an autonomous holy city but the temporal dimensions are also important to consider. As I will argue, time in Touba is not homogenous and consists of multiple temporalities. While Mourides herald the city in accordance with cosmological tenets, as a timeless, immutable heaven on earth *à la* Eliade, Touba is in fact a dynamic conurbation where time appears linear and progressive, as in any city, and its development is inscribed within a particular urban temporality.

Touba also makes time. Rituals in and visits to Touba have a horological function, creating a sacred rhythm, marking the passage of time for Mourides. The city is timeless within the Mouride *imaginaire*, yet there is an ongoing mediation between two notions of time, with 'the eternal and timeless being presented as superior to the time-bound world of finite existence' by Mouride worshippers (Eade and Sallnow 1991: 14, see also Bloch and Parry 1982). Nowhere is this mediation more visible than during *Le Grand Magal*, which takes place every November, on the eighteenth day of the Islamic month of Safar.

While the event indexes an important historical moment (marking Bamba's exile at the hands of the French) it is characterized by liminality and timelessness for Mouride disciples. The city is always bathed in a certain timeless transcendental garb for *talibés*, but this sentiment is reinforced during *Le Grand Magal*. Rites accentuate liminality for devotees who, all dressed alike in their *boubous*, frequently allude to their equality before Bamba and take part in lavish meals which create a sense of eternal unity and enduring camaraderie where differences are effaced. The city is transformed as all Mourides celebrate the urban vision of their founder.

Le Berndèèl is an important ritual during the festivities. It consists of communal religious meals offered by hosts to their families, friends and neighbours. *Dahiras* also celebrate *Le Berndèèl* offering free fare to attendees, 'representing Mouride hospitality and sharing all that is good' as Coumba put it. To prepare these meals vast amounts of food must be bought, including cattle to sacrifice at this event. One *marabout*, now deceased, *Cheikh* Bethio Thioune, bought and slaughtered five thousand cows annually to feed his disciples to make manifest his *baraka*. *Le Berndèèl* is a lavish banquet for all to participate in and rejoice in the 'triumph of life over death' (Bakhtin 1968: 282). The feast celebrates the Mouride order as an ageless, permanent, collective united through faith across time and space. As Hamidou,[6] another informant, pointed out 'to eat at the *Berndèèl* is to celebrate all the Mourides and most of all for us all to celebrate Bamba together'. Bloch and

Parry describe how the exaltation of the 'eternal, undivided group' renders obsolete death for the individual and as a result allows for the imagination of an 'idealised ... permanent social order' that exists timelessly (1982: 34–5). Interestingly, devotees who cannot attend the event often cook special meals in their homes across the diaspora, thus imagining themselves as part of a perennial pious order.

In Touba during *Le Grand Magal*, the holy city is transformed into a space of revelry, with some clear carnivalesque dimensions, as Senegalese from across the nation, and of all religious affiliations, attend the festivities. I met Tijanis, Layènes, Qadiri and even Christians, who capitalized on *Le Grand Magal* not only to trade or forge business alliances but dance and carouse, which is accepted as part of festivities by all. This creates a hybrid public sphere within which piety is not necessarily constructed in strict opposition to a plurality of possible 'aesthetic modes of celebration', as observed by Pnina Werbner (1996) in her classic ethnography of 'fun spaces' among British Pakistani Muslims (see also Schielke 2009 on Egyptian youth during Ramadan).[7]

Out of season Touba is quiet and seems empty, but the streets are bustling during the pilgrimage – the sounds of *qasaid* (religious songs) fill the air and religious processions snake down the streets as onlookers admire the displays. Baye Fall[8] colourfully dressed in their patchwork *boubous* may be seen in the streets chanting together or on their knees flagellating their backs and heads with their heavy clubs. The markets are brimming with people, sounds and scents. In the cattle fair, congeries of animals bustle for as far as the eye can see, whilst buyers and sellers loudly haggle over prices.

Besides this multisensorial intensity and despite the timeless aspect of rituals that celebrate the ideal of sacred space, urbanity is reinforced during *Le Grand Magal* itself, with certain activities ensuring that the city continues to develop rapidly as part of global trade networks. Circuits of exchange are connecting and reconnecting traders, entrepreneurs and other businesspeople. They enter into tacit trade contracts based on mutual faith and trust, the guarantee consisting perhaps of devotion to the same *marabout*, belonging to the same *dahira* or family alliances.

I observed as attendees sought partners, financiers and means to expand their businesses. Aboubacar,[9] for example, liaised with a business contact he had been put in touch with to extend his fish export business into Spain. Not all traders were Senegalese and I encountered Pakistani and Indonesian entrepreneurs for instance. These businesspersons attended to forge or renew trading alliances. Some attendees solicited services from those who had administrative or political ties, such as aid with acquiring legal documents necessary for foreign travel or requisite for business purposes. Mourides settled old debts and sought out personal favours outside of ritual spaces, in the markets and other public spaces.

The markets of Touba are vital to the city's growth and are situated centrally, close to the main mosque. Both legal and illegal activities have contributed to the market's ever-expanding range. Contraband is hawked, fake visas and false passports are peddled and, in addition, fictive companies set up their headquarters in Touba to launder money and engage in other nefarious activities. Although

Touba's *marabouts* have their own security forces that cater to their safety, there is a general lax attitude from religious leaders towards the policing of urban space, especially during *Le Grand Magal*. Local police turn a blind eye to illegal enterprises in the marketplace, as these after all are part of the city's attraction for some and have contributed to its success as a trade centre. The state dare not interfere in the Mouride city, wishing to maintain political stability and the support of Mouride leaders. As Diop points out, it is also in *marabouts*' interest to keep traders happy as after all the market is the beating heart of the city (Diop 1981: 91). Business conducted therein is vital to the livelihood of many disciples, who can then in turn transfer some of their earnings to their *marabouts* through sacred donations.

Disciples roam the markets buying a wide range of items from food to mementos to electronic goods to prayer mats and more. The vendors who make money from such sales recirculate capital in turn, buying items for themselves or their families. They also distribute funds to family, spend money on services, pay back debts, invest money into new business ventures and more. Many disciples come from overseas with money earned in France, Italy, Belgium, the United States and even China, which they spend in Touba on food or items to trade, or houses they are building and above all blessings from their *marabouts* who then in turn spend disciples' donations on goods in Touba. This creates a never-ending cycle where cash is converted into sacred capital and back again thus contributing to the growth of the city and its economy.

Mobility of Mourides and the 'movements of capital, goods, labor, and ideas' (Melly 2017: 4)[10] is thus key to Touba's urbanization. Bava (2003) has also noted that the religious mobility of Mourides and their capacity to engage in peregrination intertwines with the way in which religious routes also become means of trading and establishing new business contacts. Such mobility, and above all the capital made from movement, is transubstantiated into fixity as devotees invest in Touba, a time-space that remains stable in their symbolic and ritualistic universe. Touba provides the image of a safe, secure, timeless centre which 'grounds' Mourides, especially for the large number of them who, as migrants in the West, live often in insecure and precarious conditions (Bava 2003; Riccio 2003).

Diplomats and representatives from Islamic organizations from across the globe attend the *Magal* under the guise of paying their respects to Bamba. When I attended the *Magal* in 2009, I was informed by my Mouride hosts that politicians' primary objective was to consort with important *marabouts* and other attachés to enter into deals and exchanges. I was told that, behind closed doors, political accords were established and alliances were affirmed, though the media did not focus on the latter. Numerous representatives from local and foreign broadcasting corporations, such as the BBC and Al Jazeera, joined the seething throngs that year and filmed the religious rites occurring in and around the mosque. The film *Touba*,[11] released in 2013, likewise only paid attention to religious activities.

More recently at *Magals*, I have noted that social media has become central for the younger generations who upload photos on a daily basis to websites or use these to discuss their attendance, tweeting messages and photos with the hashtag #18Safar[12] and #grandmagal. Various newspapers[13] have detailed that traffic during festivities has become extremely high on mobile networks. For instance, in 2016 an increase in traffic of 112 per cent was witnessed on Sonatel's[14] 2G and 180 per cent on its 3G network. The company increased the number of BTS antennas[15] during last year's *Magal* from the habitual 134 to 384 to cope with the demand and profited grandly. This indicates again how religious and economic forces have developed conjointly.

Vukonic (1998) has attested that the economic impact of religious tourism is incontestable, yet *Le Grand Magal* has scarcely been recognized in academic literature as an economic driver, as scholars have focused on sacrality, reifying dichotomies that juxtapose religion with materiality. Instead of adopting an approach based upon such binary presumptions, it is necessary to analyse how religion creates urban spaces. Touba is a major commercial center and *Le Grand Magal* provides a clear economic stimulus,[16] boosting employment opportunities. Globally, the pilgrimage benefits a long list of companies and a study conducted by Guèye in 2017 suggested that the 'global impact of the *Grand Magal* composed of direct, indirect and induced impacts amounted to 452,000,000 USD distributed as expenditure in the national economy' (2017:1).

Conclusion

I have shown in this chapter how the initial development of Touba has been historically linked to the politics of charismatic rivalry and inheritance among Mouride leaders and how religious urbanization could be seen as a process of 'spatial fixation' of circulating sacralized capital. Processes of land accumulation and transformation thus need to be understood against a backdrop of intense competition for social and sacred status as the *baraka* of *Marabouts* is externalized through religious urbanization and monumentalization, in turn attracting growing membership and followers, leading to heightened prestige for religious leaders.

My ethnography also suggests that *Le Grand Magal* is not solely a religious ceremony that only has implications for the Mourides and that Touba does not merely comprise an *axis mundi*, connecting disciples vertically to the heavens (see Ross 1995). In that sense I tend to disagree with Coulon (1999: 197) on the 'peripheral' character of most places of pilgrimage, applying it to Touba and *Le Grand Magal*. Coulon states in an Eliadian tone that 'The *Grand Magal* of Touba is an excellent example of the phenomenon whereby a ritual space of a peripheral nature is created within a national ensemble' (Coulon 1999: 208). As I have indicated in this chapter, Touba can be seen as a globalized metropolis, connected horizontally to a host of locales and publics, through political, social and economic linkages, therefore it is *central* to economic and socio-cultural processes producing and reproducing religious urbanization.

Moreover, Guèye has described how as a result of this expansive urbanization of Touba 'le rêve de Cheikh Amadou Bamba ... a été à la fois réalisé et trahi'[17] (Guèye 2002: 491). As he points out, the mosque, the university, the extensive religious library, water adduction, the sacred well (known as '*les puits de la miséricorde*'), the many Coranic schools and so on, all fit within the founder's vision, and it is mass urbanization that has allowed for these structures to be built as part of a coherent socio-spatial *imaginaire*. However the city has become in many ways, and simultaneously, an uncontrollable entity in its own rights, especially with the growth of informal activities in a context of weak legal enforcement. Yet disciples do not view Touba through this particular lens. As I have described in this chapter, religion not only creates urban spaces, it mediates them. *Le Grand Magal* and its rites serve to veil such views of Touba, creating a sense of time and space that is eminently sacred. Religious rites here produce and reproduce a unifying *esprit de corps* and ensure Mourides continue to view Touba and their religious order through the lens of this symbolic system, fashioning an ontology that pervades perception.

This powerful process is also crystallized in Touba's sacralized monumentality. The central mosque, for instance, engirded by a plethora of other religious *lieux*, functions as an arena for religion to be enacted, belief to be affirmed and a model of the Mouride cosmos to be manifested and reified. Tensions and contradictions are concealed in this process, allowing a religious ideology and collective memory to exist in the imagination by being corporealized and spatialized. This explains why disciples and their leaders use a specific spiritual lexicon to describe the metropolis and their pilgrimage experiences, whilst omitting to mention the mundane activities that take place in Touba – a holy city often heralded as an alternative to the immorality, disorder and urban 'chaos' of Dakar. Thus, like beauty, 'holiness exists in the eye of the beholder' (Verschaffel 2012: 36).

Chapter 6

BUILDING CHURCHES FOR THE CITY-TO-COME: PENTECOSTAL URBANIZATION AND ASPIRATIONAL PLACE-MAKING IN THE 'RURBAN' AREAS OF SOUTHWESTERN BENIN

Carla Bertin

Introduction

Dynamics of religious spatialization in the Global South have mostly been studied in city contexts, with a growing scholarship focusing on the expansion of African Pentecostalism and its consequences in terms of urbanization as well as cultural, social and economic change. While the implications of religious urbanization in 'megacities' such as Lagos, Kinshasa or Accra are clearly significant (Coleman and Vásquez 2017; De Boeck 2013; Katsaura 2019; Marshall 2009; Ukah 2013b), in this chapter I want to explore the overlooked interplay of urbanization and 'Pentecostalization' in rural environments, taking as case study the socio-spatial changes at work in Benin. My ethnography, conducted in a cluster of villages in southwestern Benin between 2013 and 2017 reveals a process of 'rurbanization' which began in the last decade or so and which has been rendered legible by new residential and commercial constructions, and more occasionally by lavish multistorey concrete villas, which often remain uninhabited. Pentecostal churches are dotting this emerging 'rurban' landscape and have acquired a particular signification in terms of 'modernization' and 'development' amidst this changing environment. However, this process is not homogenous as the appearance of these churches varies: some seem fragile, precariously built with walls and thatched roofs made of dry branches while others have roofs made of corrugated iron sheets – a sign that the congregation is beginning to expand. In the villages where I conducted my research, there are also churches made of mud and beaten earth (*terre battue*) which blend in well with the walls of surrounding family huts. Other churches have concrete walls, and visible openings to facilitate the construction of an additional second level. Most of the churches were small in size and membership, with congregations between ten and fifty people.

In most cases, the façades and interiors of these churches were never truly completed and, in a way, these churches seemed always 'in flux'. Typically, new churches were built, at first, with simple walls made of stacked-up branches, without doors, after which more elaborate thatched walls were erected, to be replaced by mud walls that lasted until the construction of concrete walls could start. These Pentecostal churches were thus clearly shaped by a changing materiality, ultimately oriented towards the projected creation of the multistorey concrete 'church of the future'. This state of constant liminality is not disabling for local believers, however. In fact, at each of these stages of construction and development, the church remains used as a collective place of community, prayer, deliverance or choir-singing, a place to connect with the pastor and deacons, with new 'brothers and sisters in Christ' and to connect with God.

The construction of Pentecostal churches in southern Benin contributes to the transformation of rural areas gradually turning into 'rurban' spaces – a process taking place within a wider transnational urban corridor linking Abidjan, Accra, Lagos and Ibadan. Key in this transregional geography is the development of 'rurban' interstices between these megacities, shaping new patterns of circulation and flows of people and things, and at the same time driving renewed engagements with the changing landscape of the 'village' (Geschiere and Gugler 1998; Geschiere and Socpa 2016). Situating the construction of Pentecostal churches in Beninese villages against these wider dynamics of urban/rural change, this chapter explores the relationship between Pentecostal spatialization, local vernaculars of progress and the social construction of the future. I argue that the socio-spatiality of the church 'under construction' is a concretization of local epistemologies of 'development'. It is, in other words, the embodiment of a 'movement forward' intimately connected to Pentecostal modes of experiencing and envisioning the future.

My analysis of the linkages between temporality and Pentecostal place-making engages with recent anthropological literature which interrogates the multiple social and cultural dimensions of living future time (Appadurai 2013). Some of this literature puts an emphasis on how the future is made tangible and legible by people's experience of particular socio-temporalities linked to hope, expectation, uncertainty or despair (Cooper and Pratten 2014; Ferguson 1999; Miyazaki 2006). While contemporary Pentecostalism has often been studied through the lens of temporalities in relation to processes of discontinuity, social change or rupture with the past (Meyer 1998; Robbins 2007, 2010), I want to argue that Pentecostal rearticulations of the past cannot be fully understood without considering the relationship between Pentecostalism and the future. These Pentecostal aspirational dynamics in relation to place-making through church-building connect with notions of individual success and collective development that challenge the rigid boundary between 'sacred' and 'profane', religious and secular. Here, material and religious transformations are entwined and these urban aspirations in village context can simultaneously impact the fields of economic, social and religious relations.

Examining the linkages between Pentecostal understandings of the future, development and rurality in Togo, Piot (2010) draws a number of parallels between the world of 'new' churches and that of NGOs, as both groups of actors seek to reconfigure power relations and people's relationship to past and future temporalities. According to Piot, both grammars of development involve a strong tendency to shift the gaze from a past that 'haunts' the present, to the promise of an open future. Piot speaks of a 'nostalgia for the future' reflected by the new 'agentic world' of development, shaped by narratives of rupture, linked to tropes of crisis and a collective longing for 'an intercession that might be life-transforming' (2010: 66). He also draws on Guyer (2007) to argue that a millenarist narrative of the End Time constitutes one of the ways in which Pentecostalism has distanced individuals from the near future and developed a new sensitivity to the far future.[1] This narrative has anchored them in the everyday and oriented them – and their hopes – towards a remote future, where one cannot but wait for the arrival of what is (prophetically) promised. In this chapter I want to suggest a different link between experience of the future and the social process of waiting among religious communities. In fact, in rural Benin, despite all the efforts made by their members, Pentecostal churches often remain under construction for a long time. These liminal, interstitial space-times between the initial foundation of the church and the completion of the construction process have become part of a process of aspirational place-making in the context of an expected future that is slow to arrive. These modes of waiting are neither based on a passive way of engaging with the present, nor fixated upon 'a miracle' in the far, more remote future. Rather, waiting constitutes an *active* way to live this seemingly 'empty' period while the church is under construction. The Pentecostal agentic work on waiting as well as the collective ability to endure allows church members to face the uncertainty resulting from stalled construction sites.

This chapter thus addresses how the church under construction can be considered as a space-time crystallizing different affective experiences related to the temporalities of religious transformation. To do so it will first look at the context of religious territorialization and urbanization in southern Benin, drawing upon examples of church planting pioneers and their socio-spatial trajectories. Then it will explore how the material liminality of the unfinished church is shaped by social and religious aspirations, idealized in the form of the multistorey concrete church. Finally the chapter will be discussing 'modes of waithood' and how these tie up with ideas of faithful endurance.

Church planting and the Pentecostal future in village context

During my fieldwork I observed the well-attended burial of a Pentecostal villager – in a context where such ritualized practices have become increasingly challenged by Pentecostal doctrine (Noret 2004). This particular burial was special, however: Edmond, the – relatively young – deceased forty-year-old man had been known for his contribution to the construction of the local church affiliated to the Nigerian megachurch Deeper Life Bible Church (in short, Deeper Life). That day, many of those present were external to the village, including Deeper Life pastors from neighbouring regions who came to pay homage to the deceased, honouring the memory of someone described to have been actively involved 'in the work of God'. Edmond had immigrated to Nigeria for work a few years back, leaving his wife and children in the village (whom he nevertheless visited frequently and to whom he was sending money on a regular basis). Some members of the church he used to attend in Nigeria also came to the funerals, following a long journey by truck.

Edmond, during one of his visits to the village, acquired two plots (*carrés*) that were part of the family estate but whose ownership had been contested by some of his kin, who wanted to sell the land. Despite his kin's resistance, Edmond nevertheless managed to develop both plots. One plot was used for his own house, the other was donated to the church and today these two constructions face each other. The decision to donate land to the church was directly linked to a vision he received from God while he was attending a Deeper Life church service in Lagos. The vision enjoined him to return to his village 'to plant a church' and instrumental to this was the cross-border networks of Deeper Life pastors and leaders which subsequently facilitated the creation of this new rural place of worship – or *agun* ('temple' or 'community').

'The building became precarious and it had to be knocked down in 2009', the church pastor recalled during the eulogy. 'And once again, Edmond offered his help when there was not enough money to rebuild our church. He died in Nigeria. But even in Nigeria, his concern was that evangelization should move forward here, in his village!' His younger brother then paid tribute to Edmond evoking the fact that a solution to the family conflict over the two plots of land 'was miraculously found' the very same day the church building was inaugurated. He added: 'Edmond wasn't rich, but he will be in Paradise in a big concrete, multi-storey house. I've dreamed it!'

This vignette illustrates the key role of Pentecostal actors who, by being both 'local' and mobile, become involved in the transformation of village space, like Edmond whose 'work for God' and legacy were publicly honoured during his funerals. It also suggests that the construction of the church progresses through different stages, each raising a number of issues, such as family conflict over land ownership or financial problems, against a wider backdrop of ambition for material prestige. The 'ideal church', the multistorey building made of bricks, mirrors the longed-for residential house, still unusual in rural Benin, and which features in the dream of Edmond's brother. As we shall see, this question of materiality brings us back to the theme of environmental transformation and the link between the process of church building and local idioms of 'development'.

In Benin, land, and even more so in the case of family land, has an important symbolic value. Real estate is one of the first investments socially mobile Beninese make from their savings. However, when it comes to land transfer, tensions over family land may at times erupt. Edmond, for instance, faced a number of difficulties, since his ownership of the land was contested by some extended family members and thus the land became '*terrain litigieux*'. In Benin, one can often see, inscribed on large signs or in thick painted letters the notice '*terrain litigieux*' indicating the presence of conflicts for land, very often family conflicts, over inheritance or over unilateral decisions to sell.[2] In rural context, church planting can thus be impacted by these conflicts over land ownership and transmission. When someone sets up a church on a plot that is part of their family land, the ownership of the plot is then transferred to the religious community, often a national or international Pentecostal denomination. There is here a transformation of the socio-spatial configuration of the village, as land ownership moves from the domestic sphere to an extra-familial, often translocal/global religious community.

In addition to land ownership, it is also important to note that residential construction is highly valued. For instance, villagers who have moved to the city and have become economically successful, are expected to build a house in their home village for themselves and/or their family. In that sense, for urban migrants a house is a marker of success and prestige but also evidence of a continued allegiance to the community, cementing a commitment to the village as a space of primary loyalty and thus of eventual return (Geschiere and Socpa 2016: 168). The development of places of worship in village settings by urban migrants is both an act of evangelization and socio-spatial change, a process through which an ancestral connection to the village can be converted into a commitment to a collective future.

The Pentecostal evangelization of the rural district where I conducted fieldwork started in the early 1990s with the setting up of branches of the Pentecostal denomination, *Union et Renaissance des Hommes en Christ* (URHC). One of the first churches in the village I studied was established in 1992 by a young man, Frank (twenty-five), and his small evangelizing group. Until 2002, his parish was affiliated to the URHC and since then has been attached to an increasingly influential national Pentecostal denomination, the *Mission Evangélique des Affranchis* (MEA).[3] As often the case, it is in Cotonou (the economic capital of Benin), where he was a public school teacher, that Frank converted to Pentecostalism. After becoming jobless, he left the city in the 1990s, to return to the village where he planted a church.

The way Pentecostalism links city and village through processes of mobility and return deserves more attention. During the 1980s and 1990s, with the explosion of Pentecostalism in Africa, it was cities that predominantly served as a base for Pentecostal evangelization. In the case of southern Benin, most of those who set up the first churches in villages, and who are today often deacons or parish leaders, had worked in nearby towns, such as Ouidah, or most often, Cotonou, where they converted. Pastors working in these smaller rural parishes are often circulating religious actors who reside in cities and come on Sunday for church services. Deacons are more local and are typically chosen among the village church members, with which they have closer relationships than the pastor.

From the mid-1980s to the early 1990s many urbanites, like Frank, returned to their village of origin in a context of socio-economic crisis largely linked to the imposition of structural adjustment programmes by the IMF and the World Bank (Banégas 2003). Drastic cuts in public budgets led to wage arrears, job losses and mounting unemployment, and young people were particularly hit by the crisis. The *'retour à la terre'* ('back to the land') process concerned unemployed civil servants but also young graduates who could not find work and therefore went back to rural areas (Bierschenk and Olivier de Sardan 1998).

While for many, the return to the village[4] was perceived as a 'step back' in order to regain some stability in the face of uncertainty, economic insecurity and crisis, Frank and many other church planters construe their own return differently, justified almost exclusively by the task of evangelizing the village. As a young convert, Frank was involved in an evangelization group linked to his church (the URHC) in Cotonou. During the early 1990s, he enjoined the members of his group to help him undertake an evangelizing 'mission' in his village. He also managed to convince both his parents to become Pentecostal through the URHC church he attended in Cotonou. His elder brother, a customs officer at the time, was living in Cotonou and had bought some land close to their family home in the village, where he undertook two types of construction projects. The first consisted of a series of small mud houses where his parents and other members of his family could live. At the time of the fieldwork, Frank lived there with his nuclear family and his mother (his father, too sick, returned to Cotonou): this complex of small houses was seen as the new 'family house'. The second building was an imposing two-storey house which had still not been completed twenty years later, at the time of my fieldwork, mostly due to lack of funds. This was meant to be a place for Frank's elder brother to live after retirement, but, now retired, he still lives in Cotonou.

In 1992, Frank's elder brother, who has two wives and several children, agreed to Frank's request to use a non-built-up part of his land to hold religious services, initially attended by their parents and the first converts in the village. Frank was able to convince his brother, a *'grande personne'*, a respected figure in Cotonou, to fulfil his social obligation towards his village and family and help him in his mission. His brother's unfinished, yet imposing, villa which dwarfs surrounding village houses, today stands shoulder to shoulder with the Pentecostal church made of beaten earth. While Frank did not have the resources to buy a plot in the village, nor to embark in the construction of a large house like his brother, he played an influential role both within his family and the wider village community in his mission to 'plant' a church, where he now has a leading role as secretary.

While this transformation of rural space through church planting is part and parcel of a wider process of religious expansion driven by national and international Pentecostal churches, evangelization is also bound up with individual aspirations and transformation of power relations in both kinship and village spheres. The parish offers new spaces and roles for villagers (treasurer, secretary or other titles for deacons) to increase their status in the eyes of the local religious community and beyond. Frank, a returned urbanite, who played a key part in the pioneering construction of a Pentecostal church has accrued a lot of prestige. In 2015, converting his religious/symbolic capital into political capital, he was elected as member of the village council emphasizing, during the campaign, his moral probity and his important church responsibility and management experience.

Involvement in the planting of a church in the village thus transforms the spatial and temporal perspective of those, like Edmond or Frank, who reconnected with or returned to their villages during the 1990s. The village is here no longer situated in an ancestral past to which one returns (or is forced to return), but is relocated in a future to which one can aspire – a future where one can become a respected religious leader and play a key part in the spatial and religious transformation of rural society, including the diffusion of moral values through, for instance, the open rejection of 'traditional' practices deemed sinful (polygamy, consumption of the liquor made from distilled palm wine during rituals, etc.).

Pentecostal materiality and aspirations for 'development'

For church planters a key step is to assess, once a location for a church has been secured, what materials to use for the construction based on resources initially available. There is typically a chronological progression in the types of material used for building churches: first are used the most fragile materials such as straw, followed by tree branches, which are then replaced with beaten earth, and eventually concrete bricks. This range of material possibilities thus produces a heterogenous landscape of religious urbanization in village context.

This succession of building material used illustrates a spatialization process which is linear as it progresses towards an ideal 'end-form', that is, buildings made of concrete such as villas, still rare in village settings and most often seen on the outskirts of Cotonou. This process is often interrupted, mostly because of lack of resources, and thus the 'suspended spatiality' (Gupta 2018) of unfinished houses is a common feature of the 'rurban' landscape in Benin. This spatio-religious movement finds an echo in the way locals speak of and experience the future, and express their aspirations towards success and development.

In *Fongbe*, the lingua franca of southern Benin, the word that translates 'future' is *nukɔnmɛ*, literally meaning 'in front of'. The most common word used by people to speak about the future is *nukɔnyiyi*, meaning 'moving forward' (or '*aller de l'avant*' in French), suggesting not only a (spatio-temporal) orientation – a projection – but also implying movement across space. The future as 'moving forward' conveys an idea of positive mobility: if one advances, one has a (good) future. In a range of cultural contexts, an improved, more productive future is often linked to the wider trope of mobility (see Hage 2009 about migration to Australia; Jansen 2014 about Bosnia; Premawardhana 2018 about Mozambique). In Benin, the idea of forward movement implied in *nukɔnyiyi* relates to a mobility that is one-way and linear and, according to the context in which it is used, the word may also refer to the notion of evolution, progress or 'development'. Progress towards the future is achieved in different ways, for instance, through the physical mobility of individuals when they migrate to cities and/or abroad. As this chapter suggests, mobility towards the future is also realized through place-making – in particular the construction of houses and Pentecostal churches.

Churches are not the only buildings under construction that represent models of success and development through their multistorey, concrete aesthetic. The example of Frank is here again relevant. Between the church and his family home lies the imposing villa owned by his elder brother. In this case, while the 'aesthetic of the future', that is, the concrete structure and its four floors are visible, the house, which has no doors or windows is still unfinished. Moreover, and perhaps more importantly, the house is also empty – devoid of furniture, objects and people. This particular aspect of unfinished constructions has been analysed in some of the literature on housing, 'homing' and transnational migration (see Boccagni 2020). Caroline Melly, describing the large 'half-built houses' in Dakar whose construction was financed by members of the Senegalese diaspora talks of these 'houses-in-process' as having become 'latent possibilities and future articulations rather than present impossibilities' (2010: 57). Melly thus shows that unfinished houses are not in that sense truly incomplete: they are a way to assert the possibility of migrants' future participation in city life, they constitute a place-based claim for urban territoriality. These 'houses-in-process' – 'not-yet-houses' or 'inside-out houses' as she also coins them – should not solely be conceived in terms of domestic living spaces, as they embody the ongoing commitment of migrants and diasporic actors in relation to their homeland and more particularly their right to a *future* participation in the urbanity of Dakar. Here studying the process of construction allows us to think in terms of present perspectives and future aspirations.

Like the Dakar unfinished houses described by Melly, Frank's older brother's villa was something more than an uninhabited place. In southern Benin, large and lavish houses are linked to future aspirations to success and development. This is particularly evident in the material culture of posters hung inside many village huts, and which show stereotypical American/Western suburban scenes featuring a large house, a car and a family. When asked about the large houses in their region, villagers often emphasize the fact that they were not only the materialization of the success of the individual who built it,[5] but contributed equally to the 'development (*nukɔnyiyi*) of the village'. In these local tropes of development, the house's architecture, height and in particular its materiality – made of concrete – are significant elements.

Similar tropes apply to the construction of the Pentecostal churches in village settings. Like in the case of Senegalese migrants described by Melly (2010), those who invest efforts and material as well as social resources to plant and/or build a church, are expected not only to play a role of authority in the future Pentecostal community (taking on the role of deacon for example), but also within the village, for instance through local/council politics. A recurrent view is that the construction of these churches directly contributes to the 'development' of villages, especially when it comes to churches made of cement – an important material symbol of progress (*nukɔnyiyi*).

Choplin notes, in her study of the production, circulation and consumption of cement in the West African urban corridor, that cement (used to make concrete) is the 'most important and valuable symbol of urban production and accumulation' (Choplin 2019b: 4), embodying 'an avatar of modernity' – comparable to the place that glass occupied in Walter Benjamin's description of urban modernity (ibid.: 14). Imagined through its 'reassuring' resilience and toughness, cement

Figure 6.1. The villa and the church. Photo by Carla Bertin.

thus crystallizes subjective attempts to overcome the precarity, uncertainty and complexity of the African metropolitan experience (Choplin 2019a: 13).

This symbolic value of cement (see also Archambault 2018), materializing success, modernity and collective development – partly explains why Pentecostal actors are so eager to invest in concrete churches. Concrete buildings 'stand out as signs of the modern and the good' (Taussig 2004: 162). The durability (and practicality) of concrete is also of course a key characteristic here, especially in terms of maintenance: after the rainy seasons concrete buildings do not have to be repaired like mud houses do, and this has implications on how materiality is construed in relation to a projected, long-term future but also in relation to more predictable, temporal rhythms. In the context of an uncertain present, concrete allows people to imagine a future, to move forward (*yi nukɔn*). The 'concrete aesthetic' of cement shapes a process of place-making anchoring the church within a *longue durée* and is thus at the heart of process of 'religious rurbanization'.

This materiality also has a deep religious meaning. The size of a church, even unfinished, reflects the ambition and aspiration of the Pentecostal community but also potentially mirrors the grandeur of God. The church is a marker of territorialization, a sign of developmental transformation through urbanization in a context of ancestral rurality within which a new – blessed and spiritually powerful – Pentecostal society is being carved up. Like in many other African societies, rurality has in Benin often been construed, in particular by Pentecostals, through the moral geography of the 'pagan bush' – echoing older colonial tropes central to the nineteenth-century missionary 'developmental' project (Coleman and Vásquez 2017: 42). In the region where I worked, villages with no new constructions and/or with mud houses not visibly maintained were often seen by Pentecostals as 'underdeveloped', 'stuck in the past' (*gudoyiyi*, literally: 'going backwards') because they were detrimentally influenced by evil forces and witchcraft. One of my key informants, Simon (thrity two), a successful moto-taxi driver, was considering using his savings to buy a plot and build a house but was not planning to invest in his native village:

> My village is full of run down (*délabrées*) houses, meaning that witchcraft is stronger there than anywhere else. My family is very good at that. You should see the state of constructions in our village. Nobody had the strength to construct anything here. I will build far away from there.

In the end, Simon bought a plot in a peri-urban district, in the sprawling corridor linking Ouidah and Cotonou, reflecting a recent trend observed in several other African urban contexts (Choplin 2019b: 5; Melly 2010). In Simon's native village, the only construction built in concrete is in fact a Pentecostal church – a branch of a national denomination comprising three other parishes scattered across Benin. Pastor Claude, who founded the church in 1997, told me how with the presence of the church 'the village could now develop', describing local evangelization through church-planting as a force of moral transformation and *nukɔnyiyi*. This village parish, set up in 2007, was continuously evolving throughout the duration of my fieldwork. While the number of worshippers (around twenty women and five men) remained stable, the building seemed to be in a permanent state of construction and reconstruction. In 2016 the first cement bricks had been laid around the structure made of branches. The congregation would gather inside the church for services and other activities even if it was made of a (dual) evolving materiality – with one structure undergoing destruction, while the other was in construction. This gradual replacement was heralding a slow movement towards a Pentecostal modernity, with the changing church materiality representing the ideal of a new projected society, rendering 'present' the power of God's promises (Engelke 2007). Church planting in the (spiritually risky) rural context is here also linked to the idea of a pioneering territorialization allowing the 'unblocking' of the village, enabling born-again individuals and communities to break free from ancestral curses and the weight of 'tradition' (Meyer 1998).

Liminal agency and enduring waithood

Despite an intense desire for a projected, liberating Pentecostal 'rurban' modernity, many of these churches remain unfinished mostly because of limited resources, that is, lack of capital to purchase and transport cement as well as metallic materials needed for the roof. While the choice of materials and a desire to urbanize reveal

Figure 6.2. The church of Pastor Claude. Photo by Carla Bertin.

an aspirational place-making among Pentecostals, the prolonged, and never-ending delayed completion of the construction process shapes a spatio-temporal experience of liminality and in-betweenness. Unlike concrete, the temporality of construction is thus shaky, unpredictable and often 'crumbling', mostly shaped by socio-economic factors or crises such as droughts, and so on. Between the acquisition of the land, the laying of the first stone, the foundational stage of construction, and the eventual completion, several years can often pass. This was the case for instance of the district headquarters of the main association of Pentecostal churches. The land bought in 2009 remained undeveloped until 2016 when the start of construction was initiated with collective prayers led by pastors from several local parishes belonging to the district association. Foundation pillars were soon erected but because of a lack of funds and internal conflicts, the project abruptly stalled.

When they occur, material transformations, even if slow and unpredictable, are almost always the result of collective labour of 'ordinary' members – most of whom are women. Although women rarely become leaders, they are the most likely to inhabit, on an everyday basis, the religious space. They remain in the church after the service has ended and often organize church activities or meetings of microcredit groups, *tontine* (rotating credit) associations or buying clubs.

I witnessed several instances of collective construction work in one of my villages of study. During one of these, members of the local church were all called

Figure 6.3. Collective prayer. Photo by Carla Bertin.

to level the ground floor of their *temple*, whose new brick walls had been recently erected. They were to transport soil in large buckets to pour onto the floor, before flattening it in order to prepare it for the cementing process. At dawn, around thirty church members came, almost exclusively women. After several hours of work transporting the soil from a nearby plot and flattening the ground, one of the parish deacons gathered the women together, telling them: 'You have given up the fields and the market to obey the Commandments of the church! May the Lord bless you a hundredfold! May you be freed from obstacles!'

In Benin, women are indeed particularly involved in small trade and agricultural work. However, while Sunday services, weekly church meetings and church maintenance/construction work are socially demanding, affecting the time women can dedicate to economic activities, religious labour is considered productive, moving individuals forward, towards the direction of a blessed future. Waiting here is transformed into a particular form of agency and the seemingly empty time linked to the unfinished construction of the church yet-to-come is reworked and negotiated. In that sense the 'enduring attitude of expectant waiting' (Guyer 2007: 414) is not a passive state of affair and as recent 'ethnographies of waiting' (Janeja and Bandak 2018) have shown, endurance can be bound up with a range of affective experiences. Endurance, 'this ability to snatch agency in the very midst of its lack' (Hage 2009: 101), thus challenges 'stuckedness' as a 'sense of existential immobility' (ibid.: 97). Similarly as Appadurai (2013: 127) suggests,

Figure 6.4. Collective building. Photo by Carla Bertin.

hope, as a key element of endurance, can be a "force that converts the passive condition of 'waiting for' to the active condition of 'waiting to'".

'Waithood' was regularly discussed during women's meetings and Biblical stories were often quoted at length, especially when it came to problems of infertility, financial or marital issues. Recurrent stories included feminine characters who could not have children but were rewarded by a divine intervention for their faithful wait, like in the New Testament story of Elizabeth who was well beyond child bearing years and who gave birth to John the Baptist (Matthew 11:11). The ability to wait was religiously praised and seen as key to success and integral to the achievement of personal goals – construed both as something to be cultivated and as potentially rewarding. Waiting entails an attitude of hopeful endurance but also, and perhaps more importantly, because it is socially demanding it involves an active loyalty to the congregation – in a context where church leaders are concerned about the potential attraction of other religious groups present in the region.

In Sunday sermons, waiting and endurance are hailed as virtuous with pastors often reminding church members that the promises of God operate on a particular temporal plane, the *Kairos*, different, even if interrelated, to the earthly one, the *Chronos*. Waiting thus relocates the believer within a Godly temporality – '100 years for us is 1 day for God; only God knows when to give you what you are looking for' was heard during a Sunday sermon. Waiting is also framed within the Pentecostal temporal experience of faith which, as Marshall (2009: 66) argues, relies on an 'urgency of the present, as the only time we have left in which to realize the redemption of the past and the possibility of salvation'.

The hope of a liberation from *blocages spirituels* consists of a wait 'full' of religious work – involving prayers, meetings, religious services and collective labour oriented towards the material transformation of building or maintaining the church. Here, to be able to wait is to be 'blessed a hundredfold', far from being synonymous to a blind and passive obedience to a distant future. Waiting and endurance have thus become 'proactive' attitudes and, as Reinhardt points out in his ethnography of a Pentecostals in Ghana, what he calls the 'waiting of faith' is the 'normative horizon from which the Christian subject should think, feel and act upon the present' (2018: 114). The 'waiting of faith' is 'not stationary but a complex pattern of affective and ethical motion, paradoxically self-fulfilling in its very non-fulfilment' (Reinhardt 2018: 114). My study echoes Reinhardt's ethnography: I found that the capacity (and will) to wait is considered a grace, a 'gift from God' but, at the same time, it is 'learned', can be seen as a skill that matures over time and which involves experience and practice.

In the Pentecostal churches of rurban southern Benin, women spend a long time, several hours a day, praying for success and a good future. 'Endurance waiting' has become a strategy to provoke and orient divine intervention, so that answers to prayers can be granted. Furthermore, choosing to participate in the building of the church instead of working in the fields is a choice these women make in order to 'detach themselves from obstacles' blocking their *nukɔnyiyi* as 'forward-movement' to a liberating future. While endurance waiting is thus an active driving force that constantly addresses the impatient tendencies for doubt, uncertainty or despair, waiting can also, in the Maussian sense, be seen as mode of deferral between exchanges, as part of a wider moral economy of reciprocity binding believers and God (see Coleman 2004). Donations and offerings are, in that context, part of the collective work of building, maintaining and expanding the materiality of the church. In addition to volunteered time and labour, these financial contributions from church members are particularly crucial since city-based church headquarters send little or no money to their village branches to cover staff salaries, pastors' subsistence/travel expenses and the cost of maintaining or expanding a building. However, as Reinhardt (2018: 116) argues 'the gift, like prayer, is a relational, future-making act permanently threatened by the possibility of vanishing', hence the importance of faithful and hopeful waiting as well as an enacted belief in God's supreme temporality when promises of positive transformation and *nukɔnyiyi* are slow (or fail) to materialize. 'Trustful waiting' (Rey 2015: 42) is key here: 'You have to trust God, because what God says will always be realized', to quote a Pentecostal leader discussing the infertility problems of a church member. The 'economy of blessing' is clearly made of 'sacrifice and selflessness, patience and perseverance' (ibid.: 350).

Conclusion

In this chapter I have explored the ways in which the creation of Pentecostal churches contributes to the social and material circulation taking place between city and village, driving a slow process of urbanization in rural Benin. This religious urbanization crystallizes a world of promises and future aspirations, both social and religious. 'Villagers', mostly male, who have been socially mobile like Frank or Edmond, and who have spearheaded church planting, can lay claims for recognition within their communities, and can gain prestige and influence through their subsequent role in the social and religious space of the church. As private/family land is converted into religious space, and relocated within a wider Pentecostal public sphere, theses aspirations create affordances, strategically and effectively transforming the local. While Burchardt and Westendorp argue that immaterial 'urban religious aspirations' are 'realized' through 'practices of being in the city, belonging to the city and experiencing the city' (2018: 164), I showed that these aspirations are also at the heart of a process of Pentecostal place-making linking the 'city' to the 'village' through urbanization, a process which involves a particular take on the future for a range of local actors. While most Pentecostal churches in my study area have national and international branches, it is indeed mostly local actors who have played a key role in constructing new churches in village settings.

I also showed how the process of construction is linked to local understandings of the future and tropes of development. This process is slow, interrupted and mobilizes religious tropes of endurance and waiting. Seeing how people relate to these apparently invisible, empty temporalities allowed us to capture the ways in which a congregation can live and construct a common future. Unfinished churches in that sense render tangible the multiple ways in which Pentecostals articulate their present and their future.

Vokes and Pype (2018) draw on the idea of the chronotope to challenge the idea that new technologies in Africa are simply vectors of innovation, modernity and development. These technologies are instead inserted within complex temporalities, beyond the dominant idea of globalization as time-space compression. Similarly, these multistorey concrete churches reveal materialized forms of 'mobility towards the future', of 'success' and of 'development' that are more complex than dominant narratives of modernity and (Western-centric) forms of globalization.

It is useful, in this sense, to think of the church under construction as a chronotope that incorporates different driving forces of affect linked to the future, within a wider quest for a 'forward-movement'. The first brick allows the idea of the future to be grasped; it is a materiality upon which the members of the congregation project their aspirations, aspirations which go beyond the simple question of Pentecostal conversion. The collective effort to form a Pentecostal society is intimately linked to local notions of success and development, which themselves have much to do with the materiality of urbanization. Central here is the symbolic value of cement, used to produce concrete, the hegemonic materialization of the urban. The incomplete nature of such construction projects, 'ruins of the future' (Gupta 2018: 69), involves a form of active waiting during long periods when scarce resources and conflicts do not allow for these projects to 'move forward'. In order to fully understand the social meaning of these place-making processes and their link to local grammars of the future, there is a need to shift one's attention from dwelling to constructing.

Chapter 7

THE TERRITORIAL TEMPORALITIES OF URBAN RELIGION: PENTECOSTALISM, NEIGHBOURHOOD CHANGE AND PLANNING CONTROL IN LAGOS, NIGERIA

Taibat Lawanson and Gareth Millington

Introduction

When African cities grow or transform from within, urban management systems are often ill-equipped to respond to the challenges and complexities that accompany such developments. Religious denominations and places of worship are increasingly being identified as significant actors in the creation of urban forms, actors that sometimes challenge or contradict the stated goals of land use planning in many African and Asian cities (Bouma and Hughes 2000; Hancock and Srinivas 2008; Meyer 2002). At the same time, examples of the influence of religious movements in residential neighbourhoods abound in many cities globally with faith communities shaping local everyday life, deploying infrastructures and providing material and symbolic resources to members and residents (Day 2017; Fawaz 2009; Hancock and Srinivas 2008). Recent scholarship on the nexus between religion and urban space in Nigeria include Adeboye (2012), Katsaura (2019), Larkin (2008) and Obadare (2018), all of whom highlight how the activities of faith-based organizations influence urban cultures and practices. Ukah (2013a, 2016) brings an alternative and offers a welcome emphasis on political economy in his study of the RCCG (Redeemed Christian Church of God) Redemption Camp, a large Pentecostal urbanizing enclave situated just outside of Lagos (see also Asamoah-Gyadu 2019). Ukah argues that the camp is part and parcel of an 'entrepreneurial' religious vision, highlighting RCCG's integration of market logic with evangelism. This, he suggests, is the *business* of 'doing God's work'. Accordingly, 'the church's attempt to construct a city out of dense forest area, based on a profit driven understanding and practising of faith ... follow[s] the path of neoliberal urbanism' (Ukah 2016b: 258). However, while it is important to pay attention to spectacular peripheral enclaving, this chapter argues that there is also a need to interrogate the interface of religion and urbanization at a smaller scale, and in more central parts of the urban landscape, and this with a view to gain a more comprehensive understanding of how cities across the globe are evolving in pace with revivalist (Christian) movements. Using as a case study the inner urban neighbourhood of Onike in Lagos, this chapter seeks to understand the growing local presence of yet another iconic, global Nigerian Pentecostal Church – the Mountain of Fire and Miracles Ministries (MFM). In particular, we place the church's territorial strategies – accomplished over three decades – and its 'moralising' influence over urban space under critical scrutiny. As we shall see, a key question is whether this example of religious urban enclaving constitutes a form of 'popular urbanization' – in the sense of a strategy through which an urban territory is produced, transformed and appropriated by institutions and/or forms of self-organization beyond the state (Streule et al. 2020) – or a Pentecostal-inflected mode of 'pacification', gentrification and displacement.

Key urban policy documents, produced by the likes of UN-Habitat, pay scant attention to how faith-based organizations (FBOs) such as Pentecostal churches like MFM or RCCG are shaping the city and developing infrastructural projects in sub-Saharan Africa. Where religion is mentioned, it is associated with the dangers of radicalization and as a cause of segregation and social conflict. Religion is often presented as an obstacle to development, as a barrier to modernization. Jones and Peterson (2011) comparably point to how, in the related field of development, the work of FBOs is viewed instrumentally, in terms of what they contribute to the 'real' development work of NGOs. Similarly, in this chapter we do not perceive Pentecostal Christianity as incidental to urbanization. Rather, we favour an approach to this topic that focuses not on religion 'in' the city, or religion 'and' the city but upon the entanglements of religion and urban change. Such a perspective sees religion as an active agent 'preparing and pushing' in processes of urbanization as well as reacting and adapting to changing urban conditions – becoming, in the process, part-and-parcel of urbanity (see Rüpke 2020). In this sense, we see Lagos as a post-secular city (see Beaumont 2008b; Beaumont and Cloke 2012) that is illustrative of changing dynamic relations between governance, capital and religion, although our evidence points less towards collaboration between faith-based and non-faith-based partners and more towards Pentecostal territorialization.

In Lagos, Nigeria's premier city, urban growth has resulted in changing morphology and land use reconfigurations that are not only visible in terms of expansion but also at the community and neighbourhood scale. This reconfiguration is often without regard for extant planning regulations. For example, there have been significant transitions from residential to commercial (Computer Village, Palm Avenue), residential to mixed use (Allen Avenue/Opebi, Adeniran Ogunsanya) and residential to 'institutional', particularly religious, use (Oregun, Gbagada). Moreover, neighbourhoods such as Gbagada, Ilupeju, Oregun and Onike have experienced the gradual incursion of FBOs that have resulted in forms of enclaving, aesthetic transformation and a change of land use. However, the development control lexicon captures religious land uses under 'institutional', alongside schools, libraries, hospitals and government buildings. As a result, these change-of-use transformations can go largely undetected and unaddressed, not least at the policy level, and in this chapter, we also want to explore how these changes relate to a range of socio-spatial dynamics and tensions inherent in religious territorialization. In order to do so, the chapter first examines the linkages of urban development, planning administration and religious institutions discussing the potential relevance of our case study in the context of megacity Lagos. It will then proceed to explore the temporalities and patterns of socio-spatial change in Onike, and the role of MFM in these gradual local reconfigurations. The chapter finally explores how MFM actors engage with both local residents and town planning agencies and the implications of these interactions on socio-spatial inclusion and urban governance.

This case study research draws upon a mixed methodology, involving an analysis of the urban development patterns and the operative urban planning regulatory processes in the Onike area, which was then complemented by in-depth interviews with representatives of the Lagos state Physical Planning Authority and the Lagos State Urban Renewal Agency. Fieldwork was also conducted between July and October 2018 in the Onike neighbouroood, and involved discussions among residents and local church members and a geo-spatial mapping of the spatial footprint of MFM.

Planning and Pentecostalism in the spatial configuration of Lagos

Characterized as 'arguably the most Pentecostal city in the world' (Anderson 2004: 4), Lagos is undergoing intense structural changes as a direct consequence of increased spatial expansion of new forms of religiosity and its economic reverberations. These changes filter down to the everyday life of residents, whose lives adapt in accordance with Pentecostal influence on the spaces, infrastructures, rhythms and ambiences that comprise the urban fabric. Much of the impetus for the transformation of Lagos has deep roots in the irrepressible and socially strong form of Pentecostal Christianity that has come to characterize social life in southern Nigeria since the 1970s (Marshall 2009; Obadare 2018; Ukah 2016b). There has also been a shift in the Pentecostal movement from 'humble' egalitarian fellowships to entrepreneurial/bureaucratic churches, sometimes under the sway of powerful, charismatic – some might say authoritarian – personalities (Martin 2002). Examples other than MFM include RCCG, mentioned earlier, and led by Enoch Adeboye, Living Faith (or 'Winners Chapel') led by David Oyedepo and Christ Embassy led by Chris Oyakhilome.

It has been argued that the quasi destruction of state capacity in Nigeria since 1986 – under World Bank/IMF structural adjustment policies – created a void, a social space of 'radical insecurity' (Marshall 2009), in which religion, especially Pentecostalism, could compensate for a shrinking and/or failing state (see also Lanz and Oosterbaan 2016). Nowadays in Lagos, the ruins of twentieth-century public investment in the city co-exists alongside with recent religious, market-driven and informal, or popular, forms of urban development. Lagos is thus a privileged site where these developments can be observed, with the spectacular boom, since the

1990s, of Pentecostal megachurches encouraging the creation of a new kind of citizen and 'born-again' subject (Marshall, 2014; Osinulu 2014) and reconfiguring a physical and aesthetic environment that anticipates a new socio-spatial order as Ukah (2004) aptly showed. These Pentecostal churches have been spatially remapping the city through the active appropriation of secular spaces (classrooms, civic halls, hotels, restaurants, cinemas, motor parks, sports stadia and racecourses) as sites for prayer meetings, healing and deliverance services and Sunday worship (Adeboye 2012). Growing from this has been the gradual infiltration of residential neighbourhoods with religious land uses – a form of both everyday and 'sacred urbanisms' that is analogous to religious enclaving (Bhardwaj 1994). Enclaving is described by Gilsenan (1982: 394) as: 'Not only one building being constructed on an alien model, but an entire system of urban life in its economic, political, and symbolic-cultural forms being imposed upon already existing towns and cities that have been organized on quite different bases'. Enclaving is also associated with an 'aesthetics of imagination', 'which stretches from subjective and collective forms of religious differentiation to overt material manifestations' (Nielsen, Sumich and Bertelsen 2021: 898). Religious enclaving cuts across many neighbourhoods in Lagos, resulting in a situation where *religious organizations* such as Pentecostal churches – as opposed to and sometimes in opposition to existing residents – materially and symbolically anchor their presence in the urban landscape, and reorchestrate these places in particular ways, often at variance with extant planning regulations (Coleman and Elsner 1995).

Religious urbanization and scale: Enclaving as popular urbanization or gentrification?

Like all forms of urbanization under (late) capitalism, religious urbanization occurs at different scales simultaneously; from spectacular developments such as prayer camps that contain hospitals, banks, schools, housing and so forth to the 'piecemeal' (Sawyer 2014) colonization and/or institutional enclaving of existing neighbourhoods such as Onike, the focus of this chapter. And yet, these ostensibly distinct modes of Pentecostal urbanization are 'two sides of the same coin'. In other words, the piecemeal is no less remarkable than the spectacular. Onike is where the historic headquarters of the MFM church are located. MFM is known for power-prayer and spiritual warfare (Butticci 2013) and is one the fastest-growing Nigerian Pentecostal churches with hundreds of branches across Africa and the African/Nigerian diaspora. Its church auditorium in the Onike neighbourhood can accommodate several thousand worshippers, but similarly to other Lagos-based Pentecostal churches such as RCCG or Winners' Chapel (and even some Muslim organizations), MFM has established a large gated satellite space, 'Prayer City', at the periphery of Lagos where larger events are organized (Butticci 2013).

Although we focus on the neighbourhood level, this analysis is relevant to Brenner's (2019: 47) argument that spatial scales are no longer conceived as fixed, pregiven arenas of social life; rather 'the full spectrum of spatial scales, the neighbourhood, the local, and the regional to the national, the continental and the global, are now being recognized as historical products, at once socially constructed, institutionally mediated, politically contested, and therefore malleable'. In this sense, the spatial interventions of MFM in Onike are examples of Pentecostal attempts to (re)define the scale of neighbourhood in relation to an interscalar mesh of 'spatial fixes' rooted in long-term (spiritual and financial) investments in the built environment (see Brenner 2019; Harvey 2012). The interscalar Pentecostal urban imaginary involves competing churches conducting urban (and spiritual) planning at local, metropolitan and global levels and realizing these plans, in part, through the material built environment. It is in this sense that religion is not simply a question of belief, but a material phenomenon central to understanding contemporary urbanization (in Lagos and elsewhere, see Garbin and Strhan 2017a). Although we focus on the local here, our analysis is not bounded; rather, it adheres to the critical maxim that there can be 'no "specificity" without "generality"' (Goonewardena 2018: 460). In other words, this chapter does not present an isolated case – rather, it constitutes a small part of a wider research problem that attempts to understand religious urbanization as a confluence of complex, interrelated spatial scales and multiple temporalities.

In terms of urbanization, the influence of Pentecostals on the urban fabric – its physical structures, metabolisms, aesthetics, social relations and subjectivities – is a challenge to Western-centric approaches that understand neoliberal urbanization primarily in terms of *state* (re)territorialization (e.g. Brenner 2019) and *market* liberalization (Peck, Theodore and Brenner 2013). While both factors remain salient, something else is occurring in the example we discuss in this chapter, the fact that *religious* actors act as entrepreneurial agents amid the post-colonial wreckage left by state planning and gaps in governance structures, in the context of rapidly rising urban populations. Classic political economy is not the overriding context of contexts within which these urban processes unfold, rather it is a *religio*-political economy that comprises the 'context of context' (Brenner and Schmid 2015: 161). Recognition of this is informed, among others, by Obadare's (2018) understanding of the close political and economic links between Pentecostal pastors and government and Ukah's (2011) ground-breaking analysis of RCCG's many corporate links and 'market-friendly' aesthetic. However, recognition of this does not necessarily constitute or warrant a 'Southern reframing' of urban analysis (Parnell and Robinson 2012: 597), neither should religious urbanization be defined as 'pockets of resistance and shelter against retreating states under neoliberal restructuring programmes' (Lanz and Oosterbaan 2016: 489), but rather 'as a *constitutive force* of urban modernity and of neoliberal urbanism' (ibid., added emphasis). Our sensitivity to the religio-political economic context enhances the theorization of recent transformations in Lagos by illuminating the multiple drivers of urban change, in particular the accumulation strategies of entrepreneurial Pentecostal religious institutions who work both with and against the state and/or the market.

Moreover and in the sense that our data reveal evidence that Pentecostal enclaving leads to a rise in rent values and the displacement or inconveniencing of existing residents and traders, it is tempting to characterize what is occurring in Onike as an example of 'religious gentrification'. Such a phenomenon, were it to exist, would challenge most existing literature that understands gentrification as a *secularising* process – for example, Ley and Martin's (1993) study of Canadian cities. While there have been some studies linking Islam with neighbourhood-level gentrification – for example, Abaza (2004) finds that in Jakarta, gentrification and religious habitus are becoming strongly intertwined among middle-class urbanites – religion tends to be presented as the dependent variable, whereby religiosity goes up or down *as a result of* gentrification (e.g. Cimino 2013). But as Abaza (2004) and Weng (2017) highlight, religious organizations can be decisive agents in processes (and outcomes) that in some ways resemble gentrification.

But what exactly is gentrification? In a useful operational definition, Savage, Warde and Ward (2003) argue that gentrification is the coincidence of four processes: (1) the displacement of one group of residents with a concentration of new residents of a higher social status; (2) the transformation of the built environment in terms of exhibiting distinctive aesthetic features and evidence of the emergence of new local services; (3) the gathering together of persons with a shared culture, lifestyle and consumer preferences and (4) the economic reordering of property values. However, while useful, this definition leaves out the issue of pacification or domestication. As Atkinson (2007: 1911) describes it, pacification involves a process of 'scripting public spaces and framing the range of behaviours deemed acceptable'. The use of the term dates to Zukin's (1995) analysis of New York's Bryant Park during the late 1980s and early 1990s, where a park with a reputation for drug dealing and homelessness was brought back into 'control' when private actors were given responsibility for its redesign and management. But as Koch and Latham (2013) point out, in addition to acting against inclusive urban spaces, pacification (or domestication) can be understood more positively 'as a fundamental part of how people come to be at home in cities' (ibid.: 19). This way of thinking undergirds a critical investigation of gentrification, by asking '*how* spaces are being domesticated and the kinds of *ethos* that underpin a given space or set of interventions' (ibid., emphasis added). It also points to the ambivalence inherent in any attempt at the pacification of urban space.

However, as Asher Ghertner (2015) points out, gentrification theory is not equally applicable across the globe and scholars should not make the implicit assumption that urban examples or processes in, say, Lagos can be understood simply as a variation of a more general trend covered by the umbrella term 'gentrification' (ibid.: 552–3). As such, it is not only economic pressure that causes displacement but also extra-economic force and/or state violence (ibid.: 553). Asher Ghertner's conclusion, relevant here, is that 'gentrification [in the Western definition that focuses on private ownership] *is* taking place in Mumbai, Rio and Luanda, but it is happening in those areas of these cities that are *already privatized*, where diverse tenure regimes have already been flattened' (ibid.: 560, emphasis added). Indeed, this is relevant to our case study of Onike, where original owner under pressure to sell purchased from the traditional land-owning families who bequeathed customary titles. In this sense, tenures had already been privatized before MFM arrived. The custom in Lagos is for these titles to be predated to before 1978 when the Land Use act introduced statutory land holding across the country.

As stated in the introduction, another important question to consider is whether enclaving caused by religious urbanization is a form of 'popular urbanization'. This is defined by Streule et al. (2020: 652) as 'a specific urbanization process based on collective initiatives, self-organization and the activities of inhabitants'. Their aim is to move beyond debates hindered by the shortcomings of the term 'informalization', another term that is relevant to but not well-suited to understanding the complexities of religious urbanization. One obvious similarity between informal and religious forms of urbanization, as we shall show, is how both are accomplished through a 'complex continuum of legality and illegality' (Roy, 2005). The *popular* dimension is how to Pentecostalite forms of urbanization are how it *resembles* a 'process that is based on self-organization and collectivity, includes aspects of informality, illegality and social struggle, and develops incrementally by constant improvement of houses and neighbourhoods' (Streule et al. 2020: 655). Moreover, Comaroff adds that Pentecostalism makes its appeal to the masses through a variety of forms: 'Commerce, government, education, the media, the popular arts – nothing [including the city itself] seems too trivial or debased to offer grist to the spiritual mill. The task ... is to put "God-in-everything," so "anything-can-be-holy"'. Popular urbanization can be distinguished from informalization because, as Streule et al. (2020: 653 added emphasis) explain:

> The 'popular' aspect refers to a wide range of actors producing urban space ... with a shared interest in producing urban space for themselves as well as their community. These social groups can often be defined by categories such as kinship, friendship, origin, *religion* or political affiliation.

Popular urbanization is a strategy 'through which [an] urban territor[y] [is] produced, transformed and appropriated by the people'. We might see the actions of MFM, an organization funded by the tithes, offerings and donations of its members, as autonomous in that it is engaged with the production of an urban space that differs in kind and ethos 'from spaces produced through other related but distinct urbanization processes' (ibid.). Although Streule et al. point to the utopian dimensions of popular urbanization, they concede that such strategies can be driven by self-interest and pervaded by power hierarchies (ibid.). They do not however point to how these aspects may, in effect, *contaminate* popular urbanization, in the process creating displacement and their own forms of resistance and non-consent. Just like gentrification, popular urbanization – as a concept – does not capture *everything* that is happening in Onike. However, both notions offer some analytical purchase on urban change in this Lagos neighbourhood.

MFM (Mountain of Fire and Miracles) in Onike and the time-spaces of religious territorialization

The MFM purchased a single plot of land in 1994 and have grown to become the largest landowner in Onike, appropriating 36.8 per cent of the neighbourhood space for various uses (See Figure 7.1). Before providing more detail about this gradual territorialization, it is important to note that urban planning in Lagos is a complex process involving a range of different public bodies. The Yaba District office of the Lagos State Planning Permit Authority (LASSPA) exhibits jurisdictional authority over Onike, while urban development is managed within the framework of the Lagos Mainland central model city plan (2013–30). The Lagos Ministry of Physical Planning and Urban Development, through its various agencies, is tasked with initiating, executing and monitoring urban planning and spatial development in the city. Development control is the purview of the LASSPA, which is responsible for issuing development permits and monitoring compliance with operative physical development plans. The Lagos State Building Control Agency (LABCA) is tasked with building control, construction state certification and removal of illegal buildings. As indicated earlier, religious land uses are subsumed under the broad categorization of 'institutional' land use, and town planning officials often encounter challenges with FBOs, in particular Pentecostal churches. Eleven documents are required to kickstart the planning approval application process (land title documents, survey plan, architectural, structural, mechanical and electrical drawings, tax clearance, traffic/environmental impact and land use assessment, geotechnical reports and receipts of relevant assessment fees and charges) and each building is granted approval according to its intended use. In an interview, the Yaba district officer for LASSPA distinguished between 'traditional' churches and the newer Pentecostal churches:

> In this area, it is the traditional churches that have complete approvals. St Dominic's Catholic church has approval for all buildings on their premises; for example, the church building has approval for institutional land use, while the bookshop has approval for commercial land use. Many of the [Pentecostal] churches start the approval process, but when we ask them to bring a particular documentation, they usually abandon the process.

Failure to abide by planning rules has caused tensions in and around and in some religious enclaves focusing around the eclipse of the original use of buildings in a neighbourhood by what is often seen as 'invading' religious organizations (Ajadi 2017; Williams and Fagite 2017).[1] When large congregations gather in Onike residents complain of the impact on mobility, traffic and circulation, and deplore the regular transformation of a serene neighbourhood into a bustling and noisy commercial hotspot, with the presence of dozens of petty traders setting up temporary structures to take advantage of increased foot traffic (Oni 2017).

MFM members offer an alternative view, claiming that in addition to revitalizing dilapidated streets and buildings, the church has provided a once crime-ridden area with a new moral infrastructure – that, in other words, MFM has brought security and 'respectable' life to neighbourhood. The scope of this pacification is expressed by the recruitment of local 'area boys' (or gang members) who are typically policing informal street markets, sometimes through extortions and

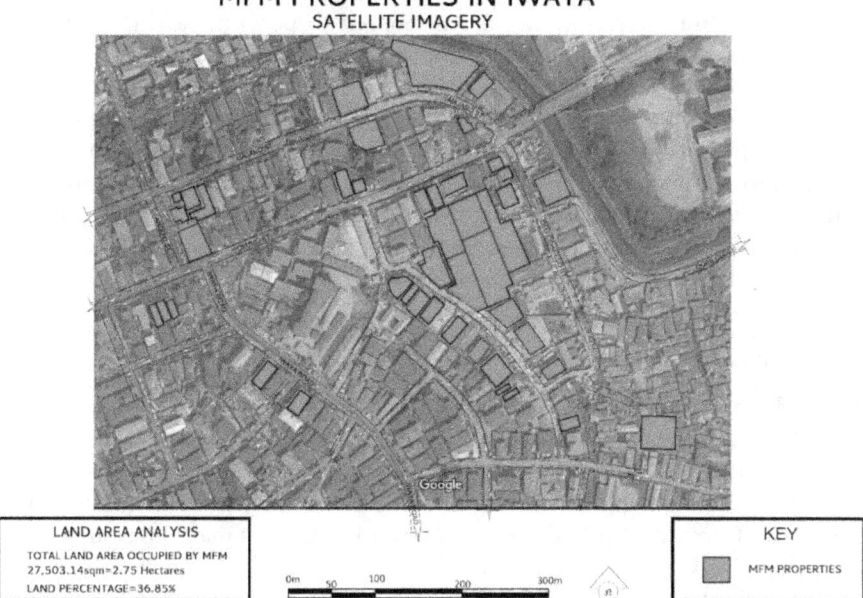

Figure 7.1. Satellite image of Onike neighbourhood (MFM properties highlighted). Courtesy, Google Maps.

rackets (Agunbiade and Olajide 2016). In one of our conversations in Onike, Joe, a former 'area boy', explained the transformation of the area:

> Before MFM this street was not this busy ... the area was very swampy. You know there were lots of witches and wizards, and crime. But since the church came in, lots of things have changed. Many of the area boys, they have become born again. We were part of the gangs and got lots of respect. The gangs still respect us but they know we are not part of that life anymore. You know this place is close to the University of Lagos, and there are lots of cults. There is no pastor that doesn't know us in this church. They know we used to be area boys, but now born again. There used to be lots of cults in this area, but none of that anymore since MFM. (Quoted in Garbin, 2020: 10)

Joe's narrative operates at several scales, from the born-again individual, to the street, to the revitalized neighbourhood. The trope of the swamp is revealing. In a West African context, water is often associated with the destructive, bewitching energies of marine spirits (Butticci 2013). The control of the environment and anxiety over permeability shows to what extent the idea of a 'second mapping' (Robbins 2014) impacts the Pentecostal place-making and particular conceptions of urban space, especially those occupied by 'malevolent forces' (Garbin 2020: 11). The campus of the University of Lagos, adjacent to Onike, is also 'remapped' by

Joe as an area conquered by 'occult economies' (Comaroff and Comaroff 2001), where 'cults' and secret societies are rumoured to perform sacrificial violence and encourage drug use and sexual promiscuity. As Marshall (2014) explains, the staging of rebirth and instanciations of renewal that are common to neo-Pentecostal churches lead to the production of both redeemed individuals and spaces on the one hand and 'a life-and-death struggle to wrest people, places and destinies from the satanic enemy' on the other (ibid.: 95). This is not simply about spiritual *belief*; rather, recourse to the supernatural – in this urban context – should be understood as a technique or practice *of power*, 'a form of socio-political action on the world' (ibid.: 105).

Timeline and patterns of change

The study shows a rapid growth of MFM properties in the study area from one plot in 1994 to over twenty-eight plots in 2018 (See Table 7.1). Interviews with residents reveal that the church has a deliberate strategy for acquiring plots and properties in the area, thus driving the pattern of land use from residential to institutional (religious). Currently, MFM owned and/or used properties make up 38.6 per cent of the total land area. This situation evokes the classical 'invasion and succession' urban ecological model, which characterizes 'invasion' as a process through which one group or institution encroaches on the territory held by another group or institution and succession as the completed process of invasion. Invasion thus entails the idea of conversion from one use to another, but also the replacement of established populations by newcomers, accompanied by the development of new local institutions and urban forms (Park et al. 1925). The Onike socio-spatial configuration also points to an 'acupunctural' strategy of land use change in central locations, using the existing city as a medium for 'expansion'. This strategy exists alongside, rather than in contradiction to the centrifugal, dispersed production of space of the large and peripheral religious prayer camps (e.g. Ukah 2016a).

Table 7.1. Periods of Land and Property Acquisition by MFM in Onike Area

Year	Local Activity
1994	MFM acquired its first plot of land in Onike.
1995–7	MFM acquired four plots of land at Olasunbo street.
1998–2005	MFM acquired four plots of land to make up eight plots for the completion of the Main Auditorium (prayer/worshipping space).
2005–12	MFM acquired about eight plots to build the 'MFM house', the 'Blue Roof' building (MFM Football Club and general administration) and the 'Purple House' (MFM's global headquarters).
2012–18	MFM acquired four plots of land towards Ajanaku street, leased four plots, bought six other plots to build the 'Music House', bookshop, mechanic workshop and other spaces.
2020 (fieldwork)	MFM has plans to acquire more properties for expansion and is targeting collapsing buildings so they can be demolished and rebuilt.

With close to 70 per cent of properties acquired less than ten years ago, it is evident that MFM now pursues an aggressive quest for land/property acquisition (see Table 7.2). Several long-term residents we interviewed talked at length about this gradual territorialization and were critical of the local presence of the church, with one mentioning the practice of 'sending scouts to put pressure on people to sell their properties'. In addition to the acquisition of existing properties, the church has also appropriated public space for its own use. For example, Remi Abuah Street does not exist anymore since it was converted into a part of the main church auditorium, a situation that exacerbated the flood vulnerability of Onike by blocking the drainage pathway, as we will discuss later. Ajanaku Street also

Table 7.2. Showing Transition of Land Uses to MFM Owned/Leased Property in Onike.

Year of property transfer to MFM	Previous use	Current official use	Specific use
Before 2000	Residential	Commercial	Printing press
Before 2000	Residential	Commercial	Vehicle workshop
Before 2000	Residential	Commercial	Vehicle workshop
Before 2000	Residential	Institutional (religious)	Church auditorium
Before 2000	Vacant space	Institutional (religious)	Children Church/Deliverance activity
Before 2000	Residential	General purpose	Admin office extension
2001–10	Vacant space	Commercial	School
2011–15	Vacant, Marshy Land	Commercial	Church hall
2001–10	NITEL Building	Commercial	Guest house
2001–10	Residential	Commercial	Music school
2001–10	Residential	Institutional (religious)	Youth Church
2011–15	Residential	Institutional (religious)	Children Church
2001–10	Residential	General purpose	Church Service Centre
2011–15	Residential	General purpose	Headquarters (Admin Offices)
2011–15	Residential	General purpose	Music library
2011–15	Residential	General purpose	Office extension – Sports and counselling
Since 2015	Residential	Commercial	Event Centre
Since 2015	Residential	Commercial	Vehicle workshop
Since 2015	Residential	Commercial	Bible School and children playground
Since 2015	Residential	Commercial	Mechanic workshop/car park
Since 2015	Residential	Commercial	Music school
Since 2015	Elementary School	Institutional (religious)	Teenage Church
Since 2015	Residential	Institutional (religious)	Church Service Hall (under construction)
Since 2015	Residential	Institutional (religious)	Prayer ground
Since 2015	Residential	General purpose	Car park
Since 2015	Residential	General purpose	Toilet
Since 2015	Residential	General purpose	Vacant/car park
Since 2015	Residential	General purpose	Car park

ceases to exist because the church acquired four plots to develop a car park and fenced off a pedestrian path which was one of the ways through which residents could previously access their homes. It is instructive to note that there was no push back on these developments from the state or local government, nor the resident's association. As Streule et al. (2020: 668) point out, the state can often only respond to popular urbanization by tolerating and negotiating the consolidation of new or refashioned settlements. This is largely because, apart from wielding growing political influence in wider society (Adogame 2012), MFM is seen by many as a benefactor locally, providing funds for road works, security and other community level interventions. In this way, MFM's urban strategy combines the quest for greater political influence with efforts aimed at winning popular consent for their interventions in the urban landscape. As MFM becomes more associated with governmental authority and their redevelopment of Onike has negative consequences for residents and traders it is a tension they struggle to maintain.

There is scant reference to the development of religious contained in the Lagos Mainland Model City Plan, even though this practice is now prevalent across the urban region. In fact, religion is only mentioned five times in the 643-page document. Under the proposed land use strategy, permissible land uses for religious purposes are referenced under two categories: 'mixed use' spaces relating to culture (including theatres, musuems, cultural centres, religious centres) and 'community spaces' relating to the religious (churches, mosques, faith centres and other religious institutions) (Lagos State Government, Mainland Central Model city plan – 2012–2032: 632).

The current situation, where over a period of twenty-four years MFM have grown in piecemeal fashion to own over a third of property in Onike – without real institutional or state attention – points to a blindspot in the design, planning and development of Lagos. The appropriation of land by MFM since 2010 in Onike represents significant land use change which has not been challenged by government authorities. Apart from the shift from residential use to religious related activities, there is also a transition from core religious uses to general/commercial land use functions, such as an event centre, guest houses, childrens playground, mechanic and book shop, all of which are owned and operated by MFM (see Table 7.2). In fact, of the twelve buildings acquired since 2015, only three are used for core religious functions (such as place of worship or religious education). This places the activitities of the church firmly within the ambits of 'enterpreneurial religion' (Lanz and Oosterbaan, 2016) and points to the church's desire to consolidate their presence in economic and urban terms through their anciliary services, while at the same time engendering a 'totalising' way of life in Onike centred around the economies, activities and ethos of MFM.

Many land use conversions undertaken by the church were implemented without obtaining relevant planning approvals. The planning approval process usually takes between three to six months. However, the planning approval process cannot proceed until all documentation is complete, hence when the process is stalled, often times, the church abandons the process and goes on to build without authorization. An assessment of MFM planning applications at the Yaba district office revealed only six applications, some as old as six years, four of which were incomplete. A field search to authenticate the status of these applications revealed that all the buildings are already completed and in use by the church, irrespective of application status (see Table 7.3).

However, when querying the low number of applications by the church, the district officer explained that Pentecostal churches (MFM inclusive) sometimes circumvent the process by applying for residential building permits, rather than 'institutional' (the correct statutory designation for religious buildings). Hence, it was impossible to verify the actual number of applications that have been submitted for religious purposes.[2] The general manager of Lagos State Physical Planning Permit Authority (LASPPA) explained that while the buildings around the main auditorium have been bought by the church they were not purchased using the name of the church. Indeed, we learned that applications are sometimes

Table 7.3. Mountain of Fire Planning Permit Applications at Yaba District Office of LASSPA (2010–18)

Year of Application	Address	No of Floors	Applied Use	Status of Application	Current Use of Property	Outstanding Documents
2012	Remi–Abuah Crescent, Onike Yaba	2	Institutional	Abandoned	Main auditorium	– Architectural drawing – Mechanical drawing – Electrical drawing – Technical report – Clearance letter
2012	Prof. Ayodele, Awojobi Avenue, Onike	4	Institutional	Under Processing	Teenage Church	– Planning technical report – Clearance letter
2016	Remi Abuah Crescent, Onike	2	Institutional	Under Processing	Main auditorium	– Clearance letter
2016	Muyideen Bello Street, Onike	3	Residential	Approved	Main auditorium	None
2016	3, Remi Abuah Crescent Street, Onike	4	Residential	Approved	Music school	None
2018	1, Olu–Osifeso Street, Onike	4	Institutional	Under Processing	Church/Event Centre	– Planning technical report – Clearance letter – Geotechnical report

Source: Lagos state Physical Planning Permit authority – Yaba District office

submitted in the names of individuals (often the previous owners) rather than the representatives of MFM. According to the district officer, the reason for this is that 'they wouldn't be able to meet special application regulations and the approval orders which churches belong to'. Indeed, applications for building permit by religious entities require more documentation and a more extensive chain of approval than residential applications made by an individual. MFM, it appears, have circumvented the planning process in establishing their enclave in Onike.

Since Onike is a dense urban area, vacant land is almost impossible to obtain. As such, in relation to new development, another practice of MFM is to acquire run-down residential buildings, demolish them and proceed to obtain fresh building approvals. As the district office stated, 'because change of use is not allowed in Lagos state, many of the churches buy old structures, obtain demolition permits, so that they can then apply for new development permits'. This is corroborated by a local resident who is also a church member:

> When the church buys property, if it is one they can easily demolish [like] all these old buildings, they demolish and fence it immediately.

Often, MFM construct buildings at variance with what was approved by LASPPA, largely because LASPPA's jurisdiction ends at the point of planning approval. The responsibility for development control and ensuring compliance with approved development permit lies with the Lagos State Building Control agency (LABCA). The difficulties in overseeing the transition from planning approval to development control is largely due to bureaucratic bottlenecks in the planning administrative framework of the Lagos state ministry of Physical Planning and Urban Development. The thirty district offices of LASPPA are required to submit monthly planning permit approval reports to the central office of the agency located at the ministry of physical planning and urban development. This office then collates the reports and forwards the same to the central office of the Lagos State Building control agency (LABCA) which then disseminates to the thirty district offices under their jurisdiction for further action. This process is completed manually and can take up to three months, a period long enough for making significant progress in actual construction. Hence, in addition to taking advantage of the 'rent gap' (Smith 1987) by purchasing decrepit dwellings in central urban locations such as Onike, the church also capitalizes on the 'bureaucratic gap' that exists due to institutional division of labour and Lagos State's continued reliance upon the 'material regime of paper documents' a term coined by Hull (2012) in his ethnography of post-colonial bureaucratic governance in urban Pakistan.

Religious appropriations of space in Onike

The MFM-driven 'regeneration' of Onike could be seen as the expression of a religious ethos mediated by the appropriation of urban space (Knott 2012). The church inprint is evident across the entire neigbourhood through signature red brick and glass detailing on new buildings, as well as the cream and purple colours the church uses to brand all its buildings – a particular aesthetic which is well known by most Lagosians. This has considerable impact on the sensory experience of Onike. The visibility and sonic presence of MFM in the neighbourhood shape the multisensoriality of the local landscape while creating distinctive urban rhythms. As Larkin (2018) puts it, the aesthetics of urban infrastructure can become a formal *expression* of experience and also one of the main ways that urban change can be *integrated* into everyday experience. The ubiquitiy of the religious branding – the logos and colours of MFM – constitutes also a promise of further 'expansion', of increased territorialization, implicitly connecting local, peripheral and global scales. All of this heralds a new relationship between citizen, infrastructure and urban space (see Lemanski 2020) – albeit a relationship which, in Lagos, is mediated through Pentecostal Christianity, the state and the market.

As indicated earlier, MFM is now the primary purchaser of land in Onike. According to an estate surveyor, there has been an increase in land value of about 160 per cent between the 1980s when the area started to be populated, and 1995, when the first MFM building was acquired (See Table 7.1). This value has steadily increased further over time, with a marked peak when the church started to expand locally, acquiring multiple dwellings and plots at a time. Through the data we collected among land surveyors and planners, we can estimate that land prices within Onike have increased more than tenfold from the 1990s, a similar trend observable to a lesser extent with plots situated at the edge of Onike.

The mapping of the study area revealed that 80 per cent of previous owners of current MFM properties were individuals and 15 per cent were family-owned properties, all acquired via outright purchase as opposed to long rental lease. According to one former resident, many property owners in Onike felt compelled to sell to the church as they were approached with an offer far above the market rate, 'making it difficult to refuse'. This was corroborated by the estate valuer who told us that 'property prices around MFM have been influenced by the presence of MFM in that [landlords] all want to sell their property to the church because they know the church will pay more money than an individual buyer'. Here it appears that part of the strategy of MFM is to deliberately raise property values in Onike so that they have a monopoly over future sales in the area, making Onike too expensive for other investors. This attests to the economic resources (and power) of the church – resources which, they understand, if invested in the built environment in this fashion, will increase the value of their existing assets in the area.

As mentioned above, MFM operates as a benefactor to the residents' association, often donating to help develop small collective projects such as street gate construction and maintenance, flood control and community/social gatherings. As one might expect due to the growing local influence of MFM, many locals have joined the church. One resident who has joined the church a few years back, has a positive view of MFM's impact, emphasizing improvements to security and infrastructure in Onike:

MFM is not disturbing anybody in this area, it has developed this area, for example now no thief can disturb this area because MFM pays for the security, and they keep a close watch even at night. Look at this road now, MFM tarred it and it is not the first time, no government is worried when it comes to this area because of MFM's input. So this area developed, if not for MFM, I don't think even in 20 years' time this area would ever have been developed.

However, MFM maintains a distance from non-church residents and businesses by choosing *not* to send representatives to monthly Residents' Association meetings (usually attended by homeowners and tenants). In this sense, while MFM invest locally to win popular consent for its transformations, by not attending local meetings they implicitly signal that real influence no longer lies with locals but with the church. In this manner, MFM departs from more progressive forms of popular urbanization premised upon 'collectivity, engagement and mutual self-help' (Streule et al. 2020: 668).

The management of flooding risks in the neighbourhood further illustrates the local impact of MFM but also its role in terms of local governance and decision-making. The 2010 Iwaya North Urban Regeneration Draft Plan identifies MFM as a major contributor to the flooding vulnerability of the area. This was due to the construction of the large fifty-thousand-seat auditorium (Ojo 2007) which was built *across* an existing street, linking two properties purchased by the church. The report states:

> By closing out Remi Abuah street to construct the Main Auditorium, the natural drainage flow had been blocked, effectively rendering the highlighted areas as critical points for flash floods (Iwaya North Urban Regeneration Draft Plan 2010: 372).

Despite MFM being responsible for exacerbating flood risk, residents have no alternative but to appeal to the church to intervene in flood mitigation, as suggested by the chairman of the Resident's Association who praised MFM's 'generosity':

> Well, the MFM Pastor has always been so generous to us, when we have anything to do that is beyond our means, we sometimes go to MFM for assistance and when they can, they help. Though we have presently presented a case for them to construct another drainage to complement the one we have done ourselves, but up until now we haven't heard from them. We also are expecting them to help us drill a bore-hole at least as a form of extension of charity to the neighbourhood. MFM is already in charge of maintaining and cleaning the canal regularly which has helped in reducing flooding when it rains.

Here we see how MFM is spearheading a process of territorial appropriation in Onike not only through property ownership but also by gaining control of decision-making and resource allocation and, where necessary, by making small, gestural improvements in the form of infrastructural investments or repair intended to maintain local consent for their redevelopment of the neighbourhood. Even when MFM creates problems such as flooding (in breach of state planning regulations), it is the church that residents appeal to for a remedy rather than the state (MFM is thus recognized here as the *de facto* controlling authority). MFM's influence in Onike has similarities to popular urbanization in that it is premised on the social networks (and financial resources) of the church and should therefore be considered an example of an alternative 'process [of urbanization] that is not dominated by the state' (Streule et al. 2020: 659). However, just as it is possible to interpret MFM's brand of religious urbanization as the construction of a territory of resistance against a weak or ineffective state and/or demonic forces, it is important to recognize that their reterritorialization of Onike does not bring equal benefit to everyone.

Fieldwork revealed that the church impacts neighbourhood activities at least twice a week (for Wednesday and Sunday services) with what is perceived by some locals as excessive noise and traffic. This impact is also felt in surrounding communities of Iwaya, Akoka and the University of Lagos Campus. The church claims that services at the MFM headquarters in Onike are the largest single congregations in Africa with attendance of over 120,000 at single meetings (Olukoya 2003). Even though the church has moved large meetings to the MFM camp on the outskirts of Lagos – called 'Prayer City' and built in 1999 [see Butticci (2013)] – and there are approximately ninety other MFM parishes across the city (Ojo 2007), there is still significant foot and automobile traffic at Onike for church services, in particular during the monthly 'Power Must Change Hands' service (the title of which clearly draws upon popular and populist sentiments). MFM's Pentecostal influence dominates the rhythms of Onike and, ironically, while Pentecostals often stress the power of the Holy Spirit to 'unblock' the path to prosperity and success, their practices are viewed by some as a detrimental force creating congestion and obstruction:

> The moment they [MFM worshippers] get out, pedestrians block everywhere and there is no movement of vehicles. The church buses and other vehicles can then leave after one hour and that is particular about Wednesday and Sundays ... During their services, UNILAG allow them [MFM] to park. For me, sometimes this affects movement on campus. When a non-church member wants to get out, he might spend 30–45 minutes just to get to the gate!

The parking facilities provided by MFM being inadequate for the huge number of worshippers who attend church services, UNILAG (the University of Lagos) has indeed allowed MFM members to use designated car parks on the University campus during Wednesday evening and Sunday morning services (in return, MFM is one of the major donors to the university, from the Central Research Laboratory to the Human Resources Development building and donations of prizes and funded scholarships). The heavy traffic situation around campus is exacerbated by the 'pop-up' shops situated along the roadside in Onike and immediate surrounding areas, selling items from Bibles and Holy Water ('Mana water'), to fruits, vegetables and snacks.

The inconveniences linked to MFM's presence in Onike has led many residents to move out of the area, with the 'soft power' of regular congestion and excessive noise constituting a 'blockbusting' of sorts (see Gotham 2002):

> Many people left the area when the church started. At that time, some landlords you know did not want to sell, but when the noise pollution and traffic was too much they were just forced to sell. (Interview with estate surveyor)

It was indeed during the early days of MFM in Onike, before the construction of the new and larger auditorium, that its sonic presence was perceived to be particularly problematic. At the time, because of the limited indoor worshipping space, 'MFMers', by their hundreds, followed services from the streets, broadcasted through powerful loudspeakers. The deployment of 'sonic energies' by Pentecostal churches, especially in the African context, is part and parcel of the embodied, multisensorial experience of the divine (see de Witte 2008; Garbin 2012). But it is also clear that this Pentecostalite sonic religiosity has the potency to destabilize the boundary between public and private domains within the urban landscape, as it plays a key role in the appropriation of (contested) space and is bound up with the idea of 'spiritual warfare'. Additionally, the presence of praying crowds was limiting local resident's movements in and around the areas and, as a church member we interviewed admitted that 'people started selling their property when they couldn't cope', a view confirmed by several long-term residents we spoke to. However, the position of the Residents' Association is rather different, with the chairman – mindful of the need to maintain a cordial relationship with MFM – striking a resigned, but conciliatory tone:

> As for the noise, we are used to it, we have seen them as a religious body, and that is what comes with it. We are not disturbed in anyway.

Concluding remarks

The land appropriation practices of MFM highlights how large-scale real estate investment by neo-Pentecostal religious organizations is an important vector of urban change in Lagos. By establishing and expanding their material, visual and sonic presence in the urban community of Onike, by offering incentives to existing landlords to sell and converting residential land uses via *in situ* redevelopment, often without recourse to extant planning regulations, MFM is actively shaping regeneration and land governance in the area. However, this dimension of religious urbanization, in comparison with the construction of large prayer camps – or 'cities' – on the periphery of the metropolis, is yet to receive sustained critical academic scrutiny, especially from within urban studies. Read in conjunction with work on prayer camps (e.g. Ukah, 2011; 2016) and translated to a multiscalar approach, this case study reveals how from prayer camps to the inner-urban neighbourhood, attempts by competing churches to establish an all-encompassing

Pentecostalite aesthetics (Meyer 2014) to everyday life in the city are well underway. The built forms, soundscapes, 'iconicity', activities, temporalities and subjectivities that accompany these changes can be all-ecompassing, reconfiguring boundaries between public and private, and are thus variously accommodated and resisted. Here, our case study raises questions for further study: what are the limits to Pentecostal religious urbanization? To what extent is the piecemeal 'colonization' of Onike being replicated elsewhere? Have other, competing Pentecostal churches such as RCCG 'abandoned' Onike since MFM have expanded?

Enclaving of the kind caused by MFM in Onike is a phenomenon similar to gentrification in many ways. Returning to the composite definition provided earlier (Savage, Warde and Ward 2003; Atkinson 2007), it appears from our study that residents are displaced but not necessarily by residents from a higher social class (which in the context of Lagos is a rather different issue than that circumscribed by Savage, Ward and Ward in relation to cities in the West). Rather, displacement is caused by changes in land use away from residential towards institutional and commercial activities connected to MFM and a growing concentration among residents of MFM members (either new residents or as 'converts'). However, it is not the case that residents are replaced by those of a higher social standing. In Onike they tend to be replaced not by residents but by a different use of space (i.e. religious rather than residential). There is an aesthetic transformation of the built environment, certainly, and evidence of services and commercial activities geared towards MFM visitors. There is also the gathering – in accordance with service timetables and commercial opening hours – of thousands of people sharing Pentecostal values. There is an economic reordering of property values in the neighbourhood, fashioned by MFM who establish a monopoly over purchases and drive up the value of their own assets (as opposed to this being an effect of the 'invisible hand' of the market). Our example points to how MFM exploit a rent gap, following classical gentrification theory, when they purchase run-down or out-of-use buildings in the neighbourhood; and a 'bureaucratic gap' where they take advantage of time lags caused by the regime of 'paper governance' (Hull 2012) and begin construction before planning approval is granted.

The appropriation of space in Onike by MFM also operates against a moralizing and redeeming (discursive) backdrop: the domestication/pacification of 'swamps' and demonic spirits and the idea that an area previously infamous for its high crime rates is now safe for visitors and residents. Some studies suggest that neoliberal governance is generally approving of gentrification (e.g. Shmaryahu-Yeshurun and Ben-Porat 2020) and while to an extent this is true in this instance, planning authorities are critical of the practices of neo-Pentecostals and recognize that the church is influencing land use change and patterns. The local district office frowns at the church's failure to adhere to planning regulations, but there is no evidence of any decisive action taken in the past or present to abate it. Individual officers working in a state capacity express frustration but what our case study demonstrates is Obadare's (2018) point that the democratic process in Nigeria post-1999 cannot be understood without recourse to the emergent political power of Pentecostal pastors and/or the commensurate *popular tendency* to view socio-political (and urban) problems in spiritual terms (ibid.: 1). Obadare's concern, relevant here, is to understand 'the deep imbrication of politics and spirituality and the contradictions that arise [from this]' (ibid.: 2). Urban change in Onike over the past three decades is, in its own small way, testament to this emergent relationship between politics, spirituality and the city.

Whilst there are similarities with gentrification, there are also aspects of MFM's investment in Onike, especially in how the church might is a *collective* effort, that is reminiscent of what Streule et al. (2020) term popular urbanization. Yet what our example shows, much more so than examples chosen by these authors, is how popular forms of urbanization are controversial, contested and have ambiguous relationships with state governance and market processes; how although religious urbanization is welcomed and makes urban life more secure for some, others suffer or perceive a series of impositions and injustices. In order to win consent for their redevelopment and ward off opposition and resistance, MFM agree to fund small community projects in Onike and, as such, provide an alternative form of authority to the state. In short, the notion of popular urbanization is applicable to religious urbanization, but Streule et al. (2020) take an overly positive view of the nature and effects of popular urbanization, naively categorizing religion as a force that acts against or ameliorates the effects of neoliberalism, rather than acknowledging how Pentecostalism often blends directly with neoliberal enterprise (Comaroff 2009). In our view, religious enclaving of the kind exemplified in Onike lies somewhere between gentrification and popular urbanization, providing an exemplar of neither but displaying tendencies towards both.

Part III

MORAL SUBJECTS, REMORALIZED SPACES AND THE
POLITICS OF KNOWLEDGE

Chapter 8

THE DARK SIDE OF THE CITY: URBANIZATION, MODERNITY AND MORAL MAPPING IN ZAMBIA

Johanneke Kroesbergen-Kamps

Introduction

Soon after my arrival in Zambia in 2011, I read a newspaper article about a cabinet minister and member of parliament who confessed in a local Pentecostal church that he had been a Satanist. He was subsequently dismissed (*Zambian Watchdog* 2011). My research soon revealed that Satanism was a recurrent topic in Zambian churches, not only within the many new Pentecostal ministries, but also within the Reformed Church in Zambia, a classical mission church to which many of my then students at Justo Mwale University, a school for pastors, belonged. Narratives about Satanism often allude to 'sacrificing' family members to Satan, causing road accidents and illnesses and harming Christians in general. I also discovered that most of the people who confessed, through public testimonies, that they had been Satanists were not successful adults like the MP, but adolescents, and mostly girls. In Zambia, these stories are taken very seriously, and in this chapter I will explore how they are connected to the production of the city as a moral spatial matrix.

Between 2012 and 2018 as part of my research on modernity, power and the performance and discursive production of Satanism in Zambia (Kamps 2018), I collected and analysed around a hundred testimonies of individuals describing themselves as 'ex-Satanists' as well as newspaper articles containing accusations of Satanism. These testimonies circulate widely across the urban public sphere in Zambia and, related both to traditional notions of power and to contemporary imaginaries of modernity (Kamps 2018; Kroesbergen-Kamps 2020a), they are particularly persuasive to a Zambian audience.

Stories about Satanism started to spread in Zambia against a backdrop of a growing, but uncertain and unpredictable economy, paralleled by the increasing dominance of (neo-)Pentecostal theology. For a decade, from 2004 to 2014, Zambia was one of the world's fastest growing economies (CIA World Factbook 2021). Urban areas, in particular Lusaka, profited the most from this new prosperity, and the pull of the city became strong for the rural, impoverished population – giving Zambia one of the highest rates of urbanization in Africa. The greater opportunities that the growing economy offered coincided with the increasing popularity of Pentecostal prosperity theology centred on the idea that wealth is a blessing from God. In many Pentecostal churches, an outward display of wealth in the form of designer clothes and luxury items, for instance, is perceived as the mark of a 'true Christian' and for many in Zambia, the interplay of Christianity, wealth and the city has become aspirational, insofar as it is integral to a desired better future for the nation.

Like the case for other African cities, Lusaka's social geography is highly divided, with the coexistence of central business and administrative area and poorer, ever-growing peri-urban settlements known as 'compounds' where most Lusaka's residents today live. Large shopping malls, mostly developed for South African retail brands like Pick 'n Pay, Shoprite or Edgars have also sprung up on all the access roads into Lusaka. These places, which crystallize desires for consumption and globalization, are where members of an emerging Zambian upper and middle class do their shopping.

To many contemporary residents of Lusaka, these promises of global modernity, prosperity and consumption are ubiquitous. The billboards that punctuate the urban landscape communicate the prospect of international travel, of owning the newest smart phone, of drinking the trendiest beverages. The city promises a better life to those who come seeking their fortune, and there are many who do.[1] However, the prospect of wealth may be visibly close in the city, but it remains out of the grasp of many of its residents. In Lusaka, 70 per cent of the population lives in informal settlements, often in unsecure housing and with a lack of infrastructure and basic services (UN Habitat 2007: 18).

While many migrants move from one urban area to another, for example from the Copperbelt to Lusaka, migration from rural to urban areas is very common as well. Families are often important footholds into the city for younger relatives as children, adolescents and young adults may be sent to live with members of the extended family based in the city to improve their lifechances, for example through the opportunities for education that Lusaka may offer them (Girard and Chapoto 2017). Churches represent another strategic network for those with urban aspirations as they can often be a way for rural residents to experience urban life first hand, for example when a choir goes on tour to an urban congregation. Churches have thus the ability to act as connectors between rural and urban life, bridging the gap between the village and the city (Ilubala-Ziwa et al. 2020).

In testimonies about Satanism, images of life in the city are abundant and thus deserve closer scrutiny. These narratives often rely on the construction of urban imaginaries and tell us a great deal about the role the city plays in people's world views and attitudes. As I will argue in this chapter, the Christian narratives about Satanism reflect how the city is perceived as a blessing, a space of opportunities on the one hand but also as a threatening, risky space on the other. Although wealth and a modern lifestyle are desired and arguably even prescribed from the prosperity gospel standpoint, there is some level of anxiety about the societal changes brought about by urbanization and modernization. Here narratives about Satanism offer symbolic resources to navigate emerging tensions linked to these transformations, plotting a moral map with boundaries delineating safe and threatening urban spaces. In this sense, insofar as they produce cartographies of desired and feared urbanities and carve up morally charged landscapes in the midst of rapid socio-spatial transformations, these narratives are intimately linked to processes of religious urbanization.

In order to address the interplay of popular/religious imaginaries, narratives about the occult and urbanity, I will first explore ideas about urban life, in the context of Lusaka, and how prosperity gospel and spiritual warfare theology can be important religious sources that imbue the city with meaning, constructing urban life as a moral project. I will then provide a more detailed analysis of the Zambian narratives about Satanism focusing on one representative narrative from my large dataset of testimonies to explore the connection between Christianity, wealth, city life and tropes of urban modernity. The testimony describes many consumer goods which are used as instruments for Satan's plan to attack Christianity. These goods are, as I will argue, all linked to local understandings of Western modernity, urbanization and globalization, and express the anxieties that arise in Zambia's changing society. For their audiences, the testimonies provide a map to help them navigate the city, to discern where the threats of urban life lie and how to negotiate them.

Spiritual warfare and the city as moral project

The prosperity gospel teaches Christians that wealth is within reach if their faith is strong enough and if they have a pastor, a man or woman of God, who takes a mediating role in accessing the (material) blessings God can provide. During my fieldwork of several years in Zambia, I attended many church services in the Reformed and Presbyterian churches as well as in a number of Pentecostal churches. I have heard time and again the promise that 'this year will be the year of financial breakthrough or of victorious living'. The preachers of the prosperity gospel emphasize that God's blessings are available in this world and that one does not have to wait for death and heaven to access the 'good life'. In an African context, this attention to the good and abundant life, which is an important concept in African traditional religions as well, finds much acclaim (see Ilo 2018). Through this focus on material success in the now, African Pentecostalism seems to have a more this-worldly orientation than the mainline Christian churches, even if *'future-worldly'* (Kroesbergen 2020: 300) may be a more apt characterization given the importance of 'sacred waithood' and 'faithful endurance' (Bertin in this volume; Rey 2015) among Pentecostals.

Another key component of African Christianity that is prevalent in Zambia is the emphasis on spiritual forces that may harm or 'block' one's progress. If the successes promised in church fail to materialize, this is often blamed on the actions of entities endowed with spiritual power: a possessing spirit or a demonic attack, the spell of a witch, or the actions of the devil himself. This attention for spiritual forces is, like the prosperity gospel, both an element of Pentecostal theology and a link with African traditional world views. Spiritual warfare refers to the idea that, while God is able to intervene in the world and in people's lives, there exists also an almost equally powerful counterforce of darkness. Through spiritual warfare, often taking the form of rituals of prayer and deliverance, these forces of evil can (and have to) be 'pushed back' in order for the Kingdom of God to materialize in this world (Hunt 1998).

The cosmology of spiritual warfare that originated with American Pentecostal-Charismatic authors like John Wimber and Peter Wagner has a cross-cultural appeal and is highly compatible with the demonization of traditional spirit and deities in African post-colonial context (Meyer 1999). Harmful spiritual entities like witches and spirits that used to have positive connotations, such as the spirits of ancestors, have been relegated to the ranks of the devil in an African Pentecostal 'witchdemonology' (Onyinah 2004).

While spiritual warfare theology and the prosperity gospel are not necessarily urban phenomena, Pentecostal churches often operate from urban centres, and their message of imminent blessings is intimately connected with the promises of the urban – better life opportunities and wealth as well as the ability to 'unblock' a path to progress and social mobility. From a spiritual warfare perspective, personal struggles are seen as individual battles in the global struggle between forces of good and evil. Spiritual warfare, in the form of overnight prayer wakes or prayer walks, often takes place in cities and draws upon potent urban imageries (see Kirby 2017b). Thus the city is not just a specific place on the map, it is also an idea, a meaningful imaginary space, textually and sensorially performative (De Boeck 2011: 324). In that sense, Christianity, the city, material wealth and the forces that may be hindering the fulfilment of prosperity, including occult and Satanist energies, are part of a same web of meaning.

In contemporary Zambia, the threat of Satan and Satanism is perceived to be everywhere: in school, in hospitals, on the road, in markets and even in churches. Satanism is often portrayed as a demoniac organization to which people can be initiated knowingly or unknowingly, willingly or unwillingly. This organization is believed to operate from an underwater or underground world, which can be accessed in the night through dream. Once initiated, Satanists are assigned to cause chaos and 'sacrifice people' – for instance through road accidents, fatal diseases like AIDS or unexplained afflictions and injuries. Being successful in sacrificing people allegedly brings rewards like financial success and access to commodities and an advancement 'in the ranks of evil'.

People who identified as ex-Satanists usually give their testimonies in the deliverance services of Pentecostal churches, but also during all-night prayer meetings that are popular with the youths in mainline churches. In Zambia, stories about Satanism gained in popularity in the 1990s. Soon testimonies, rumours and accusations spread in churches and newspapers and a moral panic surrounding Satanism peaked around 2007. By this time the phenomenon had become disruptive, and some schools – especially boarding schools – experienced collective panics, causing concern among pupils, staff and parents.

While narratives about Satanism come in many forms,[2] one of their most common characteristics is that they reveal the importance of urbanity – they mostly refer to urban professions, urban spaces and consumer goods available in cities, whether these narratives circulate among urban residents or not. This discursive setting provides powerful insights onto the imaginaries of the urban lived experience and reveals how the city is conceptualized as a moral space within which forces of good and evil are locked in a permanent struggle. In a way, narratives about Satanism form part of the wider religious discourse of spiritual warfare and prosperity gospel that is shared between churches – a 'collective habitus' (Rey and Stepick 2015) – and the city constitutes its privileged ecology.

These narratives and the world views that sustain them suggest to what extent living in the city becomes a moral project. While these stories label certain objects and places as dangerous, unhealthy or detrimental to one's economic, social and moral status, they also equip urban audiences with resources to negotiate these risks and dangers. Although the city is a space of hope, of promises and opportunities, the imaginary of the city is therefore not unambiguously positive – it is deeply ambivalent. In the following, I shall link these moral maps of urban life to anxieties and tensions related to contemporary changes in society drawing on the analysis of the 'exemplary' testimony of an ex-Satanist.

Narratives about Satanism in Zambia: Naomi's testimony

In the 1990s, anthropologists like Peter Geschiere (1997) noted that ideas and narratives about witchcraft and harmful spiritual agents did not wither with the advent of modernity in contemporary post-colonial Africa. These stories, for instance those about witches, Satanists, vampires (e.g. White 2000) or 'penis snatchers' (e.g. Bonhomme 2012) are often set in urban, 'modern' contexts. Here the idea is that witchcraft 'operates' as an explanation for afflicted human experiences, in a context of increased socio-economic challenges and protracted crisis often caused by global forces.[3] Some elements of this approach have been criticized for not trying to fully understand informants on their own terms, especially when stories about witches or the occult are interpreted as some sort of coded messages about the Western-centred category of 'modernity' (see Green and Mesaki 2005; Marshall 2009).

Although there are clear similarities between Satanism and older notions of witchcraft, and both phenomena have been conflated in academic studies,[4] Satanism in Zambia is more than just another name for witchcraft. While witchcraft in Zambia has a more rural focus, linked to problems such as crop failures and lightning strikes, Satanism, on the other hand, belongs more to the 'modern' world of the city. Stories about witchcraft generally involve relatives, in particular relatives living in the village, whereas Satanists can harm anyone and seem to be particularly active in the city – stories about Satanism often involve shopping malls, boarding schools, hospitals and politicians.[5]

Zambian narratives about Satanism are generally spread through church services, Christian pamphlets and faith-based radio stations. While I have collected many of these narratives about Satanism, some short, some very extensive, in this chapter I will use one testimony as my main source. It is an 'exemplary' testimony, representative of many testimonies shared in churches and, like most testimonies, it is given by an adolescent girl and follows a storyline that all extensive testimonies share (Kamps 2018: 128).

In the most general terms, testimonies of ex-Satanists are a variant of the narrative of redemption described by Dan McAdams (2006). Redemptive narratives are religious or secular stories that describe blessings born from death and suffering, and stress the long-term benefits of negative experiences (McAdams 2006: 16). Testimonies of ex-Satanists are full of negative experiences, especially if heard from a Christian perspective, and often they end on a positive note: the experiences of the past have made the ex-Satanist a strong Christian who is able to warn or encourage others. In Pentecostal churches, such narratives of redemption are often used as illustrations for the power of God to turn one's life around. Testimonies given in churches may describe how someone who struggled financially found a job, or how a medical condition improved after prayer. For audiences, these testimonies give hope that the blessings promised by prosperity gospel preachers will soon materialize for them as well. Within the genre of testimonies of redemption, the narratives of ex-Satanists form a special category as their stories do not so much give evidence of the blessings coming from God as of the reality of God's enemy, Satan. In this way, they are connected to the second core aspect of the African Pentecostal imagination discussed earlier, namely the spiritual warfare theology. As confessing ex-Satanists, the people who give these testimonies embody the reason why every Christian should be vigilant at all times as Satan can corrupt anyone.

The testimony I will discuss in this chapter is narrated by Naomi (not her real name), a seventeen-year-old girl based in Zambia's Southern Province. I have two recordings of her story about getting involved with Satanism and subsequently finding her way back to the fold of the church. One is a testimony in which only Naomi speaks, while the other is an interview with a male presenter. An audience is implied by both the questions of the interviewer and the way in which Naomi directs her answers and her testimony to the listeners. From her testimony it is clear that Naomi's perspective is coloured by the teachings of the Seventh Day Adventist Church, for example when she explains that the devil tries to shift the day of worship from Saturday to Sunday. However, the audience of this testimony is much wider. I received the files from a student at the Reformed/Presbyterian theological university where I taught and from a Pentecostal friend. Testimonies are commonly shared among friends and colleagues and therefore have an audience that is not restricted to a single congregation or denomination. The idea of spiritual warfare that forms the framework of these testimonies is present not just in the Pentecostal churches since many congregants of mainline churches believe in the power of Satan to wreak havoc in their lives and in the need to gain divine protection to counter this ever-present threat.

Most Zambian testimonies of ex-Satanists follow the same script, regardless of ethnic background or Christian denomination. They narrate an experience of (involuntary) initiation into Satanism, of assignments in which kin or random, unrelated people are 'sacrificed' (i.e. killed), of a final 'failed assignment' and a subsequent deliverance and/or conversion to born-again Christianity. Such testimonies are reminiscent of Christian conversion stories and as Nicolette Manglos (2010: 413) notes in the context of Malawi 'the conversion experience is central to how Pentecostals understand themselves as miraculously 'healed', emotionally and physically, and empowered to live a devout, moral life'. As I have argued elsewhere (Kamps 2018: 85), Satanism is indeed conceptualized as an affliction rather than as a regrettable 'choice' in terms of spiritual 'orientation'.

Naomi recounts how she grew up in difficult circumstances, moving from town to town to live with various relatives: a grandmother, a grandfather and finally her mother. Her testimony starts with an experience of initiation, which is typically never sought after but happens in a dream or through receiving a gift of clothing, accessories or food. Often the ex-Satanist is not even aware at the time of being 'initiated'. Naomi says that her involvement started at school, through food. In African ideas about witchcraft, food, especially ready-made food bought at the market, is seen as potentially dangerous (Steinforth 2009: 47). Throughout sub-Saharan Africa, stories are also told about the dangers of receiving gifts from unknown benefactors (Bonhomme 2012). By the time Naomi gives her testimony, she has realized that the food she received at school had made her into a Satanist.

In the standard format of testimonies, the initiation is followed by assignments, which are duly rewarded with riches or status. In Naomi's story she was used to cause accidents and to seduce men over a period of two years. She is therefore warning her audience of the danger of products tainted by satanic forces: foods from the supermarket, cosmetics, electronics, music, cars and so on. For her services, Naomi said she received the rank of 'princess' in the underworld. As in most testimonies, there comes an assignment that the protagonist cannot execute, often because they are asked to sacrifice an especially loved family member. Indeed, when Naomi was asked to sacrifice her mother and her sister, she refused and felt under increasing pressure, but then she heard a voice she ascribed to God: 'The voice said: "Why do you want to kill the innocent child? Why shed the innocent blood, what has she done to you?" Then I started crying.' In her testimony Naomi recounts how she fled and was taken up by another family. She then underwent deliverance and returned to the Seventh Day Adventist Church.

Almost all testimonies shared in a religious setting have this structure of initiation, assignments, failed assignment, deliverance and eventually redemption through renewed Christian identity. But the question remains of how and why narratives about Satanism in Zambia almost always have urban characteristics and produce a discourse about urbanity and urban life – a question I will address in the following section.

Satanism and the city

A central locational feature of most testimonies is the so-called underworld, an alternative reality, often located under the sea or ocean,[6] and which, in Naomi's narrative, includes a range of references to urban life and urbanity. When the interviewer asks her to depict this underworld, Naomi responds that 'it is a place like Lusaka'. She describes houses, churches, schools, universities, roads, vehicles, petrol stations and factories. This underworld is also equipped with modern technologies as with references to monitors, large screens and 'tracing computers' from which the inhabitants of the 'normal world' are held under surveillance.

It is not only the setup of the underworld that is reminiscent of urban life, the people in the underworld are connected to it too. In the underworld, Naomi meets other Satanists: identifiable pastors, prophets and elders, politicians including ministers and presidents; and famous Zambian and international musicians, professions that are most often targeted with accusations of Satanism (Kroesbergen-Kamps 2020a). These accusations, which often erupt after a tragic event such as the disappearance or murder of a child, can lead to riots, violence and looting. The idea behind these accusations is that to become successful in a certain profession, one needs special spiritual help, which can be acquired through human sacrifices. This notion is not new. Roles of chief, healer, hunter and trader – which all bring superior status or wealth – have always been connected to 'spiritual help' and to rituals which ensure this help (cf. Van Binsbergen 1981). Under the influence of Christianity, the spiritual world which provides this 'help' has been demonized and has become associated with Satan, with an 'updated' universe of 'suspicious' roles and professions adapted to a modern context.

All of these new professions are related to the urban world. In the postcolonial African nation-state, to a certain extent politicians and the government have taken up the role and the power that used to be in the hands of local chiefs.[7] Villagers in Zambia and other African countries often see politicians and government officials as outsiders, signifying a structure of power alternative to village politics (Kaspin 1993). Teachers are educated in the city, and then can be posted anywhere by the government upon graduation. Because they are new in the community, have been educated in town and in many rural areas they are among the few persons receiving a salary, teachers are viewed as belonging to the urban world more than to the world of the village. The businessman and the commercial farmer have connections to towns as well and their relative wealth and trade links beyond the village in way 'alienate' them from village life. Furthermore, and perhaps surprisingly, pastors are often accused of involvement in Satanism. While on the one hand narratives about Satanism are very useful for pastors as evidence of the reality of (and need for) spiritual warfare and also of their own power to deliver those affected by it (cf. Kamps 2018: 149ff), suspicion or accusations of Satanism can also be directed against them. These accusations against pastors are generally an urban phenomenon, with those accused often leading Pentecostal churches which are more prevalent in cities than in rural areas.

Even in an urban context, it is believed that exceptional success still requires support from extraordinary powers. Members of the 'old professions' that needed spiritual help – chiefs, hunters, diviners and traders – were expected to act on behalf of the community, and their means of acquiring spiritual powers were more or less accepted as a fact of life. Satanism, on the other hand, is the name – obviously given from a Christian perspective – for illicit ways of accessing spiritual powers in an urban, rather than a rural, world. The contemporary professions associated with Satanism are seen as representatives of a state and economy that 'will eat its own children' and whose power and success do not trickle down to the members of the larger society, but are used for personal gain. Accusations of Satanism reflect a loss of faith in the ability of leaders to act on behalf of the community. In this urban world of meaning, the globalizing discourse of Satanism is used to express suspicions of the (illicit) accumulation of power, wealth and other forms of success. Witchcraft and Satanism may be seen as two distinct phenomena in Zambia, one more urban that the other, but my analysis shows that they are addressing similar issues of inequality and 'unfair' gain or loss.

It is not just the 'big men' in the city that are perceived as dangerous. Katrien Pype, in her Kinshasa ethnography (2015) writes about the way in which Pentecostal ideas about the battle between God and Satan have become attached to certain locations, thereby dividing the world into safe and dangerous zones. Among Kinshasa Christians, in particular Pentecostals, rivers, cemeteries and the bush are hazardous spaces because of their connection with 'traditional' ideas of the spirit world. Naomi's testimony, in which a river is the entrance to the underworld, follows this pattern. In other testimonies graveyards are mentioned as meeting places of Satanists and, again, places where one can access the underworld. The bush, which is an important space in the rural imaginary in Zambia as well as in the Democratic Republic of Congo (Pype 2015: 83), is however largely missing from Zambian testimonies about Satanism. Other categories of places that are identified as dangerous by Kinshasa's Christians are sites connected to practices deemed sinful – (secular) dancing, drinking and adultery – busy streets, sites linked to sorcery practices and traditional healers, political and educational institutions. Both the home and the church are constantly under threat of demonic or satanic influence as well – the vision here is that the city, like the body, is potentially porous and 'open' to evil attacks.

Specific urban locales are connected to Satanism, and those mentioned in Naomi's testimonies include schools, roads or urban markets, the latter seen to be dangerous, mostly because the items sold there may have been produced in the underworld. In her testimony, Naomi lists numerous goods, from processed foods to cosmetics and from clothes and fashion apparel to CDs and cars. Buying and using these products can cause all kinds of problems – illnesses, changes in behaviour, problems in relationships, demon possession or financial troubles.

Moreover, churches are said to be particularly targeted by Satanists. For instance, it is said that by changing the sermon of a pastor, the devil brings more people into his own ranks. Another strategy often mentioned is to make church members fall asleep during the sermon so that they do not hear God's word.

Naomi says: 'Wherever the pastor wants to preach, the devil comes there, he'll start massaging you. He'll be massaging you and massaging you until you feel like dozing. Dozing till you sleep and you'll say, "Ah, what were they preaching?"' As a Seventh Day Adventist, Naomi views the churches that worship on Sunday as more or less influenced by Satan. However, her testimony indicated that even her own church is not safe, with the pastor described as letting the devil influencing him through the purchase of brand-new shoes – made in the underworld – 'making him good looking and attractive'. Here, because of the deceptive 'tainted shoes', the character of the pastor – 'boasting' and rendered arrogant – as well as his message have changed. He is no longer preaching the true word of God: he is said, instead, to be misleading his congregants.

Modern materiality in question

To understand the link between the production of dangerous spaces in testimonies and the moral world of urbanity there is a need to take a closer look at the trope of modernity. While a Western-centred, teleological vision of modernity has been challenged by scholars who draw upon concepts such as 'multiple modernities' to highlight its profound performative instability and ethno-centrism (Comaroff and Comaroff 1993: xi; Eisenstadt 2000), I would argue that modernity, however, can constitute a category with an 'emic potency'. Evolutionist theories may have lost their attraction in the social sciences, but they have long influenced (and may still influence) Western dealings with Africa (see Ellis 2011) and, consequently, the way in which Africans perceive modernity. As Karen Tranberg Hansen writes in her study of second-hand clothing trade in Zambia (1999: 207), 'unlike anthropologists who have been taught to be wary of the predictions of modernisation theory, few Zambians have qualms about the promises of modernisation'. James Ferguson (1999: 84), who writes about 'expectations of modernity' on the Zambian Copperbelt also notes that 'modernization theory had become a local tongue, and sociological terminology and folk classifications had become disconcertingly intermingled in informants' intimate personal narratives. ... That which once presented itself as *explicans* was beginning to make itself visible as *explicandum*'. Thus, the concept of modernity has become part of a larger discourse of expectations for an attainable future, which encompasses a range of iconic (developmental) totems, such as infrastructure, healthcare provision, education, supermarkets, but also Christianity and the nuclear family. The space where this modernity materializes and realizes itself is the city, constructed in opposition to the village. From this perspective, the places singled out in the testimonies of Satanism make a great deal of sense and they are connected to both local Zambian images of modernity and to global flows of commerce.

In an article about modernity and consumerism in Botswana, Wim van Binsbergen discusses the biography of Mary, a young woman from a village who moves to Francistown, one of Botswana's largest cities. Living in the city changes Mary, and one of these changes is that she is taught by her colleagues to use lotions, creams and cosmetics, which are less readily available in the village (1999: 189): 'Her calloused hands and feet soften, ... she learns to use cheap body lotion after every bath, comes to insist on the use of toilet paper and disposable menstrual pads (instead of improvised thick wads of toilet paper grabbed at the factory toilets), becomes expert at the names, prices and directions-for-use of hair-styling products.' Most of the products mentioned by Van Binsbergen as crystallizing the making of a modern embodied (urban) subject are, in Satanist testimonies, named as potentially dangerous.

Additionally, the clothes typically mentioned in the testimonies are not the traditional *chitenges* women wear in the village, but Western-style suits and other off-the-rack articles. Some brands are singled out: Naomi mentions that CK (Calvin Klein) stands for 'Christian Killer'. For most Zambians, Western ready-to-wear fashion is available in the form of second-hand clothing, known locally as *salaula* (see Tranberg Hansen 1999). These clothes are also connected to an elsewhere, they are often donations from Western countries and it is not uncommon to see Zambians wearing T-shirts made for German or Dutch local sports clubs, for instance. These clothes, with their (to the wearer) meaningless letters and words, sometimes inspire anxiety. I once visited a youth camp in a rural area where an evangelist was preaching about Satanism. He asked the youths who had worn clothes 'with words they did not understand' to come forward to be prayed for, since these clothes could well have initiated them into Satanism. All the youths came to the front.

As with clothes, traditional Zambian foods and drinks, such as maize porridge (*nsima*) and local beer (for example *chibuku* or *thobwa*) are never mentioned in testimonies. Rather, satanic edibles are processed foods and imported soft drinks, which are available in the supermarkets and markets in town. While these can be found to a lesser extent in rural areas, in the city they are almost omnipresent. Another category of 'satanic products' involves containers – or media support – of other goods, for instance movies, music and other entertainment products, but also household utensils and ornaments, which are popular gifts at kitchen parties. The 'kitchen party' is a Zambian combination of the traditional initiation ceremony (during which a bride-to-be is given advice on how to act as wife) alongside a Western-style bridal shower (Rasing 1999), a party for female relatives and friends who bring kitchen gear and household utensils as gifts.

All of the products that are seen as possibly satanic are generally imported goods, produced and processed abroad in countries with strong links to the West, and connected to a modern, urban, lifestyle. These are the products that can be bought in the new South African malls, rather than in the shops owned by Chinese traders. Many of the products that are singled out in testimonies as potentially threatening are the ones that are consumed by upper- and middle-class Zambians to perform a Western-style modernity.

Moreover, in Zambia, Christianity and modernity are often conceptualized together in opposition to traditional/ancestral forms of rurality. Yet in villages, the church is also seen as a potential connection to the city, and as indicated earlier, there is a pride among villagers to be able to go to Lusaka with a church choir or other church group. It is within the city that the main increase in predominantly Pentecostal churches has happened in recent years. These city churches often preach a message of prosperity and present themselves as operating on an international scale. While in the village there is not usually enough money available to make this a viable message, in the city, one can at least hope that the riches and blessings will really come.

Like consumer products and the church, the home is another place that is spoken about in testimonies and has, in a certain way, an urban quality. Many testimonies, including Naomi's, discuss an assignment to kill a loved family member. Some have argued that the sacrifices in these narratives are allegories of living with extended families (see for example Meyer 1995 and 1998). However, in the testimonies that I have collected the sacrificed family members are often part of the nuclear family – a family form promoted in Zambia by missionaries and social welfare officials connected to the mining industry.

While the nuclear family remains an ideal, a domestic model preached by churches, praised by the government and some sections of the media, it is far from the lived reality of many Zambians (see also Ashforth 2005, for South Africa). This situation is partly due to the influence of the AIDS epidemic, which has caused children to live in households headed by relatives or elder siblings. In fact, in urban areas only 45 per cent of children live with both parents (Central Statistical Office 2015b: 25). In addition, parents in rural areas sometimes send their children to live with relatives in the city, hoping for better education and employment prospects.

The ex-Satanists who give their testimony are often, like Naomi, adolescents who are sent from household to household and always feel out of place, never at home.

Schools and markets, the church and the home: they are all displayed in the testimonies of ex-Satanists like Naomi as dangerous spaces related to the imaginary of the modern city. In this way, testimonies provide a moral map of the city, which both locates evil territories and implies the need to carve up protective spaces. But what does this process of moral mapping suggest about the imaginary of the city that ordinary Zambians hold? What lies behind the fears of certain places and products in the city, and the actions that spring from these fears? In the concluding section of this chapter, I address these questions.

Conclusion: The dark side of the city and the mask of modernity

In testimonies about Satanism, the city is imagined not only as a place of hope, but also as a source of threat and a dangerous place, and as a result, city dwellers have to navigate different interrelated imaginaries or maps of the world. I also have argued that the constant threat of spiritual evil is intimately related to expectations of development. In these expectations, modernity is an important emic term. Unlike anthropologists who shun the evolutionist connotations this term may evoke, ordinary Zambians understand modernity as the final stage of a process of development. On the surface, this use of the term 'modernity' is linked to the infrastructural reality of the city and contrasted with the idioms of 'tradition' and rurality – 'the village'. Christianity is also a part and parcel of this concept of modernity – the ideal Christian has left tradition behind to become educated, rich and influential. While to many Zambians, modernity means material prosperity, this prosperity comes with other changes as well – and it is these changes that are addressed in the testimonies.

In the city, everyone seems to want a piece of modernity: to look fashionable, to drive a car, to have access to education and healthcare. In the testimonies, this desire is intimately understood. It is education that leads Naomi into Satanism. In many other testimonies, rings, necklaces or skirts are the objects that involuntarily initiate one into Satanism. The desire to 'look good' is also key here and it is no coincidence that Naomi mentions the shoes of the pastor as a satanic influence. Within Zambian Christianity, prosperity preachers are influential in almost all denominations. For this type of Christianity, blessings of wealth, success and status are a proof for one's good standing with God. A pastor needs to display this visual evidence of his blessed status to be recognized as a man of God within his congregation. Pastors (and congregants alike) will therefore try to look as smart as possible. Many products that the testimonies identify as dangerous are not only associated with modernity, and life in the admired Western world, but also with appearance. Clothes and apparel can make one look stylish and fashionable. Creams may adjust the colour of one's skin, and weaves can give one a completely new hairstyle. All of these products can be seen as *masks* that can dramatically change one's appearance.

The testimonies raise the question whether these changes in appearance can transform one's identity as well. The Chewa, a tribe from Zambia and Malawi, have groups of masked dancers called Nyau. The masks and costumes of the dancers hide their features – supposedly no one knows who the dancers really are. But the masks do more than that. When the Nyau are dancing, they become the mask that they wear. Testimonies about Satanism warn their audiences that, in a similar way, wearing certain clothes or a certain type of make-up may make you a different person as well. What you wear or eat, the friends that you have and the places that you go to, all of these may come at great cost and may change who you are. As Green-Simms describes in her ethnography of 'postcolonial automobility' in West Africa, the boundary between the car and the self is highly porous with the car acting as an extension of the self (2017: 195). This porosity may also work the other way around as well: if the car is satanic, maybe the driver will change as well.

Naomi's testimony is quite clear about the costs of wealth: 'When you sacrifice a 25-year-old man, it means you will have 6.8 million euros.[8] When you sacrifice three people, you get a taxi. When you kill your mother, you are supposed to be given a Toyota Canter. You kill your wife, your child, including your mum: you get a 12-room house.' Naomi is also clear about the influence of cosmetics on one's identity. About the popular weaves that many African women and even children wear, she says:

> The more that you plait that child, she'll be in time a Satanist, you see? When she looks in the mirror, she doesn't see herself. She sees a demon, beautifully

decorated and she thinks that she looks like that. That child will think: 'Ah, these things look good on me.' The next time they will come to you and cry: 'Mommy, plait my hair.' And the more she will be saying again and again, and the more the demons will enter in that child. And that is where you will find the child, if she was humble, she will become too stubborn. She was respecting the daddy, but she changes immediately, doing strange things that you say, 'This child, now there is something wrong.' But you won't discover what is wrong with the child. What is wrong is the wig that influences the child.

Like the pastor with his shoes that make him too confident and cocky, the child (and woman) with a wig will become stubborn and unwilling to accept authority. Becoming a person dressed in modern clothes has changed their identity.

This new identity is like a caricature of Western urban modernity: improved standards of living go together with an egotistical form of individualism, a boastful identity in which ties with the family are severed and no respect is given to those who deserve it. The material prosperity and individual autonomy brought by modernity are desired, but at the same time the consequences of development and modernization for personal identity and public morality are feared. Behind many narratives of Satanism lies the question: if I go with modernity – if I buy this soft drink or lipstick – will I still remain the same? Or will I have become a Satanist, who doesn't care about his or her family? This makes urban locales like supermarkets, hospitals, roads, schools and churches ambiguous spaces that embody the desire for betterment as well as the threat of losing oneself to evil influences. Robert Orsi in his discussion of urban religion (1999: 44) states that urban dwellers experience the questions 'who am I?', 'what is possible in life?' and 'what is good?' through the spaces they inhabit. In Zambian cities these questions seem especially pressing, and testimonies of Satanism engage fears that enjoying the experience of the city – its professions, its spaces of opportunity and commerce and the products that are found there – may involve not just an increase in well-being but also a loss of identity.

Stories about Satanists are thus stories about urban Christians in Zambia. They are powerful narratives in which desires and fears are engaged, and they function as cautionary tales against an unquestioned acceptance of modern identities. The imaginary of Satanism offers people living in Zambian cities a vocabulary to make sense of their fortunes, desires and fears. The churches that sponsor the narratives about Satanism offer city dwellers a community and shared practices that lift up secular desires in a Christian – in particular – Pentecostal framework of meaning. They state that, yes, the city is a dangerous place, but through prayer and acts of spiritual warfare this space can be brought under control and redeemed. Ultimately, even the ex-Satanists who give their gruesome testimonies have been delivered and brought back into the fold of Christianity. These churches provide a literal moral map to navigate the dangerous spaces of the city, and a figurative moral map of rejected and approved identities. In this way, they provide Zambian Christians with symbolic resources to handle social change and navigate urban modernity.

Chapter 9

RELIGIOUSLY MOTIVATED SCHOOLS AND
UNIVERSITIES AS 'MORAL ENCLAVES': REFORMING
URBAN YOUTHS IN TANZANIA AND NIGERIA

Hansjörg Dilger and Marloes Janson

It is very important to have schools that provide Islamic teachings. Many students come from homes where the parents are divorced or have died. Often, the students are not watched at home and watch too much TV. Only very few parents come to school and report if there are problems at home or if a student does not perform well. If we knew about these issues we would follow-up and provide counselling.
– Education officer of the Africa Muslims Agency, Tanzania

We expect the government to support us, but actually we are our own government. We send our children to school, but the public schools are so bad that we are going into debt to afford private education. Because NEPA [the National Electric Power Authority, which is popularly known as 'Never Expect Power Always'] is unreliable, we buy our own generators. Since the government is not providing us with security, we secure ourselves by trusting God.
– Pastor of Mountain of Fire and Miracles Ministeries, Nigeria

The first statement was made by the education officer of the Africa Muslims Agency (AMA) in Tanzania, which has established schools and other development-related projects in the country since the mid-1990s. Similarly to Nigeria, there is a widespread sentiment among the country's population that government schools are no longer able to provide 'good education' to their students. At the same time, the statement by the AMA leader echoes the perception that religiously motivated educational institutions are essential for the ethical self-formation of young people in urban environments, which are perceived as morally and economically challenging.

The second quote were the words preached by a pastor of Mountain of Fire and Miracles Ministries (MFM), one of the fastest growing Pentecostal churches in Nigeria, which is also present in Tanzania. His sermon reveals that religious organizations have stepped into the vacuum that was left by the eroding state, thereby resonating the words of the iconic Nigerian novelist Chimamanda Ngozi Adichie that 'religion has become our [African] answer to a failed economy' (*Guardian*, 19 February 2005; quoted by Gandy 2005: 51).

This chapter explores how the educational initiatives of new religious actors have become 'enclaves' of moral reform in the wake of privatization and class formation in urban Tanzania and Nigeria. Taking the two quotes above as a starting point, we argue that moral subject formation in Christian and Muslim institutions of secondary and higher education is inseparably intertwined with the embeddedness of these organizations in translocal networks, their role in the reconfiguration and segregation of urban space and the transformation of the post-colonial state from the 1990s onwards.

By the mid-1990s, many of Africa's polities had lost their quality of 'stateness' to the extent that international and national talk emerged of 'collapsed' or 'vacuous' states, today more generally known as 'fragile' or 'disabled' states (e.g. Bayart 1993; Chabal and Daloz 1999; Ferguson 2006; Olivier de Sardan 2014). Within this context of 'fractional' statehood, religiously motivated organizations[1] began operating as alternative religious communities, equipped with all the necessary instruments – ranging from electricity, to health clinics and educational institutions – of a functioning state.[2] Furthermore, this 'new' type of development organization combined a focus on material progress with the fostering of spiritual and moral well-being among – and often attempted conversion of – their beneficiaries (Bornstein 2005; Thomas 2005: 233–42). In this context, Thomas (2005) speaks of a 'virtue-ethics' approach to development,[3] which provides an understanding of 'how Faith practices articulate the connections between "religious" and "economic" spheres of activity' (Coleman 2011: 33).

In this chapter, we focus on education, which is commonly regarded as the *sine qua non* of social change and economic development in Africa (e.g. Fichtner 2012; Stambach 2006), and which has opened up new opportunities for moral as well as political and market engagement by Christian and Muslim actors at all educational levels against the backdrop of liberalization and privatization since the 1990s (Dilger and Schulz 2013: 370). Whereas anthropology has largely treated education and religion separately (Stambach 2006: 4–8), our chapter studies them as interconnected, thereby shedding light on how educational interventions contribute to public life through moral modes of subject-formation (cf. Bornstein 2005; Stambach 2006, 2010a). The case studies presented below – based on participant observation in classrooms and on campuses, qualitative interviews and informal conversations with students, parents and other relatives, teaching and administrative staff and management, and an analysis of curricula and other printed and online material – explore the implications of these recent religiously motivated investments in the educational domain with regard to the socio-moral transformation of urban space. By means of a comparative ethnographic study of the missions of a range of Christian and Muslim educational institutions in urban Tanzania and Nigeria, we argue that in the context of compromised state education and inadequate infrastructure, religiously motivated initiatives provide youths with the tools and material spaces to negotiate the socio-moral unpredictability of urban living and to convert themselves into moral citizens according to the values of the religiously motivated organizations that run these institutions, as well as civic virtues.

Studying moral enclaves comparatively

A comparison between Tanzania and Nigeria is particularly interesting as they are both former British colonies, characterized by high ethnic diversity and with similar ratios of Muslims and Christians, where, old, religious organizations have played an important role in social service provision, including schooling (Reichmuth 1996; Stambach 2010b). In both settings neo-Pentecostal churches and reformist strands of Islam have established schools and universities since the mid-1990s.[4] These religiously motivated educational initiatives combine secular education with the teaching and embodiment of moral (faith-specific) values – relating to issues of dress, comportment, gender, class and discipline among others. However, there are also marked differences between the two settings. Although the history of both Tanzania and Nigeria demonstrate that religion has been used and understood as a function of politics, religion has become a destabilizing force in Nigeria, whereas in Tanzania the post-colonial state has aimed to be 'religiously neutral' (although particularly Muslim reformists have questioned this claim because they have been historically marginalized in their access to social services) (Dilger 2020; Loimeier 2007: 151–2).

The divergent political instrumentalization of religion in Tanzania and Nigeria had implications for their educational systems, which have multiple political, economic, social and religious dimensions. In an effort to redress the Christian-Muslim inequality in education in Tanzania, all mission and private schools were nationalized with the implementation of socialist policies in 1969. Since privatization in 1995 the growing market of Christian and Muslim schools in the country has become a particularly urban phenomenon. Especially in the most populous city, Dar es Salaam, the increasingly commodified educational landscape is composed of a multitude of Christian and Muslim primary and secondary schools, which have become deeply embedded in – and drivers of – free market dynamics and social differentiation processes (though in highly unequal ways owing to the historical marginalization of Muslim schools in the country) (Dilger 2013). In contrast, in urban Nigeria – where since 1999 the ownership of higher educational institutions has been deregulated by the state – there has been a spectacular rise of universities funded by religious organizations who recognize tertiary education as key driver for national growth. Pentecostal organizations took the lead in this new development, to which Muslim organizations responded by establishing their own universities. Complementing the typical image of a country being torn by religious violence, the upsurge of religiously motivated universities in Nigeria's economic hub Lagos and its hinterland shows that religious difference does not automatically lead to violence; religious divergence could as well be the ground for mutual borrowing, competition and religious entanglements (Janson 2021; Janson and Meyer 2016).

The upsurge of religiously motivated educational institutions in Tanzania and Nigeria needs to be studied against the backdrop of what Beaumont (2008a) calls 'neoliberal urbanism'. The 'religious entrepreneurs'– leaders who act partly with a charity agenda, and partly as market leaders on the religious marketplace (Lanz and Oosterbaan 2016; Lauterbach 2016)[5] – who run these schools and universities have heavily invested in religious infrastructure, thereby transforming urban space. Here it should be noted that urban space refers not only to Tanzanian and Nigerian urban centres. Owing to a shortage of land in the urban centres and a tight real estate market, schools and universities have bought land in urban hinterlands as well as at the centres' margins, which, in line with the expansionist missions of the religious traditions that they represent, have become part of the sprawling metropolis.

To chart the spatial and socio-moral implications of the educational investments in (semi)urban infrastructure, we have coined the notion of a 'moral enclave', which we conceive as an educational space in the city and the sprawling suburbia where students are being trained as moral subjects by new religious actors. Our notion of the moral enclave draws on what is called 'enclave urbanism' in urban studies. AlSayyad and Roy (2006) argue that new patterns of urban citizenship are marked by emergent enclaves that rest upon protectionism and increased segregation (both perceived as well as physically manifest) of atomized communities in the urban realm. In a similar vein, the educational spaces that we discuss in this chapter set themselves apart explicitly from their highly fluid and, in their students, their families, and staff's eyes, 'immoral' urban environments. Because of these educational institutions' tendency towards boundary maintenance through exclusionary and regulatory practices of moral subject formation, education can be understood here as a practice of enclaving for the building of moral communities constituted by good citizens trained to lead a moral life.

As pointed out by Sivan in his essay on fundamentalist religious movements, the enclave places the morally defiled outside society in contrast to the community of virtuous insiders: 'A sort of "wall of virtue" is thereby constructed, separating the saved, free, equal (before God or before history), and morally superior enclave from the hitherto-tempting central community' (1995: 18). Although the schools and universities that we studied ban drinking, smoking and premarital sexual relationships, and censor dress and their students' leisure activities, the boundary between 'inside' and 'outside' is not impermeable. Religiously motivated schools and universities as moral enclaves are not just 'local' or demarcated spaces. Rather, they are also a motor of urbanization and globalization processes with regard to class formation, urban reconfiguration and the building of moral capital that becomes relevant in the students and teachers' lives beyond their educational institutions. Moreover, they are entwined with the formation of translocal networks by maintaining ties with North America and the Arab Middle East to secure funding – and where such financial ties do not exist, they appeal to students' desire to be integrated in the global community of Muslims, the *umma*, or in world

Christianity. Thus, while the focus in urban and development studies is primarily on spatially contained enclaves,[6] our emphasis is on outward-looking and globally oriented enclaves. In brief, the concept of the moral enclave prompts us to rethink the interplay between religion, urban space and globalization (cf. Burchardt and Becci 2013; Dilger et al. 2020), thereby providing a better understanding of how religious entrepreneurs 'make place' on various scales from the local to the global (Massey 1992), and how religion 'takes place' (Knott 2005: 43) through the mutual shaping of socio-moral relations 'between people and things, people and places, people and symbols, and the imagined relations between these' (ibid.: 21) in urban Tanzania and Nigeria today.

In line with the co-constitution of religious engagement and urban space, a second focus in this chapter is the increasingly privatized and marketized public sphere in urban Tanzania and Nigeria. In their mission to convert both souls and public space, Christian and Muslim schools and universities compete not only with state institutions but also among themselves and other private educational institutions, thereby becoming implicated in an 'increasingly competitive educational market' (Dilger 2013: 454). This is true even for those institutions that are run mainly as charity projects and cater specifically for the less well off segments of the urban population (as in the example of the Africa Muslims Agency's seminary below). However, while other religiously motivated schools and universities are often registered as non-profit organizations as well, they often charge considerable tuition fees and therefore appeal more to the emergent middle classes,[7] thereby distinguishing themselves explicitly from the older, more 'charitable' Christian and Muslim organizations (Beaumont 2008b: 2023) and perpetuating social inequalities (Collins 2009) through their market orientation. Competition on the educational market manifests not only in tuition fees, but also in entry criteria. Whereas state institutions screen their applicants for academic qualifications, religiously motivated schools and universities pride themselves that they also screen for 'character'.

This brings us to the third and final focus in this chapter: religiously motivated schools and universities occupy their own niche in the educational market by bidding on morality. Unlike what their label suggests, beyond providing secular education they do not (only) teach religious subjects but instead create spaces for the embodiment of religiously informed moral values. As part of their mission to educate 'good citizens', the schools and universities that are central in this chapter engage in moral and bodily surveillance of their students. For example, they have wardens on ground to ensure that students do not engage in illicit behaviour, and have implemented codes of conduct that restrict students' off-campus mobility, ensure their compliance with regulations for dress and bodily care and limit male–female interactions. Our case studies illustrate that by shifting the emphasis from religiosity to religiously informed morality, these novel educational institutions aspire to cater for the needs of the various segments of the emerging middle classes in urban Tanzania and Nigeria, who by means of their moral disposition aim to distinguish themselves both from the 'morally lax' students of state educational institutions, and the 'backward' mindset of students getting a religious education (e.g. in Qur'anic or Bible Schools). This reaffirms Simpson's conclusion that 'the desire for education [in his case mission schools] becomes a desire to be different, to become Other – and, indeed, Chosen Other' (1998: 220). This 'Otherness' is reflected in the material infrastructure of religiously motivated schools and universities: compared with the lack of facilities in many state educational institutions, and despite their struggle to obtain funding, most of the schools and universities in our case studies attempt to look 'modern' with their freshly painted classrooms and lecture theatres, computer facilities for staff and students and 'corporate' dress code. As a result, many Tanzanians and Nigerians consider the modern space of religiously motivated schools and universities a proper site for the formation of the new middle class.

To sum up, by taking the dialectic entanglement between urban space, moral subject formation and social class formation as our starting point, this chapter explores how the cityscape has mediated new forms of religiously inflected infrastructure through the building of educational moral enclaves in urban Tanzania and Nigeria. This novel infrastructure provides a fresh perspective on education as both a provider of development and a venue for the disciplining of a new generation of moral citizens striving for upward social mobility.

St. Mary's International Primary School and Al-Farouq Islamic Seminary for Boys in Urban Tanzania

St. Mary's International Primary School was founded by the late Dr Gertrude Rwakatare, the former leading pastor of a popular neo-Pentecostal church in Dar es Salaam, in the mid-1990s and is today part of one of the largest privately owned (primary and secondary) school networks in Tanzania.[8] Dr Rwakatare (*St. Mary's Mirror* 2002–3: 3) described that the founding of St. Mary's International Primary School was closely connected to Tanzania's poor educational situation at the time, and that she felt 'touched' when she 'saw buses taking [Tanzanian] students to Kenya and Uganda to acquire quality education' (ibid.: 3). In her endeavour to establish her school network, she received support from the US-based NGO Christian Working Woman as well as several members of her own Pentecostal church, which counted around ten thousand members in 2010. She also drew on her political connections, especially since she was appointed Special Seat Member of Parliament in 2007; a position that allowed her to draw attention to the needs and challenges of Tanzania's (private) educational system at a political level.

The establishment of the network's first school in Dar es Salaam in 1996 was linked closely to the selling of urban land to private investors after the official ending of the socialist *Ujamaa* project in 1985. Under these conditions, new religious entrepreneurs like the late Dr Rwakatare established their educational projects primarily on the margins of the city that had not yet been densely populated. St. Mary's International Primary School was built in a neighbourhood on the former outskirts of Dar es Salaam that until the 1980s had been used for agricultural purposes. Later, Dr Rwakatare purchased the former grounds of the

Tanzanian National Insurance Company in the immediate neighbourhood of St. Mary's International School, where she established an orphanage that provided shelter and education to about seven hundred children in 2006.

In the context of the economic hardship faced by many in the city, some of the new religious entrepreneurs like Dr Rwakatare became targets of suspicion among the urban public. There were persistent rumours in the immediate community – but also among students and teachers – that the land on which St. Mary's International Primary School was built was haunted by spirits (*majini*) (Dilger 2022: 102–03). Some of Dilger's interlocutors ascribed the presence of these *majini* to the backgrounds of the pupils themselves, who allegedly brought them from their rural homes, either for protection or because these spirits had followed them maliciously (see below). Other staff members and students claimed that Dr Rwakatare herself had forged an alliance with evil forces as a way of getting rich – a not uncommon allegation against both male and female neo-Pentecostal pastors in the city, who had accumulated significant amounts of wealth over relatively short periods of time.

In the early 2010s, the International Primary School was attracting significant numbers of students from the (partly upper) middle classes whose parents were able and willing to pay the comparatively high school fees in order to secure good education for their children. School fees for the day school in 2009 were set at

Figure 9.1. St Mary's International Primary School's courtyard with school-owned buses, 2009. Courtesy H. Dilger.

Tanzanian Shillings (TZH) 1,080,000 per year (about 355 GBP); this included school buses, meals and supplies excluding textbooks. In contrast, attending a public primary school in Tanzania has been 'free' since 2001, except for the often considerable costs for uniforms, textbooks and transport. The 1800 (day and boarding) students and their families from mostly Christian, and sometimes Muslim, backgrounds appreciated the fact that the school was employing English as language of instruction consistently;[9] that its teachers allegedly 'worked harder' than at government schools; that its buildings and classrooms had comparatively high aesthetic and material standards and that it had its own computer room and transport system. Furthermore, the school's reputation derived from the fact that it was perceived as providing 'moral education' and training 'well-adjusted, knowledgeable and responsible citizens' (Dilger 2017: 520). The morning assemblies in particular were a key site for instilling discipline and moral values in the students, for instance by singing the national anthem and the so-called patriotic song,[10] and also by screening the pupils' bodies for compliance with the school's rules for dress and hygiene (ibid.). Students were also encouraged to help enforce discipline by running for one of the offices in the student governing body (so-called monitors and prefects) who were responsible for taking attendance and maintaining silence in class, among other tasks. In the *St. Mary's Mirror* (2002–3), students described how such positions trained them for becoming 'academic giants' (ibid.: 12f.) and 'leaders in the future' (ibid.: 31).

While the school was sometimes perceived as a 'Christian school' owing to its linkage with the late Dr Rwakatare and her church, students and teachers disputed such a categorization, based on the somewhat diffuse status of the teaching of religion in the school's curriculum and the fact that students of highly diverse Christian and Muslim backgrounds were enrolled. Under these conditions, the school's Christian, and more specifically Pentecostal, orientation became central for the students' and teachers' moral self-formation in rather implicit ways. This focus became visible not only in the religious imagery displayed in the school buildings and the use of prayers and religious songs (which were equally popular in Dr Rwakatare's church) in everyday interactions in the space of the school, but also in spiritual healing from malevolent spirits, as is common in neo-Pentecostal churches in the city. At the time of Dilger's research in 2008–10, female Muslim students from wealthy backgrounds were said to be especially vulnerable to the potentially 'harmful' impact of spirits.[11] One teacher explained:

> I usually see [the possessed students] lying down, beating [themselves], crying and making a lot of noise. Maybe ... this is an Arabic problem ... It is [common among] rich people. This student [who was possessed] came from a rich family. I think that her ancestors did something wrong.[12]

The dynamics of class formation and the desire for the learning and teaching of moral values were also central to the Al-Farouq Islamic Seminary for Boys, established in 1997 and located in the immediate vicinity of St. Mary's International Primary School (though it has no further relationship with Dr Rwakatare's school). Its founding organization, the Africa Muslims Agency (AMA), is based in Kuwait and has been involved in proselytization (*da'wa*) and the building of wells, health institutions and educational facilities in Tanzania since 1994 (Ahmed 2009: 428). At the time of Dilger's research in 2010, the AMA headquarters in Dar es Salaam were run mostly by Tanzanian nationals, some of whom had pursued – in the same vein as the teachers at Al-Farouq – educational opportunities abroad, including in Sudan, Egypt, Saudi Arabia and Pakistan.[13] At the same time, the development organization depended heavily on funding from Kuwait, and central administrative decisions were made by the headquarters abroad.

Unlike St. Mary's, Al-Farouq Islamic Seminary – which is run on the ordinary and advanced secondary level and admits only boys from a Muslim background – is not directed at Dar es Salaam's (upper) middle classes, but rather the city's working and lower middle classes who usually have only modest expectations of becoming socially upwardly mobile. In 2009, the majority of the parents of the 365 registered students worked as small-scale traders, low-ranked government employees or in one of the blue-collar jobs in the city.[14] While most of them paid annual school fees ranging from TZH 300,000 (for the day school, about 100 GBP) to TZH 650,000 (about 214 GBP for the boarding school), several students and teachers received educational grants and/or free treatment at the AMA-owned dispensary; some of

Figure 9.2. Plaques on the AMA buildings show that they were built with support from various local and international donors, most notably the Kuwait-based development organization *Direct Aid* (here: the library), 2010. Courtesy H. Dilger.

the sponsored students were orphans who resided in a separate boarding section on the AMA premises. The students and teachers' impression that Al-Farouq was less competitive than other – private as well as some high-performing government – schools was reinforced by its weak material infrastructure (as manifested by the poorly equipped library and laboratory) as well as the high turnover of teachers owing to the school's low salaries. Furthermore, the students were well aware that their educational situation was generally worse than that of their peers in the more costly Christian schools in the city. As one student emphasized, these schools provided private buses for their students whereas Al-Farouq students had to use public transport (*daladala*):

> In [Christian] schools the students are brought home after school, but we ride the *daladala*. They are often too crowded. I leave school at 2:30 p.m. and often have to wait half an hour for transportation. In some *daladalas* you have to stand up the whole way home. By the time you get home your whole body aches.[15]

Despite their criticism, the students and teachers at Al-Farouq appreciated their school because of its strong focus on teaching morality and its perceived ability to turn their pupils into 'good Muslims'. In conversations, most of them described Dar es Salaam's urban environment as 'risky' and claimed that it held many 'moral temptations' especially for young men of lower social status, including the use of drugs and the risk of getting infected with HIV/AIDS or other sexually transmitted diseases. In this context, the headmaster explained, parents expect Al-Farouq's management and teachers to provide a strong religious and moral formation for their children so that they 'become good members of society' and would not 'join bad groups of people'.[16] In this regard, the school management found it necessary that the Al-Farouq secondary school continued as a unisex school. As Mr Ahmed, the school's education coordinator, remarked: 'The mixing of [male and female] students can lead to negative implications as far as Islamic teachings are concerned.'[17]

As part of their moral-religious education at Al-Farouq, the students attended Islamic Knowledge and Arabic classes as well as the noon prayers at the on-site mosque. They were also punished heavily when they performed poorly in class or when they transgressed the school's rules, for example by coming late to class, making noise in the classroom, violating the school's dress code or regulations against entering into illicit relationships.[18] In contrast to St. Mary's Primary School, discipline was enforced mostly by the teachers and management themselves, and there was no visible student governing body during Dilger's research. Furthermore, while St. Mary's had a strong commitment to nation-building and the formation of 'good citizens,' this aspect was much less pronounced at the Islamic seminary. Instead, the belonging to the global community of Muslims – the *umma* – was emphasized informally, for instance by greeting each other with '*salaam aleikum*' or addressing each other jokingly as '*mashehe*' (sheikh). This mutual reassurance about their shared faith was particularly important for some of the students and teachers who felt discriminated in their everyday interactions with non-Muslims in the city. Thus, one teacher explained that Muslims were treated differently in their everyday encounters with Christians and other people in Dar es Salaam: 'Sometimes you sense that they greet you differently because you are a Muslim – for instance, when they shake hands with you.'[19] Some students put it more dramatically, claiming that the public perceived Islamic schools as training grounds for 'future terrorists'.[20] At the same time, this did not preclude their feeling of belonging to Tanzania's ethnically and religiously highly diverse society, as one student put it:

> [Being with other Muslims] helps me to recognize that we Muslims are supposed to be as one, how we are supposed to be and live. We learn the life that we are going to live later. And this is not only for the Muslims – all human beings are one, only their beliefs are different.[21]

Thus, while the sense of being a distinct religious and moral community in the wider urban context was more pronounced at Al-Farouq than at a religiously mixed Christian school like St. Mary's, the value of living together well in a pluralistic society was also part of the moral self-formation at the Islamic seminary (Dilger 2022: 175). Hence, Muslim students became knowledgeable and confident about their faith by living in a diverse society, in which they engaged with people from different religious and ethnic backgrounds on an everyday basis and simultaneously longed to lead a morally 'pure' and 'clean' life in a spiritually and socio-economically challenging environment.

To sum up, both the neo-Pentecostal primary school and the Islamic seminary function as moral enclaves which enforce the embodiment of religiously informed values through a wide range of disciplinary practices that aim at character-building and improving educational performance. The sense of being a distinct socio-moral community of students and teachers – which is tied to notions of academic excellence in the case of St. Mary's and to perceptions of socio-economic deprivation in the case of Al-Farouq – is enhanced by the architecture of the schools, which is shaped by the divergent quality of their buildings and their being closed-off from the urban environment by high walls. At the same time, however, both schools foster the connections beyond the confinements of their educational institutions, and thus have become embedded in Dar es Salaam's booming, and rapidly transforming, educational marketplace in highly specific ways. At St Mary's, these connections include the strong commitment to the education of a future societal, and internationally oriented elite, as well as the ties with the government and religious and secular partner organizations in the United States and Europe. At Al-Farouq, they comprise the cultivation of the students' awareness of belonging both to the global *umma* of Muslims and Dar es Salaam's multicultural and multireligious population, as well as the ties with sponsors and development organizations in the Arab World and a range of Islamic educational centres in East and Northeast Africa.

Redeemer's University and Fountain University in urban Nigeria

Similar to Dar es Salaam where religiously oriented schools function as moral enclaves in a highly pluriform and allegedly morally corrupt urban landscape, we see a similar shift towards 'moral education' in religiously motivated universities in Lagos and its urban hinterland. These universities mushroomed to put an end to Nigeria's 'crisis in tertiary education' (Anugwom 2002). University College Ibadan (UCI) was the first university to open its doors in Nigeria's third largest city Ibadan in 1948, heralding Nigeria's 'University Age' (Livsey 2017). After a successful start, in the late 1960s public universities – as major centres of domestic and foreign investment – became embroiled in ethno-political rivalries and the university age started to dwindle. In an attempt to turn the tide and revive Nigeria's earlier university age, the ownership of higher education institutions was deregulated from the state in 1999. This resulted in the creation of private universities, including those associated with Pentecostal churches and, more recently, reformist Muslim organizations.

The Redeemed Christian Church of God (RCCG) is the largest Pentecostal church in present-day Nigeria. In 1983, Pastor Adeboye received a divine call summoning him to establish a 'City of God' to redeem the 'Sin City' that was Lagos, resulting in Redemption City (Ukah 2013b). This massive prayer camp along the Lagos–Ibadan Expressway signifies RCCG's prosperity gospel, which propagates the value of succeeding professionally. In order to raise its congregants into well-educated professionals, Pastor Adeboye – who holds a PhD in Mathematics and worked as a university lecturer before being ordained RCCG's General Overseer (G.O.) – established Redeemer's University Nigeria (RUN) in 2005. When RCCG needed space for its proposed 3-by-3 kilometre auditorium, the university moved from Redemption Camp to its permanent site in Ede, a town in Osun State some 200 kilometres southwest from Lagos, in 2014. The real estate market is tight and land scarce in Lagos State. Land is more affordable in neighbouring Osun State. Moreover, unlike in Lagos – an alleged node for drug traffickers, smugglers and fraudsters – in smaller urban centres such as Ede inhabitants are less exposed to night life, gambling places and beer parlours, making it a proper site for a university teaching 'morality'. Despite its distance from Lagos, Ede is well located for both private and public transport. With its modern buildings and its facilities like shops, hostels, restaurants and a bank, the architectural style of the campus in Ede resembles that of RCCG's Redemption City in Lagos, as a result of which it is considered an annex of the latter, suggesting that worship and running a university are part of the same mission. Underscoring Pentecostal churches' modern architecture, a Muslim interlocutor told Janson: 'These days you don't know whether you are entering a church or bank: they all look the same with their glass facades and high-tech architecture.'[22]

Redeemer's University's acronym is RUN and this is also part of its motto: 'Running with a vision'. Its vision is to become 'the foremost institution for producing graduates who combine academic excellence in the practice of their profession with God-fearing attributes'. According to its online prospectus, in 2017 RUN enrolled around 2,400 students who pursued degrees in thirty programmes in six colleges. That same year RUN won the UNIDO (United Nations Industrial Development Organization) Nigeria National Quality Gold Award, and in 2018 the Southwest Outstanding Private University of the Year award. Other than becoming a top teaching institute, in line with its mission to 'march on to change the world for God', RUN strives to become one of Africa's most renowned research institutes. In 2014 it won a World Bank grant to fund the African Centre of Excellence for Genomics of Infectious Diseases, which is involved in research on the containment of the Ebola virus and Lassa fever, and to establish a post-doctoral fellowship training programme. Despite its (inter) national reputation, RUN has difficulties in securing funding. Janson was told by colleagues from state universities that in an effort to generate income, Pentecostal universities, including RUN, even deduct tithes from staff's salaries, which made them criticize these universities as 'prisons' that try to control their staff.

Adjacent to the Redemption City, a few kilometres away on the opposite side of the Lagos–Ibadan Expressway – popularly known as 'the Spiritual Highway' (Janson and Akinleye 2015) – the prayer camp of *Nasrul-Lahi-L-Fatih Society of Nigeria*, which translates as 'There is no help except from Allah' and is abbreviated to NASFAT, is located. Since its establishment in 1995, NASFAT has

Figure 9.3. Redeemer's university's goals, 2017. Courtesy M. Janson.

grown into Nigeria's largest Muslim organization of contemporary times (Janson 2020). According to its Mission Statement, NASFAT aims to 'empower Muslims spiritually as well as economically'. The avenue to economic empowerment is good education. In line with its mission, NASFAT established primary and secondary schools and, in 2007, Fountain University (FU). According to its prospectus, FU had a student body of about a thousand in 2017 and offered fourteen programmes in two colleges. Janson was told by FU's senior management that compared with RUN's students, FU's students were from less wealthy backgrounds. Still, they can be considered to be belonging to the new middle class: their parents often work as university lecturers, engineers or business people. While the tuition fees of an undergraduate degree at RUN were around 693,000 Naira per term (depending on the programme), that is, approximately 1,460 GBP, with 390,000 Naira (around 825 GBP) tuition fees per term, FU was one of the cheapest private universities in Nigeria in 2017. Still, compared with the tuition fees charged by Lagos State University of 25,000 Naira, 390,000 Naira is an extraordinary amount for the average Nigerian, whose monthly income is 75,000 Naira.[23] Although tuition fees are high at RUN and FU, their management emphasized that their primary motif is not 'earning money'. According to RUN's Deputy Registrar: 'Daddy G.O. didn't establish a university to make profit. Our mission is to impact lives and to improve the moral standard of our students. In order to achieve our goal, we must fight the moral decadence of this current generation.'[24]

Elucidating FU's establishment, a NASFAT official said:

Because of the Pentecostal syndrome that keeps Nigeria firmly in its grasp, we decided to establish our own university. All big Pentecostal churches have a university, so we thought we also needed one. You can compare our mutual competition to that between MTN and Glo, or Coca Cola and Pepsi (Janson 2021: 102).[25]

FU is located in Osogbo in southwestern Nigeria. The choice for this location can be explained by NASFAT's self-proclaimed mission of competing with RUN: Osogbo and Ede are neighbouring towns. Furthermore, Osogbo has a long history of Islam: it was one of the earliest commercial centres in the region, attracting Muslim traders (Ogungbile 2011). FU's management told Janson: 'We selected our environment with the greatest of care, because environment is the mental feeding ground out of which the food that goes into our minds is extracted.'[26]

During her visit to FU's campus in 2017, Janson was welcomed by a dried-up fountain at the gate. FU's emblem is the fountain, representing a pool of knowledge. The dried-up fountain can be seen as symbolizing the fate of several private universities in Nigeria, with a crumbling infrastructure and difficulties in recruiting qualified staff and students. Aware that they had not yet reached the same level as Pentecostal universities, such as RUN, a member of FU's management said: 'You can't compare a sprinter with a runner. Pentecostal universities are sprinting and we are running behind them; the gap is still wide.'[27] To close the gap, FU has signed Memoranda of Understanding (MoUs) with four universities in the United Arab

9. *Reforming Urban Youths in Tanzania and Nigeria* 157

Figure 9.4. FU's dried-up fountain, 2017. Courtesy M. Janson.

Emirates, Malaysia and Sudan. The benefits of this international collaboration for students and lecturers are yet to be seen.

Somewhat ironically for a religiously motivated university, FU does not offer religious education. In contrast, RUN expanded its curriculum with Christian Religious Studies in 2016. However, because it recruited only one student, RUN's management decided that it was not lucrative to continue the programme. A concerned father told Janson that he was unwilling to 'invest hundreds of thousands of Naira for my children to become religious functionaries'.[28] To meet parents' wishes of their children finding a 'good job' upon graduation, RUN and FU's curricula reveal their strong professional and secularist self-understanding. Hence, the division between religious educational institutions and religiously motivated universities such as RUN and FU can be summarized in terms of Chidester's (2006: 67) divide between the teaching *of* religion and the teaching *about* religion. Whereas Bible Colleges and Islamic Seminaries teach religion, RUN and FU do not teach religious subjects but embrace a teaching philosophy that encompasses integrity, decency and virtue – moral values that are considered to be part of both a Christian and Muslim understanding of religion, as well as good citizenship. Elucidating RUN's teaching philosophy, a staff member lectured Janson: 'Our degree is awarded on the pedigree of Loyalty, Integrity, Faithfulness, and Excellence, which means LIFE to us. We are guided by a strong commitment to run with our vision by producing morally sound and high-quality graduates.'[29]

NASFAT's National Education Secretary described 'moral education' as follows: 'We instil ethics in our students by training them to show respect for their parents, teachers, and classmates, to show punctuality, and to look after their body by not eating fast food and dressing modestly.'[30] Underlining that 'moral education' involves more than teaching religious subjects, RUN's Deputy Registrar explained to Janson:

> Religion is not just reflected in our curriculum, but more in our rules and regulations. We don't allow smoking and drinking: students using alcohol or drugs are expelled. This is written in black and white in our student handbook. We don't allow trousers for ladies, except for during sports activities, and we don't allow them to expose their bodies. Male students must dress corporately, which means a jacket and tie. We have many rules and regulations, also regarding hairstyle, music choice, internet use, watching television, and the use of mobile phones. Our students are allowed to watch television only in their hostels' common room, where wardens censor the programmes they watch. Students can browse the internet only in designated areas. The moral standard for staff is even higher than for students. Their letter of appointment contains a clause about dress and mandatory participation in church programmes.

In line with RUN and FU's emphasis on moral education, students are expected to show 'good character', as expressed in their conduct and apparel. Prospective students at RUN are screened via an interview, and female students even have to undergo a pregnancy test as a response to the widespread discourse in Nigeria regarding the 'moral laxity' of public educational institutions where 'teenage mothers' are believed to be a common problem.[31] Prospective students at FU need a reference on 'good character' from an imam or religious community leader. Once admitted at RUN and FU, students must dress 'modestly and corporately', which means a jacket and tie for men and a skirt (at least below the knees) and a cap or *hijab* (covering the chest) for women. Furthermore, during term time RUN and FU students are not allowed to leave campus; should they have an emergency appointment outside the campus, they must first seek permission from both their parents and the Head of Department. All FU students carry a 'Temporary Exit Card'. Before the holidays start, they must document where they are travelling to and when and at what time they will return to campus. If they return late, they face suspension.

The RUN and FU deploy various measures for disciplining students. The provost of the Redeemed Christian School of Missions (RECSOM) told Janson proudly that in 2013 he introduced a programme in collaboration with RUN to 'rehabilitate erring students'. Those students who are suspended from RUN for engaging in 'sinful' activities such as drinking, smoking or engaging in love relationships are interned for half a year at RECSOM, which the provost described as 'a mission school where the soldiers of Christ are being trained in a military way', to participate in its harsh regime of non-stop 'prayer marathons' and fasting.[32] If after six months they have 'recovered their destiny', they are allowed to resume their studies at RUN. The FU operates an integrity point system: at the beginning of the semester, a student is credited with a hundred points, which s/he progressively loses if s/he commits offences against the regulations. For example, running late for on-site mosque programmes (which are mandatory for Muslim students and optional for Christian students) results in a deduction of fifteen points, 'indecency' is punished by a deduction of thirty points and the possession of charms leads to expulsion. 'Indecency' includes, among other things, students' love relations. Except for mixed classrooms – where female and male students sit separately – interaction between male and female students outside the classroom is kept to a minimum at both RUN and FU. The only interaction between male and female students at RUN is over lunch and dinner in the cafeteria, to which students, because of the possibility of intermixing, referred as 'Love Garden'.

Because RUN and FU enact morality rather than religiosity, it is not uncommon to find Muslim students at RUN and Christian students at FU. For instance, Janson interviewed two female Muslim students at RUN who had a Muslim father and a Christian mother and who told her that their parents had selected RUN because of its 'high standard' and because they wanted to 'instil discipline' in their daughters. A male student confided to her that he had converted to Islam in his first year at RUN: 'As long as you follow the rules, you're cool here. I'm used to going to church since my mum, who is an accountant and pays for my tuition, is a Christian.' A male Christian student applied to FU when, for the fourth time, he was not admitted at the University of Lagos. A female Christian student had more ideological reasons for applying to FU. At school she had many Muslim friends and by studying at FU she wanted to adjust the negative stereotyping around Muslims: 'I want to show that not all Muslims are into Boko Haram.'[33]

Parents' rising quest for moral higher education seems to be class motivated. During her field research, Janson heard several parents from the emerging middle class exclaim: 'Secular education is not enough for our children!' At the same time, they associated religious education with a 'traditional mindset', unable to secure their children positions in the lucrative private sector of the Nigerian economy. Against this background, religiously motivated universities such as RUN and FU cultivate an education-based middle-class identity, stressing not only the civic virtues of education but also its role in building a moral community composed of virtuous citizens who act as what RUN's management described in terms of 'arrow heads of national development'.[34]

Conclusion: Religiously motivated education and the formation of moral enclaves

Drawing on Althusserian (1971) notions of governmentality that conceive of the school as the ideological tool of the (secular) nation-state, education remains identified in much anthropological scholarship as state driven, laying the foundation for secular-modern citizenship, thereby reproducing the ingrained religion-education dichotomy (Stambach 2010b: 24). As our case studies demonstrate, religion and education have become increasingly conflated in urban Tanzania and Nigeria. The Christian and Muslim schools and universities that have been established in these countries since the mid-1990s combine their secular curricula with the mission to educate students to become moral citizens. Many of our interlocutors are seeking to negotiate the relationship between being (or becoming) moral subjects and good citizens, and education serves as a means to reconcile the two. Taking this course, studying religiously informed moral practice and education as co-constituted opens up a conceptual locus for analysing how the public domain is being transformed through socio-moral interventions, and how new governmental regimes and infrastructures have emerged in urban Africa.

The gradual withdrawal of the state from the economy throughout Africa – and the simultaneous weakening of state education due to the emergence of global initiatives for universal access to education (Dilger 2013: 454, 565) – has generated a new public sphere evolving around private enterprises, including religious organizations. According to past World Bank president James Wolfensohn, 'half the work in education and health in sub-Saharan Africa is done by the church' (quoted by Wodon 2015: 90). Similarly, a report by the United Nations Fund for Population Activities (UNFPA 2009) stated that 'there is clearly an important parallel faith-based universe of development, one which provides anywhere between 30–60% of healthcare and educational services in many developing countries' (ibid.). As a result, the novel public sphere that has emerged in both urban Tanzania and Nigeria is increasingly governed by religiously informed rules and values.

The new religious entrepreneurs who have stepped into the vacuum that was left by the withdrawing state invested heavily in education – a 'high density' sector in which the post-colonial state's presence has long been most visible (Olivier de Sardan 2014: 405). Because land is expensive in the urban centres of Tanzania and Nigeria, they have moved out of the megacities, converting semi-urban landscapes into what could be defined as 'moral enclaves': settings at the margins of the megacity – regarded as godless and dystopian – but close enough to the urban centres where capital is concentrated and from where the majority of students are recruited. What we see here is that (semi)urban space, rather than providing a conventional kind of unruliness and anonymity that permits freedom of behaviour, creates a context for the disciplining of students into moral citizens. According to AlSayyad and Roy (2006: 3), this 'doubleness' of spatial formations as simultaneously 'free' and 'protected' is a valuable analytical tool for examining contemporary urban moral geographies.

Drawing on Garbin and Strhan (2017), the above-mentioned illustrates that centre-periphery dialectical dynamics are interwoven in the contemporary religious landscapes of urban Tanzania and Nigeria, thereby affirming Sassen's argument that 'the city, a complex type of place, has once again become a lens through which to examine major processes that unsettle existing arrangements' (2007: 99). The resulting urban-religious configurations, and the moral enclaves that they contain, are not just localized: they are connected to North America and partly to Europe (in the case of St Mary's in Tanzania and RUN in Nigeria),

Northeast Africa and the Arab Middle East (in the case of Al-Farouq in Tanzania and FU in Nigeria) and global funding agencies (in the case of RUN in Nigeria). By shedding light on the translocal spatial strategies of religious educational actors, moral enclaves could thus deepen our insight into the complex, and affectively highly charged, interplay of religion, globalization and the city (Burchardt and Becci 2013; Dilger et al. 2020; Garbin and Strhan 2017; Lanz 2013).

Exploring recent educational missions, our case studies have addressed the question of what constitutes 'good education' in relation to specific urban settings in Tanzania and Nigeria. The comparative perspective not only involved primary and secondary religiously motivated education in Tanzania versus tertiary education in Nigeria, but also a comparison between (Pentecostal) Christian and (reformist) Muslim initiatives in the increasingly commodified and diversified educational market. These competitive, religiously motivated missions aim at realizing educational goals that ultimately will bring about wider socio-economic and moral transformations in the two countries' cityscapes. The case studies illustrate that the establishment of new Christian and Muslim schools and universities has become part and parcel of a larger process of moral (self-)formation, and of providing new avenues for the cultivation of moral values among urban youths. Because of their emphasis on morality, these educational establishments are also respected in the wider society; many parents, who do not necessarily affiliate with the religious traditions that the schools and universities that are central in this chapter represent, noted that if they had the financial means they preferred sending their children to a religiously motivated school or university, where 'proper morality' is being trained and embodied, than to a public educational institution.[35]

Apart from their 'moral laxity', in both urban Tanzania and Nigeria there is a widespread discourse regarding the dwindling educational standard in state schools and universities, as reflected by their poor infrastructure, lack of educational material and teachers with low qualifications. Along with the perception of the allegedly impoverished and 'immoral' urban environment in both sites, this discourse explains why 'good education' has become a strongly valued social, economic and moral asset among students, their families and the wider public. In the religiously motivated schools and universities that we studied, moral education and social class formation go hand in hand, thereby laying the foundation for a range of education-based class identities, whereby education is no longer seen as a 'public good' but rather widens and sharpens social inequalities (Collins 2009; Dilger 2013).

At a time when a public school diploma and even a degree from a state university are no longer sufficient to secure upward social and economic movement with the promise of a more successful life, many families are preoccupied with advancing their young relatives' social position (and with that also their own position). From our conversations with students, their parents and relatives and teachers, it appeared that 'good education' not only entails a strong performance in a high-quality institution that teaches consistently in English, which is believed to be essential for securing a well-paying job in the future, but also moral education that makes graduates stand out by their exemplary behaviour. This attitude explains the need to probe the subjective dimensions of education, that is, the moral values and ideals that are associated with and embodied in new educational settings (Dilger 2017; Fumanti 2006; Simpson 1998). Thus, while the emerging African middle classes are usually defined in terms of their varying economic and income-based positions, a truer depiction of their class formation is socio-cultural, as expressed through education and morality, thereby reinforcing Bourdieu's (2006) idea of education as a marker of both personal distinction and social class. In the moral enclaves that are religiously motivated schools and universities, students go through a process of subjectivation in the Foucauldian sense (1983) – which is realized through what Mauss (1973) calls 'techniques of the body' including a dress code and a code of conduct – moulding them into moral citizens and lifting them out of the urban environment perceived as 'sinful' into a higher social and moral order.

As scholars of religion, we are urged to scrutinize how well our concepts and analytical categories account for 'the fluid and mutating nature of religion' (Burchardt and Becci 2013: 18). The scrutiny of ingrained conceptual schemes prompts us to a decompartmentalized study of religion, which crosses boundaries and blurs sharp distinctions between religion and education, Christianity and Islam, religion and economy as well as public and private (see also Janson 2021; Janson and Meyer 2016). In the interlocking of these various domains, education is more than a tool for individual achievement, social class formation and national development; it is first and foremost a 'moral disposition' (Stambach 2010b: 12), which has significant repercussions for the formation of the highly diversified and fragmented public sphere in contemporary urban Africa.

Chapter 10

MANAGING THE 'SENSIBLE SECULAR': DISCIPLINING
THE URBAN IN A NIGERIAN CHRISTIAN UNIVERSITY

Simon Coleman and Xavier Moyet

In 2013, the state government of Lagos released a short film that had been sponsored by the city's governor, Babatunde Fashola. A distinguished lawyer and energetic advocate for urban reform, Fashola saw his political mission as the transformation of Lagos into a vibrant megacity, equipped with spectacular infrastructure that would reflect its significance as the economic hub of the country.[1] The film certainly expressed Fashola's aspirations. Titled 'Lagos: Africa's Big Apple,'[2] it presented images of gleaming skyscrapers, speed boats, smart hotels and an artificial marina (Förster and Siegenthaler 2018: 397; see also Okeowo: 2013). Fashola's message seemed clear: not only was Lagos already a major urban centre within Africa – 'a modern mega-city for the twenty-first century' that was 'expanding beyond its own physical limits', as the film's voiceover proclaimed – it was also becoming a serious player across a global landscape of dynamic world cities.[3]

A major problem soon emerged, however. The depiction of a glamorous metropolis provoked at least as much scepticism as excitement among inhabitants of the city itself (Förster and Siegenthaler 2018: 397). Alluring representations of a prosperous, self-consciously 'modern' lifestyle seemed to have little in common with an immediate Lagosian reality of choked and decaying roads, unequal access to sanitation and electricity and legally dubious appropriation of land by government and private corporations. The hypermobility celebrated in the film proved an uneasy reminder of a city increasingly surrendering to neoliberal impulses, marked by gated communities and exclusive island developments sheltered from the poverty highly visible elsewhere. Echoing other views expressed at the time, a popular news blog dismissed Governor Fashola's 'fantasy video' and quoted an eloquent if unnamed critic: 'Let us hear the voices of the teeming millions of Lagosians stating that their city is Eldorado on earth. Then I will take the video seriously.'[4]

The image of Lagos as African Big Apple failed to achieve widespread resonance, but Fashola's film and the reactions to it highlight key questions that motivate this chapter. At the most general level, we are interested in the material and ideological consequences of both constructing and enacting ambitious visions of city life. After all, Lagos is not only the most populated city in sub-Saharan Africa, with around twenty million inhabitants (and growing) (Ukah 2013b: 180), it is also perceived across large parts of Nigeria as a place of exciting if dangerous opportunity, a location of 'entrepreneurial hustle' (Gilbert 2018: 238) whose mobile and porous boundaries express a restless – and relentless – urban expansion. We intend to explore not merely the obvious gaps, but also the observable intersections, between idealized and actualized images of the urban. At a lower level of abstraction, we examine relations between public governance and private enterprise in a metropolitan region that both echoes and challenges Fashola's particular vision for expansion.

As we explore these questions, our ethnography leads us far from downtown hotels and waterfront developments. Our gaze moves inland towards other urban infrastructures – not contained at the centre of Lagos, but radiating from it, and ones that have taken shape over the past few decades: the predominantly Christian prayer camps that have sprouted up across peri-urban landscapes in the region. In their reflections on reimagining cities in Africa, Till Förster and Fiona Siegenthaler (2018: 395–6) observe that urban ways of living are not easily tethered to 'well-contoured spaces' of planned development, but rather 'creep into the hinterland along roads and highways, inspiring dreams and illusions about what the city has to offer'. This pattern of following arteries leading out of the city well describes the location of such camps, many of which are constructed along the famous Lagos–Ibadan expressway. The latter is a 120-kilometer route between Nigeria's first- and third-largest cities that was opened in 1978, at the peak of the oil boom in the country (Janson and Akinleye 2015: 550). Calling it an 'expressway' immediately provokes a certain irony, given that its crowded lanes, cratered surfaces and frequent accidents tend to bring traffic to a standstill. However, it has proved effective as a different kind of infrastructure, constituting what Janson and Akinleye call 'a stage for the performance of public religiosity' (ibid.). Since the late 1980s over twenty movements – mostly Christian but some Muslim – have created sophisticated camps along the highway, often spreading over thousands of hectares. In doing so they have come to fulfil Förster and Siegenthaler's prediction of relatively unregulated urban 'creep' along diffuse spaces, and yet *within* their own boundaries they graphically demonstrate the possibility of planned and controlled development. In doing so, they may perform a variety of functions – as locations of mass prayer, sites of denominational administration, providers of desirable accommodation and suppliers of both medical aid and multilevel education.

Camps maintain complex relationships to Lagos proper. Carved out of the bush, they rely on attracting regular visitors while benefitting economically and environmentally from being located on cheaper land. At the same time, they often act as vast adjuncts to church headquarters located downtown, embodying a kind of stretched urbanism that juxtaposes but also connects two very different visions of town life. Many church members may live in the bustle Lagos itself, yet regularly commute out to a location that provides a material exemplification of order and calm. While city streets in Lagos are dotted by numerous smaller churches, camps permit not only spatial expansion but also the creation of ethical and aesthetic coherence in contexts where religiously inflected jurisdiction becomes more prominent than that of the state.

Describing the oldest and largest of these camps, an article in *The Economist*[5] (2018) depicts the Redeemed Christian Church's 'Redemption City' as a form of 'anti-Lagos' – a phrase that captures the key sense of being opposed to, yet partially defined by, a metropolis that offers sinful temptation but also necessary resources. The subtitle of the article presents the camp as illustrating 'what happens when Pentecostal churches become urban planners'. These themes are closely akin to our own interests. Where we depart from *The Economist*, however, is in its additional characterization of Redemption City as 'one of Africa's oddest places', implying that its mixture of the religious and the urban, the prayerful and the self-consciously modern, is somehow anomalous or uncanny in relation to an assumed municipal norm or ideal. Such views echo the frequent (though increasingly challenged) assumptions of urban theory that 'modern urbanity, as the end product of the city's long spiritual decline, can be equated with secularity' (Lanz 2013: 21). In contrast, we suggest that Redemption City, and more particularly the wider metropolitan phenomenon that it and similar camps embody, cannot readily be comprehended by secular assumptions of development. To some degree, especially in south-west Nigeria, their establishment may recall a longer Yoruba tradition of locating divine purpose in the establishment of cities, exemplified by the city of Ile-Ife, possibly the oldest Yoruba city and said to be the birthplace of humanity (see also Ukah 2013b: 181).[6] At the same time, such locations enable powerful intersections between contemporary Pentecostal modes of envisioning space and wider economic, territorial and political logics. Despite their literally and ideologically guarded character, camps should not be seen as inherently isolated from wider urban developments in Lagos and beyond. In many ways they express in high relief processes that are evident elsewhere. Religiosity and widespread forms of 'religiocity' are not mutually exclusive.

Our focus in this chapter will not be on Redemption City or the Lagos–Ibadan expressway, but rather on a camp that is also a campus – a university complex that forms a minor city in and of itself, located a little way from Lagos and founded by the neo-Pentecostal denomination Winners Chapel (also known as Living Faith Church). Covenant University (CU) was established in 2002 in a formerly undeveloped area of Ogun State. The campus landscape we explore overlaps with that covered by Janson and Dilger elsewhere in this volume. Like them, we are interested in ways that educational practices might link with disciplined – and disciplining – transformations of urban space. Much of what we describe resonates with their depiction of 'moral enclaves' where students are trained as civic and religious subjects within closely controlled environments. However, our focus is equally on other themes that are present but mostly implicit within their chapter. Our concern is with how enclaving, apparently inward-looking and defensive from one perspective, also prepares students to be confident and effective actors in wider urban spheres. Centripetal dispositions cultivated in the context of camp life are complemented by orientations that are far more expansive.

This argument builds on a previous distinction one of us has made between two ethical approaches commonly adopted by neo-Pentecostal and charismatic churches in relation to wider culture: 'enclaving' and 'encroaching' (Coleman and Chattoo 2019). Enclaving draws a moral boundary around different practices while creating articulations among them, so that work, leisure and ritual come to be interwoven morally, socially and spatially. Despite its significance in framing conditions necessary to form the religious subject this type of ethical and material encompassment does not satisfy the spatially and ideologically expansive imperative of much Pentecostal and more broadly evangelical life. Enclaving is almost always counter-balanced by practices relating to encroachment. The latter involves attempts to move into and (re-)moralize other realms, activities and objects, but is more complex than conventional practices that overt missionization might imply. Admittedly, different social, economic, political and cultural contexts afford very varied opportunities for expansion. However, media of encroachment might include numerous modes of cultural production and consumption (music, literature, architecture, even scholarship) and nuanced engagement with public life – including attempts to reconstruct what it means to be an urban citizen.[7] This argument has already been illustrated by the 'stretched' qualities of the urban spaces we have already described, not least the idea of an 'anti-Lagos' opposed to, but ineluctably conjoined with, Lagos itself. While sitting in his office at CU one professor told us: 'This place essentially is not Lagos, but it's very close to Lagos. It has already merged with Lagos.'[8] Three positions – distinction from, proximity to and absorption within –are contained in this one sentence, and express the ambiguity of the connections being expressed. We assert that this mutual articulation of distance and proximity, rejection and appropriation, lies at the heart of much of what is taught and enacted at CU, as well as being inherent in the broader peri-urban field formed by the complex relationships between Lagos and its surrounding religious camps. In these terms, students learn to become experts in cultivating and combining 'enclaving' and 'encroaching' as active dispositions that aid them in negotiating different types of urban space.

These themes will be explored once we have provided more detail on the educational and religious context of southern Nigeria.[9] We draw on interviews we have carried out with students and faculty at CU, ranging from undergraduates to the vice chancellor, as well as literature produced by the university. Indeed, it was during an interview conducted with three faculty members that we heard the phrase in the title of this chapter. We had been discussing the university's use of online technologies: reliable provision of the latter has helped CU foster its reputation as a desirable educational establishment within Nigeria, but has presented moral challenges to Christian users who might be tempted to explore unsuitable sites. In explaining how the university manages such dilemmas in both logistical and ethical terms one professor noted to us that 'we have sensible seculars'.[10] His implication was that the non-Christian world was not automatically excluded from the campus or the lives of its inhabitants. Rather, it was incorporated while being moderated, recognized as necessary to personal development yet contained within Pentecostal frames of acceptability and action. The fact that we were talking about the internet is especially apt, given the focus of this chapter on the management and penetration of boundaries. It represents a prime means of reaching out into an exciting if risky world, forming the always-ongoing project of balancing and blending centripetal and centrifugal dimensions of a cultivated and predominantly urban Pentecostal sensibility.

Infrastructures of aspiration

In tracing the history of universities in Nigeria from the end of the colonial period into the twenty-first century, Ogechi Emmanuel Anyanwu (2011) highlights the role of tertiary education in the development of national consciousness (cf. Fumanti 2006; Livsey 2017; Stambach 2010a), but also the complicated politics of access associated with a scarce resource. In response to local demands, the British established the University College of Ibadan (UCI) in 1948 but remained concerned over the dangers of providing such sophisticated instruction for 'colonial subjects' (Anyanwu, 2011: 2). The UCI remained tiny during the last years of colonial rule, and it is not surprising that, with the establishment of independence in 1960, new public universities were perceived as powerful vehicles for both social change and individual ambition. Demand continued to exceed supply, however. Anyanwu (ibid.: 16) reports that during the 1990s political and economic instabilities, radicalization of labour unions and evergrowing calls for more access prompted moves towards deregulation of the sector. The establishment of private universities had previously been resisted by a variety of political régimes, but expansion now seemed a logical response to desires for a mass education system.

Such enlargement of the educational field brought its own problems, reflecting long-standing structural tensions in Nigeria. How could all geographical areas of the country be covered, and how might education be offered equitably across ethnic, class and religious divisions? Issues of quality control also emerged, and Anyanwu concludes that, since 2000 many universities of questionable status 'have mushroomed across Nigeria' (2011: 221). The contemporary landscape of educational provision negotiates a complex tightrope of legitimation in the public sphere. Many state-run services – whether they are offering education or electricity – are as likely to attract scepticism as trust. While the country's 1999 constitution did not declare Nigeria to be a secular state as such, it did prohibit all branches of government from adopting any particular faith as the state religion (Ogbu 2014: 135). In a country where levels of religious practice are high, secular pedagogical strategies run the risk of appearing immoral. On the other hand, traditional religious establishments are prone to offer forms of certification out of step with the demands of ambitious urbanites. All of these concerns have created a significant market niche for Christian organizations eager to promote a combination of the moral and the modern, and simultaneously to assert affinities between Pentecostalism and professionalism.[11] Promulgation of positive attitudes to education also aligns well with theological positions adopted by denominations such as the Redeemed Christian Church of God and Winners Chapel, which combine globally oriented forms of prosperity thinking with explicit celebrations of African identity and agency.

If the deregulation of the Nigerian university landscape has provided openings for well-funded religious organizations to establish tertiary-level educational institutions, it has echoed broader developments that have opened up civic and urban life to Pentecostal aspirations. Asonzeh Ukah (2013b: 179) argues that in recent decades the most dramatic transformations of the Nigerian urban landscape have been driven by religion. As the economic fortunes of the country have declined since the 1980s, prominence in public life has become more available to well-funded spiritual entrepreneurs prepared to combine ideological missionizing with infrastructural aid. Similarly, Obvious Katsaura (2020: 505) traces the formation of a 'Pentecosmopolis' in and around Lagos – a dynamic and diverse urban sphere that can operate at multiple scales and in different directions. Pentecostalism is understood here as constituting a 'polynucleated,' deeply urban Christian movement that is in a constant state of adaptation (ibid.: 505–6), engaged in forms of 'spatial aggression' (ibid.: 512) that may be exercised across church buildings, stadiums, roads, sub-cities and so on.

The Pentecosmopolitan outlook of denominations in and around Lagos is reinforced by pastor-prophets' claims to high levels of academic qualification, 'signifying a cosmopolitan and global credentialism that resonates with local trends' (Katsaura 2020: 508). Innocent Chiluwa, himself Professor of Linguistics and Media/Digital Communications at CU, notes that between 2005 and 2012 five out of the seven fastest-growing and richest Nigerian churches had established universities in the country (Chiluwa 2012: 741). Typically, such churches (including Winners Chapel) also develop 'independent world-class satellite facilities and modern media centres where activities are transmitted via satellite to members across the world' (ibid.: 735).[12] We might ask how more culturally defensive, enclaved orientations can coexist with Katsaura's Pentecosmopolitanism or such locality-transcending activities, but examining this conjunction as it plays out in both the urban spatialities and embodied dispositions of believers is precisely the point of this chapter. An initial sense of the productive intersections entailed in enclaving and encroaching is provided by the following reflection from a faculty member at CU, where he describes the key activities that led to the development of the campus in which we were sitting. Referring to David Oyedepo, the founder of Winners Chapel, he notes:[13]

> He had barely settled in Lagos, when God said 'Leave Lagos, come to this bush here.' This place was bush. I was here in 1994 and I did not see anything ... And he got here. So, how would you leave Lagos, where people will be coming, without you doing much? I mean, just take a megaphone and people will be coming to your church. You now leave Lagos and come to the forest here. So you come to the forest where you did not have people at all. The kind of people that you had here were traditionalists, people that were not going to church or mosque, and you now come to their midst and established a big church, and people are coming from Abeokuta, Lagos, everywhere to come to this same church, then

there is something about it ... I am a member of this church ... because I saw that there something unique, something different from what I have been seeing all over the country.

Despite the reference to 'something unique', there is much here that draws on recognizable Pentecostal tropes in establishing camps: the compliance with a divine vision granted to a charismatic leader; the clearing away of 'bush' associated with wildness as well as the spirits of traditional religion; the establishment of a place isolated from other distractions but also the sense of competitive and ongoing dialogue with larger centres of population. What is described is a form of urban seduction away from one space to another – and it is one that has clearly appealed to the speaker himself, since these words provide a personal testimony as to why he is involved with the church. In the account, Oyedepo ostentatiously leaves Lagos proper, but he does not abandon it entirely and nor does he deny the inherent virtues of urbanization: rather, he entices Lagosians to come to the space he has carved out on the margins of their city.

These reflections point to the cultivation of an urban disposition capable of being enacted across different media in ways that are flexible and adaptive. The speaker is referring to the origins of a church, but not only that; he is also describing the foundation of a camp-cum-city, but again, not only that; for he is depicting the emergence of a university – an institution that enables links with intellectual and social networks that reach out far beyond 'purely' Pentecostal landscapes of agency and recognition. As we shall see, the result is a space that responds, both positively and negatively, to many of the trends that have characterized Africa's urban revolution in the post-colonial period: mobility of population; porous peri-urban edges; high levels of informal organization and the challenge of poverty (see Dilger et al. 2020b: 10). In describing post-colonial approaches to urbanization Laurent Fourchard observes that non-Western cities have been excluded from much urban theory, but he also draws attention to the ways in which 'for historical reasons, African universities are too often in a subaltern position in the production of knowledge that has received worldwide audience in the social sciences' (Fourchard 2021: 9). The CU can be understood as tackling both of these issues directly: it is an enclave but also a 'univer-city'; a spatially and ethically enclosed institution that promulgates forms of knowledge intended to put it on a global map of respectable educational establishments. In doing so, it navigates complex histories and contemporary practices of exclusion and openness, both emerging from and contesting past histories of urban and university life in Nigeria. To find out how, it is time to look more closely at the university itself.

On connections and separations

A car journey northwards to CU from the University of Lagos (Unilag), situated some 35 kilometres away in the heart of the city, is often frustrating and strenuous. It may take an hour or more depending on traffic and the often parlous state of the Ota Road leading out to the campus. Eventually the Winners camp becomes visible through a distinctive wall: spikes on top, neat hedges below. A hoarding at the gated entrance proclaims: 'Welcome to Canaanland – Home of Signs and Wonders.' On arrival, drivers take a purple token from a uniformed 'Kingsguard', who is likely to ask them to state their business before inspecting the boot of their vehicle. Cars then proceed down a well-maintained road lined with trees and manicured hedges. The hurly burly of Lagos or, in local parlance, its 'wahala',[14] is left far behind. Neat garbage bins dot the landscape, as do expansive lawns and signs bearing biblical verses. Eventually another gate is reached, which must be navigated to gain entrance to CU itself, a site easily legible as a college campus with its large sports stadium, multistorey buildings, housing departments and dorms and wide avenues. Entering the site, it is easy to agree with the words of a graduate student as he described to us his initial impressions of the campus: 'After working at my father's farm for 3 years and arrived here the first time in 2004, I thought I was in London, because I have been to a lot of Nigerian universities: you do not find this kind of beautiful environment ... Beautiful structures, the environment is green, neat, you don't find paper on the floor. It was mind blowing for me.'[15]

Nonetheless, a still more striking message greets the visitor as they approach the original building of the complex: a large banner stating 'Vision 10: 2022 – A Prophetic Verdict. To be one of the top 10 leading world-class universities by 2022'. This aspiration, associated with the denomination's founder, David Oyedepo, and written in a form almost reminiscent of a Bible verse, overlays a map of the world. Crests of famous top ten universities – CalTech, MIT, Oxford, Cambridge – are also displayed, with CU's emblem taking the middle spot. Spatially insulated as it is, CU draws on the imagery of 'Vision 10' to look outwards towards other horizons beyond Nigeria itself. Nor is this Vision a mere piece of university propaganda, largely ignored or viewed only with irony by students and staff. It is the subject of collective but also individual prayer, and regular updates on progress in climbing the table are relayed to members of the university. All of our interlocutors at CU had developed a sense of their own relationship to the task of achieving its aims. As an undergraduate noted:[16] 'Everybody is working towards it, the staff, the faculty, management, student, and we believe that we will reach it.' His sense of looking forward was complemented by the views of a CU professor: 'The prophetic Verdict. It's a vision the university has, but not just through human efforts, but one God himself has given. It's already a done deal, a fait accompli.'[17] He thus juxtaposed prophecy with verdict: depicting a future vision that had *already* been accomplished. Such language might be classified as classic prosperity talk: the laying claim to an outcome that conflates present desire with future realization, and thus requires the speaker to assert perfect confidence in divine agency. But it does more rhetorical work than that. Not only does it entail a prediction that can be tested within a very short time, but also it appeals to multiple worlds of assessment. Another professor summarized the Vision for us succinctly: 'It is a prophecy and it's also in the secular realm, we are also pursuing it.'[18]

If the physical features of CU, from its neat lawns to its confident banners, make an immediate impression, the university's academic handbook – intended to be compulsory reading for all students – reinforces the message of seeking measurable, material achievement: 'On October 21, 2002, the African educational landscape was radically altered by the formal entry of Covenant University (CU) into the Higher Education context.'[19] Inflated language is common in university literature, but some of the hyperbole can be backed up by evidence. Barely two decades old, CU already has much to boast about in its efforts to become a 'leading World-class university'.[20] During its short history, undergraduate entry has been made increasingly competitive, with a grade requirement that is now higher than most other universities in the country.[21] Webometric ratings have assessed it as the best private university in the country and the second best overall.[22] Other prizes listed in the handbook include: the 'Best Maintained Educational Institution Award 2012,' awarded by the Nigerian Chapter of International Facility Management Association; the Best ICT Driven University in West Africa, 2010; and the first university in Nigeria to host two Nobel Prize winners to an international conference.

These plaudits go beyond denominational self-congratulation: they claim widespread recognition from the *non*-Pentecostal world.[23] The capacity for CU to inhabit multiple rhetorical and institutional registers simultaneously is revealed in its detailed 'Strategic Plan 2018–22',[24] which lists the hard labour required to translate charismatic prophecy into bureaucratic reality. The cover places the text 'Vision 10: 2022' over the image of a bar chart. Another introductory page refers to the 'I of 10 in 10' project – the task of 'getting the University listed among the top ten universities in the world within a ten-year period (2012–22)' – and then argues that this vision can be 'conceived as an 8-point agenda numbered 1 to 8 with 16 actionable goals' (Covenant University, 2020: 2–3). Aims such as developing research, making international contacts, contacting alumni and so on, are summarized in a table where a number of 'parameters' are linked to action plans measurable through Webometrics. These strategies contribute to (ibid.: 4) what is called 'The ReCITe Agenda: A Research-Intensive Approach for the Attainment of Vision 10: 2022'.

Any ambitious organization is likely to work through producing quantifiable projections. Their ambition also helps to justify the tuition fees paid for a private university.[25] However, at CU such figures are actively inscribed into the everyday educational and prayer routines of all who live and work on campus, not least as the 'Vision 10' agenda becomes a pervasive presence in the visual and verbal life of the campus. It becomes an ideal goal motivating the collective labour and self disciplining of all members of the university, from undergraduates to faculty. In his work on the history of the British and Foreign Bible Society, Matthew Engelke (2020: 813) highlights the importance of counting and statistics for 'the realization of its vision of a Christianity that covered the globe'. Such numbers took on a rhetorical and temporal force of their own, appearing to 'function as objective indicators of progress' and enjoining 'the society's constituency to think in absolute, certain, formulaic terms' (ibid.: 818). We shall have more to say about the CU rhetoric of planning below, but what is clear is that the idea of '1 of 10 in 10' takes on a compelling narrative momentum within an institution that teaches students to value strategy alongside vision, enumerated action points alongside flows of inspiration.

While CU is an impressive institution in its own right, it comprises just one part of Oyedepo's overall vision for a camp carved out of the bush. Planning of the university in the late 1990s began immediately after Winners Chapel had dedicated the fifty-thousand-seat 'Faith Tabernacle', at the time probably the largest church auditorium in the world. The total site has now grown to around 10,500 hectares, and houses the Winners Chapel administrative centre, a primary and secondary school and numerous other enterprises owned by the Church, including a publishing house, bakery, micro-finance bank, water processing plant, generator and gas plant. As one professor reflected: 'Does it look like an ideal city? Yes, it is like an ideal city because there is a system to take care of waste, the roads are good, they have a department called physical planning development, responsible for building maintenance, road construction.'[26] This combination of self-reliance and infrastructural efficiency is presented as a morality tale of good management in many of our interviews. A student noted:[27]

> I think of the years the religious institutions have been able to set models for the government. For us to have a space like this and everything is working in a society where it is assumed that nothing can work. Over the years, electricity is not work [sic.]; there are places where you don't have water in Nigeria, which are government's responsibility. Housing is not adequate, this is government's responsibility. And you have religious institutions coming to fill this gap, coming to show that it is actually possible, it can actually work. Since 1999 that Canaan Land has been built, there has been no power outage, for a very long time there has been no power outage, because everywhere is powered by generator, until we built our gas plant ... So, yes, we are a model for infrastructure development.

If multilayered ambition is expressed through a language of effective infrastructural provision and governance, CU makes its own contributions to the overall sense of ordered flow: alongside its relatively reliable internet connections (at least in public areas), delivery of its academic programmes occurs free of the strikes and union face-offs common in other parts of the Nigerian university sector. Things tend to 'work'; and so do people.

Yet, while CU subscribes to the camp's aesthetic of modernist efficiency, it also constitutes a social and cultural world that is fenced off in its own way. Undergraduates are limited to a handful of 'exeats' a term. When we asked CU students how often they went even to the rest of Canaanland we were told that they only visited it occasionally, possibly to go to a bank or to visit a worship programme. As a doctoral student noted of the rest of the site: 'It is a religious space, but it is outside the university. The university is independent of the Church.'[28] Generally speaking, the religious grounds are more restricted to undergraduates than they are to graduates, given that the latter are assumed to be more mature and to require less supervision. A young computer science student remarked of Canaanland that: 'It's in the same compound. It's right across from my building, that's computer engineering building. Everything is practically the same'; and yet, when we asked if he went over very often, he replied: 'Not really! Only during Youth Alive, that's when the school has a program for the youths. ... Probably two or three times I've been there'. What is expressed here is more than simply lack of curiosity: it points to a widespread quality of enclavedness that is cultivated *within* as well as beyond the camp. It embodies a significant dimension of the social and material order signified but also imposed by well-spaced-out buildings, immaculate lawns, garbage bins that continue to hide matter out of place.

This is not to say that the CU campus is entirely isolated from the outside world; rather, its 'encroachments' are both strategic and controlled. For instance, the Director of the CU Center for Research, Innovation and Discovery[29] described a project called *Limitless*, which processes plastic waste while raising awareness of environment challenges facing communities neighbouring the campus. Another programme, *Recreate*, repurposes ELTs (end of life tyres) into affordable footwear, and so – according to the stated project aims – transforms 'waste' into 'wealth'. In similar fashion, a social sciences professor described to us a 'community impact initiative' where 'especially our final year students, they will go, to clean the streets, especially the major road in this town. Clean the roads ... as part of community service, and ... sink borehole in communities around'.[30]

Although they entail action outside the campus itself, these and other projects take on similar characteristics to 'secular sensibles,' performing the rhetorical labour of blending the spiritual with the professional. As terms, both 'limitless' and 'recreate' have powerful prosperity connotations, but might equally be understood through secular registers of positivity and virtue. While the projects venture into spaces of public, civic action where government has apparently failed, they also perform ethical work on students themselves. If the latter are being trained to become, in Katsaura's (2020) terms, good 'Pentecosmopolitans', able to adapt across scales and in different directions, their 'spatial aggressions' (Katsaura 2020: 505) are also being moulded to operate more subtly than the direct annexation of land. Rather, they become translated into offerings of aid, the ordering of environments, the extension of infrastructural efficiencies. As a student told us of his experience of such projects: 'It began to become a culture in Covenant Uni.'[31]

The connections and separations described in this section have taken numerous forms and scales. We have encountered a campus that is both part of and partially separated from a camp; a mini-city that draws from yet remains insulated from Lagos; a university population founded on a Pentecostal vision but keen also to be recognized through secular indices of success. The CU looks for much of the time like an enclave, but to succeed on its own terms it must operate on numerous institutional, ethical and rhetorical registers simultaneously, and appeal to multiple forms of self-identification. This last point is illustrated beautifully in the words of an undergraduate who lists for us the elements that come together to make up his experience of what we call 'religiocity':[32]

> I'm a student of Covenant University, Ota, Ogun State Nigeria. I'm from Edo state. I'm Nigerian, proudly Nigerian. Also, I'm a Christian. I'm also, how would

I say ... urban, so I think this interview really [speaks] to me ... Because, I'm both religious and I'm urban too.

In the next section, we focus more on the specific behavioural and ethical dimensions of student life in CU. We ask how the frontstage presentation of an ultra-modern and ultra-moral campus relates to the backstage realities of living and working on campus. But we also continue to pose a question underlying the whole of this chapter: how Pentecostal boundary-making relates to boundary-blurring, and thus how borders are both asserted and bypassed in the development of a Pentecosmopolitan way of life.

Discipline, punish, encompass

At a dinner hosted by the University of Lagos, one of us fell into conversation with a colleague with extensive experience of students in both England and Nigeria.[33] On hearing of our fieldwork, the colleague joked that when she saw a cluster of English students she usually wondered if they were plotting some kind of protest. However, whenever she spotted a gathering of CU students she assumed that they were simply reading the Bible together. She spoke with a smile, yet her words revealed something significant about the hard-won reputation of Covenant as a school known for its strictness. In the context of the 'market' of private universities in Nigeria, developing a name for disciplined piety is no trivial matter: it provides an important justification for parents to send their children, secure in the knowledge that their offspring will learn the 'right' values.

Our characterization of CU as disciplined and disciplining institution echoes Janson's and Dilger's points in this volume about religious schools and universities as enclaves designed to train students as both moral subjects and middle-class citizens. At CU, the aim of training 'a new generation of leaders in all fields of human endeavour' – effectively a new professional elite for the country and indeed for Africa – is made quite explicit (Covenant University Handbook 2018: 1). We have observed how one way to create a sense of difference from other institutions is through emphasizing materialities of the modern – ranging from impressive architecture to reliable internet connectivity. Another is through controlling, but also being *seen* to control, students as they pass through the classes, halls and dorms of university life. The CU disciplinary project is not confined to undergraduates, although they are generally subjected to the most restrictions given that they are regarded as immature in their self-mastery. A professor described to us the CU rule that undergraduates must attend a minimum of 75 per cent of all classes:[34]

> Somebody in public university, you may be there, maybe for a whole semester, you may be opportune to attend class maybe thrice, and nobody is going to do anything about it, that's your choice. But here, it's not like that, there are rules and regulations on ground. There are core values on ground that guide the comportment of the lecturers, their activities, their relationship with the

students, and all of that. So many things like that, that we can talk about in terms of the difference, between here and there.

His words are notable not only for the standard critique of federal universities but also for his declaration that core values guide the comportment of lecturers as well as students. He was keen to convey the point, as other professors noted, that CU has a duty to provide exemplary governance in ways that might resonate throughout the whole of Nigerian society. Creating order at CU is also linked to the overall Visionary project – the sense of co-producing an institutional trajectory that will put the university in a prominent place in the global map of research and teaching institutions. Such projected linear progress, with its millennial undertones, entails not spiritual so much as scholarly salvation, although in fact the two cannot be separated. In the CU Strategic Plan, a graphic depicts the elements required to become a world force: around the sides of the diagram are features such as citation of research, international outlook, teaching quality and community engagement. At the centre, however, is placed 'Disciplined Atmosphere for Learning'.[35] In more informal language, a professor reflected on the position of private universities in Nigeria, and concluded: 'Yes, you must perform. And then the teachers teach better and the students are compelled to attend classes.'[36]

Discipline can take many forms, but at CU it cuts across micro-controls of the body, patterns of work and prayer and the forms of work required by the university. Much of what is required of students is summarized in the tabular form favoured by many CU documents and listed towards the end of the Student Handbook. A long list of infractions is provided in one column, with the 'tariff' for each transgression in another. For instance, absence from regular chapel meetings incurs a warning letter before more serious sanctions may be applied; possession of items ranging from hair straighteners to jeans and other 'diabolic materials'[37] prompts a range of punishments potentially leading to expulsion; further rules entail observing proper silences in shared accommodation, signing attendance registers and agreeing not to host members of the opposite sex in dorm rooms.[38] Alternatives to expulsion are offered, provided students:

> Sign an undertaking, attesting to their understanding of the terms of the alternative penalties. The students shall review some Christian literature and or other Community Services as may be stipulated in the letter communicating disciplinary measures outside lecture periods, wear special T-shirts with inscription, 'Please, pray for me to be core value compliant' during the week period and sit at designated location in the University Chapel during Chapel services and other University assemblies.

These 'substitute' punishments propel students towards a public shaming process with considerable visibility in a relatively small university community of some eight thousand undergraduates. In the past, photos of students who were suspended or rusticated from school were also displayed in the Chapel for the undergraduate population to see, though this practice is no longer carried out.[39]

If such measures seem draconian from the perspective of many universities elsewhere, we found nuanced responses to their implementation among the students we talked to. In an extended set of comments gathered anonymously and away from the CU campus,[40] an undergraduate confessed that he found it extremely hard to combine the daily 'CHOP' (Covenant Hour of Prayer, from 5.30 to 6.30 a.m.) with his demanding degree requirements, and he also looked askance at the 'MSS,' or Monitoring and Surveillance Services, whose staff go around the campus to check out whether school rules are being implemented: 'In actual fact, what they do, is that they act like a police. Because they monitor you to see whether your hair is properly done, whether your trousers are too short, whether your clothes are too tight.' Yet, when asked to characterize the disciplinary regime as a whole, he found reasons to justify its existence, not least through a language of distinction: 'The educational standard and discipline they put in the school. Even though it's a bit strenuous, the system actually works. When you see students, when you talk to students from other universities, you can really see what they are missing out on.' He added: 'Also, Covenant University is a very disciplined institution, and if you want to attend Covenant University, you really need to change the way you see life.' In such sentiments, the surveillance and retribution systems of CU become narratively conjoined not only with its Vision, but also with the decidedly marketable inculcation of a sense of exceptionality within the Nigerian educational system. Most of the students we spoke to seemed ambivalent but ultimately willing to accept such discipline in return for gaining the educational, professional and ethical capital associated with the reputation of their degree.

Anxieties over behaviour are often heightened in relation to a particular set of activities at CU: those relating to social media and the internet. The ambition of the university to be regarded as a globally competitive research and teaching institution depends in part on its provision of widely accessible digital infrastructure (cf. e.g. Awoleye et al. 2008). Its achievement of this goal is subject to front- and backstaging performances: according to some students, web connections—in common with sanitary and maintenance services—are prioritized in public spaces more than in student dorms. More problematically, providing unconfined web and social media access can appear inherently incompatible with ensuring disciplined and ethical practices of study, leading to the central dilemma of how to create a 'sensible secular' out of technologies that risk enabling access to obscene material, unsuitable and/or secret relationships and what CU faculty member Innocent Chiluwa, in a published piece on 'Online Religion in Nigeria,' calls 'random online worship' (2012: 746).[41]

Under such circumstances, there is much at stake – ethically, reputationally, pedagogically – in CU regulation of electronic media. The list of infractions and their tariffs contained in the Handbook warns that viewing of pornography is punished by expulsion – perhaps not surprisingly, given what we have said so far. Less immediately obvious is that possession of a mobile phone with a SIM card risks at least a week's suspension for undergraduates. This ban is particularly interesting because it appears to have few practical consequences: students can use laptops or tablets and have access to such social media outlets as WhatsApp and FaceBook. However, the possession of a SIM card has become a metonym for the cardinal sins at CU of losing focus and/or permitting secret (possibly 'occult') relationships to prevail over one's life. One woman notes that the regime did indeed change her personal routines: 'After graduating ... I came out after four years, I found phone a distraction for many months, until I became later used to it. I wasn't used to carrying phone, sometimes when my parents or family members are calling me, I don't even remember I'm with phone.'⁴² What the CU campus offers as an official alternative to mobile phone use has become increasingly obsolete, yet remains significant for what it suggests about the public choreographing of behaviour. Large red phones using prepaid cards are placed in public spaces around the campus and are designed to restrict both the time and the privacy surrounding conversations. Such devices are on prominent display on the campus and provide a reminder that communication needs to be regulated, though they do not appear to be used extensively.

Our inventory of CU disciplinary techniques should not be taken to imply that resistance or scepticism are eradicated on campus. Even in interviews with committed students and staff we heard of numerous minor 'offences': watching inappropriate films, smuggling in phones, stealing kisses, turning a blind eye to the failings of others, avoiding irksome prayer regimes. A degree of permitting such 'laxities' in backstage contexts may actually provide the flexibility necessary to sustain the public presentation of CU as unified institution. Over time, however, the build-up of certain breaches has led to discreet responses, such as the replacement of a security team when it had appeared to become too lax in monitoring infractions.⁴³ We also heard of students who deliberately committed offences in order to be expelled. Occasionally, however, spectacular incidents have occurred, where highly public restitution has appeared necessary. Notable among these is an episode described here by a doctoral student:

> The percentage of students who violate the rules is sometimes as high as 20 percent, and that is mostly boys. For example, in my first year as an undergraduate, and some students, especially the final year students, organized themselves to go out and party at a club in Lagos. So the information went round secretly on campus, and a lot of students geared up and went, unfortunately for them, one of them was killed at the club. The school got the information and did their investigation and found out that it was about 155 of them that went out that day, and all of them were expelled. At that point, Covenant Uni was a population of about 5,000 students, so you can imagine 150 students out.

This narrative contains tragic elements while also playing on chronic anxieties expressed at CU: the unruliness of youth, especially of young men; the public breaching of boundaries in a way that risks reputational damage; action carried out in secret and the ever-present danger of being tempted by the worst sides of urban life. In telling the story, the student emphasizes that the expulsion of the boys helped to reinforce the sense that 'Covenant Uni gave the parents and country a promise to abide by rules and regulation,' and that it has remained faithful to its undertaking:

> Covenant Uni does not respect name or title; because a majority of these students' parents were government officials, governors, ministers. For Covenant Uni to be very confident and brave enough to still expel their children, regardless of the status of their parents in the society, gave Covenant Uni a positive reputation in the society.

Nonetheless, such defensive and reactive postures, drawing on public punishment as means of reasserting purity, do not tell the whole story of subject formation at CU. There are at least two significant ways in which Pentecosmopolitan stances are developed that convert acknowledgement of ideological difference into positive virtue. One relates to the relative diversity of university's intake: not particularly in social class terms, but in relation to geographical and religious background. We do not have full access to demographic data, but a study of engineering students at Covenant (Popoola et al. 2018) records students as coming from almost all parts of the country.[44] More significant is that our interviews reveal that many who come to study have no background in Winners Chapel, or even Pentecostalism. Engagement with the university's spiritual regime regularly occurs alongside other, competing or complementary forms of affiliation. Here for instance is a dialogue we had with a younger female student:[45]

Question: Do you belong to Winners Chapel?
Response: No, not exactly, I am Anglican but by virtue of being a Covenant University student, I am trying to, just that because I have learnt to like their way of life, I have learnt a lot.
Question: Okay, but you were born an Anglican?
Response: No, actually I was born in Deeper Life Bible Ministry ...
Question: So how did it work, why is it that you have gone from Deeper Life to Anglican Church?
Response: Because I stay with my Aunt and my Aunt is an Anglican, so I had to go with her to church.

She points to a pragmatic dimension of religious affiliation that is not uncommon in urban Nigeria, but which must be taken into account when considering the seemingly all-embracing character of Pentecostal morality at CU. As a male PhD candidate noted: 'I don't know about how they did their entrance, but there are Muslims, Catholics, Anglicans, you don't really have to be from Winners to get into the school.'[46] Although we did not interview any Muslim students, we did ask our interlocutors about the presence of such non-Christians at CU. In the eyes of one professor:

> We have always had Muslim students because we do not compel anyone to renounce their religion before they can be students, but we tell them that we are

a Christian mission university, so you already know our dos and don'ts: 'These are the things we want, are you still willing to be part of this university?' And they could say: 'I do not mind, I want to be part, because of your standard and quality, Vision and everything.' [47]

In this account, 'quality' trumps religious affiliation in deciding which university to attend. Of course, expanding the potential student body helps the financial viability of the institution. There is also an implicit conversionist dimension to expanding numbers in this way, but making such a strategy explicit would be counter-productive as it would discourage 'non-Winners' parents from sending their children to the university. While there is no possibility of a public Muslim prayer space being countenanced on campus, private devotion is tolerated as long as it does not, in this professor's words, 'become a spectacle'. An example of how this accommodation might work was provided by the male PhD candidate mentioned above – himself a born-again Christian who for a time dated a Muslim student on campus, and who observed his girlfriend go to Chapel purely in order to comply with Covenant rules of public participation.

Thus if CU functions as a moral enclave, it retains the capacity to promote Pentecostal pieties alongside positive or at least sustainably negotiated experiences of coexistence with ideological Others. Acknowledging this complexity widens our understandings of the civic as well as spiritualized spaces that are being created on campus: ones where difference is encompassed within Pentecostal frames rather than banished from them. Parallels are evident here with Marloes Janson's (2016) description of the phenomenon of 'Chrislam', which has emerged in Lagos as a minority but vibrant ritual convergence between two traditions supposed to be in competition. The CU studiously avoids Chrislam's positive and public promotion of the blurring of boundaries, but it does offer an institutionalized means of embracing Christian and Muslim students under a common vision of disciplined professionalism and urban ambition.

A second form of proactive Pentecostal cosmopolitanism emerges from a concept that – like Oyedepo's Vision – is intended to permeate intellectual, cultural and even embodied life at CU. According to the university's handbook,

> The Total Man Concept (TMC) is Covenant University's custom-built Programme that constitutes the core concept of her academic programmes. This concept centres on 'developing the man that will develop his world'. It is designed to make the student become intelligently conscious of his environment and thus be able to maximize his potential.

Despite the gender-specific language, interlocutors assure us that 'TMC' applies equally to men and women. In practice, it is much more than a concept: it consists of courses and even exercise regimes compulsory for all students and designed – as one undergraduate noted – 'to make the student a total man spiritually, physically, emotionally, entrepreneurially, in all aspects of life. Just to talk about success parameters, how you should be a total man, not just academically, but also as an individual in the world'.⁴⁸ Such 'totality' is meant to provide an underlying thread of goal-orientation that cuts across subject-specific divisions as well as potential gaps between academic and other aspects of life. The teaching provides students with examples of individuals to be emulated as they learn 'how to actualise your vision' (the words of a doctoral student).⁴⁹ Thus: 'They teach us about people. Like Winston Churchill, Nelson Mandela … different successful people, David Oyedepo also.'⁵⁰ While this list is conspicuous for its maleness, others have noted the presence in the TMC curriculum of inspirational women as well, such as Oprah Winfrey. Career exemplars do not have to be exclusively Nigerian or African; they do not even have to be born-again. Similar latitude is evident in the official presentation of the TMC programme as centring 'on three components of the human personality: the spirit, the mind, and the body'. The parallels with a tripartite Christian anthropology of the person are evident; yet the student is now defined as an agent whose specific religious affiliation is no longer specified. In this sense, Christian theology is, if not rendered exactly cosmopolitan, nonetheless translated into a more generalizable lexicon of entrepreneurial agency. It has become akin to a 'spiritual sensible': a moderation of Pentecostal understandings of the religious subject in order to acknowledge – and implicitly encompass – wider frames of understanding.

Concluding remarks

This chapter began by depicting a form of urban hybridity that appeared to backfire on its creator. Babatunde Fashola's presentation of Lagos as 'Africa's Big Apple' fell foul of an obvious gap between political ambition and urban reality. We went on to discuss problems with another kind of hybrid: *The Economist*'s assumption that a Pentecostal camp such as Redemption City might be deeply 'odd' because of its mixture of religious and urban elements, as if the two were inherently incompatible in the modern world. One response to knee-jerk conflations of the secular with the urban is to state that they draw on a Euro-American genealogy of secularism whose parochiality is becoming increasingly obvious. That is an important point, but we hope also to have demonstrated how our interlocutors at CU deal in reflexive and often highly strategic ways with intersections of the secular, the urban and the religious. In doing so, they navigate multiple scales and landscapes of agency, ranging from an enclaved campus to a global landscape of competing universities. Of course, the notion of the 'secular sensible' is itself a kind of hybrid. If it seems to gain some resonance that is because of the hard ideological and institutional work that goes into making what it represents seem plausible to its community of interpretation at CU – challenging divisions between secular and spiritual forms of agency, while placing modern means of communication under Pentecostal regimes of discipline (cf. de Bruijn and van Dijk 2012c).

Although we have been discussing the ongoing influence of ritualized, Pentecostal technologies of the self in people's lives, we have been doing so without close reference to languages of prayer, spaces of worship, or practices of mission.

Rather, we have examined Pentecostalism as it is manifested through multiple and interlinked media of the urban and the pedagogical, with both exhibiting stances of enclaving and encroachment in their operation. Compared to the city-wide horizon sketched out by Fashola, the CU's spatial regime of closely monitored operations is limited to a single campus. However, in concentrating attention in this way, the university has allowed itself to become an attractive, even a seductive, destination for many who are not denominational members, or even Christians. What we are describing is not the Chrislam documented by Janson (2016, 2021), which overtly celebrates forms of ritual hybridization. Nor are we referring directly to the creation of a broadly diffused 'Pentecostalite' public sphere, as examined by Birgit Meyer's (2004) analysis of the blending of Christian discourses with those of popular entertainment. Our account comes closer to Katsaura's (2020) interests in Pentecosmopolitan forms of spatiality and sociality, where he declares his intention to examine Pentecostal models of producing 'city-ness' and urban experience (see also Warikobo 2014). Our particular concern has been to examine a space that permits both the intensification and the diffusion of Pentecostal qualities of action: an enclave that is also an attempt to encompass a global type of institution – the university – whose professional operation necessitates engagement with non-Pentecostal forms of knowledge dissemination and even creation. In encountering the CU campus, students do not engage directly with the megacity that is Lagos but they do deal with the challenges of modern urbanity: its ethical challenges and its restless gaze beyond proximate horizons to other cities, other continents, other opportunities. In the process, of course, they contribute to and benefit from a privileged form of 'privatopia' (Warf 2003: 247) in a region where gated communities abound.

We have been tracing the emergence and production of a form of peri-urban development rooted in West Africa, but it would be too limiting to argue for a theoretical frame exclusively oriented to the political economy of the urban South. The phenomenon we have been describing has historical and cultural roots that are as complex and global as cities themselves. Certainly, there is nothing new per se in towns or indeed universities based on religious foundations: both were common in medieval Europe. The great evangelical movements of the nineteenth century rooted themselves in cities around the world. The CU itself draws on African but also Euro-American models of pedagogy, and it is connected to a denomination that is creating its own form of transnational presence, not only through churches and virtual media but also via the diasporic movements of supporters who inhabit every continent on earth. Furthermore, if the neoliberal discourses of academic excellence and entrepreneurial scholarship deployed by the university – its talk of limitless ambition, markers of excellence, transferable skills and so on – sound familiar to readers of this chapter, it is because they have permeated the vocabulary of academic administrators almost everywhere.

Our analysis has still wider implications for understanding the intersections between contemporary forms of Pentecostalism and neoliberalism. At about the same time as CU was being planned, Jean and John Comaroff (1999) were writing about a 'millennial moment' during which capitalism was developing 'an effervescent new spirit – a magical, neo-Protestant zeitgeist – welling up close to its core' (ibid.: 281). Their primary interest was in the forms of magical thinking accompanying the new Protestant Ethic in its spread across Africa and Latin America: the spiritual anxieties emergent among the urban poor as they witnessed the consolidation of wealth in the hands of a few citizens, and came to view the market as an inherently mysterious – and potentially occult – mechanism of accumulation and distribution. If the Comaroffs examined populations losing faith in the possibilities of production as means of economic salvation, our work focuses on largely middle-class students who are, by contrast, learning to invest much faith and effort in varieties of labour – directed towards the professional world, their prayer lives, but also themselves. Whether misguided or not, they are coming to assume that transparent and predictable modes of entrepreneurial effort will yield results, despite the history of economic relations among nations in Africa and elsewhere. This is not the place to enter into a longer discussion of millennial capitalism as it is perceived through middle-class lenses, but we finish with reflections on the most egregious example of millennial thinking that has diffused throughout CU. Even with the best and most hopeful of (secular) intentions, it is hard to imagine how a university ranked well into the 1000s in world rankings[51] can come close to its intention of being a top-ten institution by 2022. We have already shown how this ambition has prompted decidedly non-magical action in the form of concerted planning and labour. Yet, there might just be a sense in which the rhetoric – the performative language – of Oyedepo's Vision has *already* achieved an important result, even a kind of prophetic verdict. For in the space of just two decades the university has indeed inserted itself into global fields of reckoning, calibration and accountability. It now 'counts' for something in secular as well as Pentecostal worlds, and in numerous urban, cosmopolitan realms where the two can coexist.

Chapter 11

NOTES ON AFRICAN RELIGIOUS EVERYDAY LIFE IN
AN URBAN (POST-)PANDEMIC WORLD

David Garbin, Simon Coleman and Gareth Millington

While the chapters in this volume draw upon data collected before the Covid crisis, some of the questions they raise are highly relevant to our understanding of the impacts of the pandemic on the dynamics of religious urbanization and religious everyday life in African cityscapes. In most of our case study countries, public health concerns over contagion and the spread of the virus among dense urban populations have been unevenly translated into practices of social distancing. One of the consequences of such precautions has been the reduction or banning of mass religious activities, imposed as part of a series of measures to limit public gatherings. The question of how the potential shift in the character of religious life, and more specifically in the affordances of 'emplaced' socialities that are shaped by religious urbanity and infrastructures, is both complex and inevitably contingent on particular contexts – historical, religious and political.

Whilst epidemics on the African continent are frequent (Cobbinah, Erdiaw-Kwasie and Adams 2020; Durizzo et al. 2021), there is an emerging consensus that the lockdowns and restrictions specific to Covid; 19 have caused considerable harm to residents with 'precarious short-term sources of income' (Smit 2020: 1). Indeed, some suggest 'the pandemic has had a larger economic than health impact on people living in poverty' (Durizzo et al. 2021: 9). Densely populated informal settlements have often been the focus of public health concern across the continent, especially where urban planning regimes have been inherited from Anglophone and Francophone colonial pasts (Cobbinah et al. 2020). The solution, during Covid, has not, however, been a renewed effort to upgrade living conditions but rather a turn to militaristic policing. In some cases, governments have been given 'extraordinary licence to evict, lockdown and control the movements of urban communities' (Kihato and Landau 2020: 1). For example, the policing of the daily routines of slum residents in Rwanda, Kenya and Ghana has led to the shooting and flogging of citizens who disobey rules (Kihato and Landau 2020: 1; see also Lamb 2020 on South Africa). Compliance, however, is almost impossible for those whose survival depends upon movement around the city and daily participation in dynamic, improvisational social networks as a means to obtain the necessities needed for life (Simone 2018). This context has also restricted public forms of religious activity whilst increasing demand for religiously provided infrastructure and services as well as for religious forms of authority. It has also placed considerable pressure – financial, representational and political – on the religious organizations and groups who in preceding decades have come to assume growing prominence in the structuring of everyday life in cities across the continent.

A good example of the complexities of the pandemic moment is provided by Marian Burchardt, whose contribution to this volume examines the transformative 'urban aspirations' of Pentecostal FBOs involved in the fight against HIV/AIDS in Cape Town. In a personal communication,[1] he notes how the rejection of Covid vaccines espoused by some Pentecostal churches is indeed reminiscent of their rebuffal of biomedical treatments against HIV and AIDS. The Covid and HIV/AIDS crises differ in relation to key Pentecostal tropes, in particular as far as the remoralization of urban everyday life is concerned, but in both cases the avoidance of vaccines is formulated against the backdrop of beliefs in the superiority and legitimacy of the healing power of the Holy Spirit and ways to access it, most notably through prayer.

Similarly (in a piece co-authored with Taru and Chimbidzikai) Kirby[2] – who writes in this volume about the social infrastructures of urban religion in the pluralized context of Dar es Salaam – points to a 'spiritualisation of the pandemic' and the centrality of the idiom of spiritual warfare in the response offered by churches in Tanzania and Zimbabwe. However, he and his co-authors suggest that religious groups and congregations may also constitute an important urban public health resource when it comes to delivering services and messaging, 'cultivat[ing] a sense of hope and mutual care in the face of uncertainty'. Moreover, as the piece aptly argues, the idioms of warfare should not be exclusively attributed to a set of religious attitudes since 'warfare' is the signature trope through which Covid has sometimes been framed by a host of global political figures and media commentators, "shift[ing] responsibility onto citizens as 'combatants', whether for failing to adhere to physical distancing or for their biomedical frailty".

In the context of Nigeria, Moyet, another contributor to our volume, observes that some public health measures have met resistance from prominent Pentecostal figures, such as Bishop David Oyedepo, Pastor of the megachurch Winners Chapel, who claimed during a service streamed online that 'shutting down churches would be like shutting down hospitals'.[3] This claim embodies an aspiration to 'reconfigure the totality that comprises the everyday infrastructural lives of urban dwellers', as we write in our introduction. If the crisis constituted by the pandemic forces city dwellers to seek the most effective remedies available, it also raises the question of whether spiritual services can plausibly be presented by religious groups as inherently 'necessary' dimensions of urban life, even – or perhaps especially – under the exceptional circumstances of an existential crisis. According to this view, spiritual infrastructure is just as important as its economic or medical counterparts in sustaining everyday life in the city and must therefore (unlike mere leisure pursuits) continue to be offered during a time of crisis. This is concomitant with the deliberate intertwining of the spiritual with economic, social and political dimensions of life pursued by many neo-Pentecostal churches across the continent (e.g. Marshall 2009; Obadare 2018). At the same time, it is notable that Covenant University, founded by Bishop Oyedepo and discussed in this volume by both Dilger and Janson, and Coleman and Moyet, has been assiduous in deploying and monitoring the effects of online learning on its students. As a purported leader in both spiritual *and* digital infrastructure, the university can be presented as a model for other universities to follow as they develop online learning platforms, post pandemic (Adeyeye et al. 2022).

Whatever the expressed attitudes of religious leaders, during the height of the pandemic from 2020 places of worship across urban Africa remained empty and restrictions on religious gatherings led many to remotely participate in religious services streamed online, or broadcast on TV or radio. Of course, the global deployment of religious forms of presence through electronic and audiovisual media is not novel in itself and has been well documented (Campbell 2013; Isetti et al. 2021; Vásquez and Garbin 2016). However, as suggested by Garbin[4] (discussing religious urbanization among Kimbanguists, Catholics and Pentecostals in Congo), many questions have been raised about the impact of the pandemic on the dynamics of physical contact and embodied/emplaced 'collective effervescence' given the importance of the space-body nexus in Charismatic practice and the centrality of tactile sensorialities (De Witte 2012). Adapting Harvey's 'spatial fix' concept, he has observed that pastors and religious leaders have shown some anxiety about the inability of churches, during the lockdown and/or because of the restrictions, to retain – to 'fix'– their members, also noting the detrimental impact of worshipping online on the accumulation of religious capital in the forms of tithes or donations. This raises the prospect of empty prayer venues and auditoriums. This concern needs to be understood against a wider religious field shaped by intense competition between churches and highly charismatic pastors, competition also played out in the media and popular cultural spheres, as he writes in his chapter (in this volume) co-authored with Mokoko-Gampiot (see also Pype 2012).

There are some parallels here with the observations of Kroesbergen-Kamps (2020c) whose chapter examines the dynamics of moral mapping and Christian narratives of the occult in Lusaka. She conducted follow-up research among Zambian Pentecostals, stressing the emergence of hybrid models of religiosity and religious meaning-making in times of Covid, and noting how religious leaders have had to renegotiate the articulation of vertical relations (with the spiritual world) and horizontal networks of congregants in novel ways. Her analysis draws upon Jeffrey Alexander and Philip Smith (2020: 2)'s understanding of the pandemic as 'a remarkable demonstration of a societal capacity for highspeed bricolage as familiar structures of meanings (narrative, iconography, genre, binary codes) and meaningful practices (collective rituals, interaction rituals and performances) were bolted and glued together in new ways'.

As several chapters in our volume suggest, the importance of place-making and collective worship – bringing people into close and emplaced, often praying proximity – should not be downplayed, even if believers can also be 'touched' by the transcendental, religious energies flowing through audiovisual media and new technologies. The experience of crowds and pilgrimage is often key to religious urbanity and contributes to the legitimacy of particular forms of urbanization, as Kingsbury writes in her piece on the Senegalese holy city of Touba, which has become the 'global metropolis' of the dispersed Muslim Mourid Brotherhood. The case study of Touba, like Nkamba, the New Jerusalem of Kimbanguists described by Garbin and Mokoko-Gampiot (this volume), shows how pilgrimage crowds constitute complex assemblages of formal and informal urban practices that can connect a 'holy city' to publics situated beyond its immediate urban boundaries.

The issues raised by the global Covid pandemic suggest a need to understand the contemporary dynamics and management of these gatherings and 'spiritual masses', the interplay of social proximity and density, as well as the relations between individual embodied actions and crowd behaviour. While crowds and masses were viewed by classical theorists in sociology and social psychology, including Lebon, Simmel and Durkheim, as powerful forces shaping and sometimes challenging the social order of modern society, their contemporary marginalization – often in favour of other, supposedly more 'modern' social forms, such as classes, publics, networks or virtual communities – has reflected a reluctance to challenge simplistic assumptions of crowds as amorphous, irrational and often dangerous to urban order. Implicit here is that the nature of crowds – the collective effervescence of the multitude – is inherently de-individualizing, questioning the ideal of the modern, autonomous liberal subject. What our volume shows is that the infrastructure of mass religion is essential to both crowd socialities and imaginaries of the 'megasocial', given the continued salience of mass events and a post-Covid longing for face-to-face interactions.

We hope in this short chapter to have given a glimpse of the nuances of African urban adaptations to a simultaneous crisis of health, sociality and spirituality. One of the more common popular as well as academic discourses in anticipating religious responses to Covid has revolved around the assumption that believers would revert to apocalyptic and conspiracy-filled tropes in responding to the pandemic. Variations on these tropes have undoubtedly emerged in Africa and elsewhere;[5] but such spectacular spiritual displays have only ever been part of the story. The multifaceted character of responses indicates how a 'global' threat has become assimilated – however awkwardly, controversially and sometimes tragically – into the rhythms and infrastructures of everyday life in African urban contexts.

Chapter 12

AFTERWORD

Caroline Knowles

Several chapters in this volume are based on valuable data collected as a part of the British Academy's Cities and Infrastructure Programme.[1] This programme, comprising seventeen research projects transcending the usual disciplinary silos, is a part of the Global Challenges Research Fund (GCRF), an important component of the UK's Official Development Assistance (ODA). This is worth mentioning because these GCRF projects, which have been responsible for conducting research into some of the most pressing issues affecting cities in the Global South, were defunded when the UK international aid budget was slashed in 2021 from 0.7 per cent to 0.5 per cent of gross national income. Aside from providing early indicators of what the government's conception of 'global Britain' might mean post Brexit, these research projects, like the one on which several of the chapters in this collection are based, aimed to underpin policy changes to improve life in some of the most marginalized low-income communities.

Defunding sent a wrecking ball through carefully constructed research partnerships established over years with researchers in universities and partners in civil society organizations across the Global South. It pulled the plug on important research with far-reaching consequences. The research data which guide the careful insights, arguments and analyses in this book, could not now be funded. This would be a huge loss of intellectual and policy assets, as well as eroding the social relationships upon which detailed and sophisticated research like this is built.

The timely collection of papers brought together in this volume brings a wealth of detailed empirical research and critical analysis to existing conceptions of what cities are and might become. It indisputably extends urban analytics. It brings sophisticated understanding of how African cities actually operate on the ground, hyperlocally and in translocal contexts. Extending beyond the customary list of countries and cities, the essays in this volume unfold the intersections between organized religion and city-making in Benin, Tanzania, Congo, South Africa, Senegal, Zambia and Nigeria, providing a wealth of case studies and ethnographies bringing cities in these countries alive and into the foreground of the urban analytic frameworks of the twenty-first century.

The papers show what happens when faith communities, ranging from Islam to Pentecostalism, are connected with urban planning and governance, as well as with people's aspirations and imaginaries, as new maps of cities are created, transforming neighbourhoods and people's lives in the process. In these analyses, the usual attention paid to the spaces of everyday urban lives is widened to encompass everyday religious life, symbolism and practices, appropriately expanding an understanding of what quotidian life might consist of in urban Africa. This makes religious organizations and their spatial and temporal moorings part of the dynamic development of cities, showing how metaphors of bridging and enclave are enacted together, and how reconstructed spaces both expand and limit possibilities for local communities as new forms of displacement and entitlement are created together. From these insights, an expanded understanding of everyday urban life through religious space and close encounters with how the logics of faith actually make cities, sometimes in concert with circuits of transnational capital, comes into view. This book, and the research projects underpinning it, is highly original in providing what is missing in urban scholarship: serious, empirically grounded, analyses of religious urbanism and the agency of religion in shaping cities. It shows how religious organizations are influential in making, maintaining and running cities along particular lines: issues which are hitherto poorly understood and under researched.

Alongside a better and more textured understanding of cities from the vantage point of the often overlooked or simply poorly understood domains of religion, the essays in this collection give a vivid impression of some of the motilities of urban life and the mechanisms by which cities extend beyond their formal boundaries into all sorts of territories previously seen as peripheral to city life. The expanded understanding of cities also reveals how they actually operate. Conceptions of urban infrastructure are reworked to include those which calibrate and channel the everyday ecologies of religious life. This extends conventional readings of what infrastructure is and how it operates in some exciting new directions. This book shows which city infrastructures religious actors, and, by extension their congregations, consider significant in developing and organizing urban life. These infrastructures govern behaviour and shape subjectivities, as they stand in for absent or crumbling state provision, making cities run, revealing their poetics and politics along with their pipes in the process. This conception of infrastructure, like the Cities and Infrastructure Programme which funded it, reveals emergent and experimental configurations of urban life and the resources supporting it. This open and suggestive, and expansive approach to infrastructure is one of the book's key strengths.

Overall, this book brings religion into the mainstream of urbanism's analytic frames, with new insights, possibilities, alignments and political logics. It brings together and scrutinizes interconnections between cities' physical infrastructures, their moral economies and the production of religious subjectivities and multifaceted forms of aspiration. The result is an extended and sophisticated conception of everyday urban life and the landscapes through which it is routed. This book opens nuanced and varied ways of rethinking urban space and time. It makes an important contribution to urban scholarship as well as to understanding the dynamics of religion in shaping African cities as modern and vibrant places of the twenty-first century.

NOTES

Chapter 1: Introduction

1 https://www.thecable.ng/lagos-commissioner-inaugurates-bridge-car-park-built-deeper-life-church (accessed 25 September 2021).
2 https://dclm.org/about/w-f-kumuyi/ (accessed 25 September 2021).
3 See CT TV report about the inauguration, https://www.youtube.com/watch?v=TW57CDBj1fM (accessed 25 September 2021).
4 https://www.sunnewsonline.com/how-deeper-life-church-gave-lifeline-to-gbagada-community-builds-bridge-others/ (accessed 25 September 2021).
5 Chat board: precondition for building the church – https://www.nairaland.com/4373343/deeper-life-did-not-donate (accessed 25 September 2021).
6 https://guardian.ng/property/how-deeper-lifes-30000-capacity-hqtrs-was-built-by-officials/ (accessed 25 September 2021).
7 In this model, as the city increasingly concentrates economic and (post)-industrial activities, its 'centre' implodes, acting as a spur to the expansion or 'explosion', of urbanization.
8 For a discussion of this literature see Garbin and Strhan (2017) or Becci and Burchardt (2013).
9 Also focusing on infrastructure, but in a more material rather than metaphorical sense, Katrien Pype (2016) explores the rural–urban connectivities mediated by electronic media that create 'technosocialities' between Kinois (inhabitants of Kinshasa) and the hinterland.

Chapter 2

1 In this chapter I draw on fifteen months of ethnographic fieldwork in Kariakoo where I lived between 2015 and 2016. I use the term 'residents' to denote both those that inhabit properties in the district as well as the business operators that make up the majority of Kariakoo's much larger 'daytime' population. I am grateful for feedback on earlier drafts by Erik Meinema, Joseph Tulasiewicz and members of the Centre for African Studies at the University of Bradford.
2 See Fredericks (2018: 14n13) and Guma (2020: 731–2) for an overview of some noteworthy contributions to this emerging literature on infrastructure.
3 Other examples from East Africa include Eastleigh in Nairobi (Carrier 2016) and the downtown area of Kampala. On the other side of the African continent, AbdouMaliq Simone (2011: 364) provides the examples of New Bell in Douala, Ikeja in Lagos and Treichville in Abidjan. Because these different urban outcomes are 'singularities,' emerging from urban arrangements specific to each setting, they are best understood as 'repeated instances' (Robinson 2016: 14). The family resemblances between these

sites can be explained with reference to their parallel exposure to colonial urban planning, post-colonial regimes of governance and neoliberal economic restructuring.
4 The following sections incorporate some significantly revised material which appears in an earlier article (Kirby 2020).
5 Even understood as 'infrastructure' in the most narrow and immediately recognizable sense, Kariakoo's mosque complexes provide washing and toilet facilities for worshippers, both of which are in short supply in the district. Kwa Mtoro Mosque even offers a source of free drinking water for all residents.

Chapter 3

1 'Religious Urbanization and infrastructural lives in African megacities (RUA): Moral economies of development in Kinshasa and Lagos', funded by the British Academy, https://rua-project.ac.uk (accessed March 2022).
2 Branhamism is a Christian Charismatic movement, which is well established in Kinshasa (from the American prophet William Branham, 1909–65). For more on Branhamists in Kinshasa see Pype (2017).
3 Prestige partly linked to Cardinal Malula's role in 'Africanizing' Congolese Catholicism during the Mobutu era and more recently, the political stance of the clergy and lay Catholic actors against the authoritarian Kabila regime and their campaign for free and fair elections in the 2010s. As Demart (2017: 83–90) suggests Malula's attitude towards Mobutu's rule was ambiguous at best – oscillating between implicit support from the outset and rejection of the Mobutist ideology of *Authenticité*.
4 With pastors and *évangelistes* often preaching to commuters in the city's buses, taxi-vans or near bus stops or stations.
5 In fact, as Rey (2007) and others have pointed out, Bourdieu's analysis of the 'practical logic' of religion had an important role to play in shaping his entire theory of practice as well as his conceptualization of social fields.
6 Bérée is Berea, an Ancient Greek city where the Apostle Paul took refuge and preached, as mentioned in the New Testament (Act 17).
7 Pype (2017: 123) defines *anti-valeurs* in the Congolese lexicon as referring to 'asocial actions like corruption, immodesty, and loose-ness, and are connected to the quality of one's personal relationships, be they with the nuclear and extended family, friends, neighbours, and business partners'.
8 The association between witchcraft and childhood is a relatively recent phenomenon in African contexts (La Fontaine 2016) and most of those who have studied the phenomenon in the DRC argue that it has to be understood against the backdrop of rapid societal change and transformation in the moral economy of kinship (De Boeck and Plissart 2004).
9 We spoke to school staff who were critical of the automatic adequation between 'behavioural problems' and witchcraft possession. We were also told that Maman Olangi herself warned against 'quick diagnostics' and advocated sustained periods of observation and communication with the child, instead of rushing to the "cure d'âme' therapy."
10 Mahaneim is a place mentioned several times in the Bible, where Jacob met the Angels (Genesis 32: 2–10).
11 Société Nationale d'Électricité (SNEL).
12 Official colonial category designating a class of 'evolved' Congolese, usually low-level civil servants, or clerks and so on.

Chapter 4

1. For a widely used definition see Clarke and Jennings (2008: 6).
2. Most FBOs in South Africa are associated with Christianity with which 79.9 per cent of the population identifies, according to the census of 2001 (Hendriks and Erasmus 2005: 91). The increasing visibility of Pentecostal FBOs is also linked to the increasing popularity of this type of Christianity in terms of numbers of followers.
3. Most transnationally organized FBOs also belong to this type of Christian churches. On mainline Christianity after apartheid see Bompani (2006).
4. See https://www.sikhulasonke.org.za/about-khayelitsha.html (accessed April 2022).
5. See https://www.aidsmap.com/news/jul-2020/vertical-transmission-rate-18-khayelitsha-south-africa (accessed April 2022).
6. All names of informants in this chapter have been changed so as to protect their anonymity.
7. On contemporary Anglicans for instance, see Vandermeulen, Patterson and Burchardt (2013). Historically, social services were very much part of the missionary enterprise, for instance through medical missions.
8. Also available at http://www.livinghope.co.za/about/living-hope/our-story/ (accessed 16 June 2013).
9. There was, however, a notable reluctance in Pentecostal FBOs to publicly engage with notions of 'gender mainstreaming' as these were generally associated with moralities that were too liberal and permissive in Pentecostal perception.
10. There was a shared understanding in Pentecostal FBOs that youth sexual permissiveness and HIV risk was a result of exposure to parental sex and, more generally, the adoption of 'bad' behavioural models of the parental generation. As a consequence, they could justify extending their interventions into the private spheres of domestic education and childrearing.
11. In social theory such processes of standardization and of organizations operating within the same organizational field becoming increasingly similar is captured through the concept of institutional isomorphism, itself informed by Weber's theory of bureaucratization. On the contradictory effects of institutional isomorphism in the field of HIV/AIDS interventions in Africa see Swidler and Watkins (2009).
12. Of what clients' need really consisted was in fact highly contested and subject of intense debates amongst FBO workers and beneficiaries. The result of these debates was precisely that FBO workers sometimes attempted to put the guise of 'HIV/AIDS-related activity' upon all sorts of interventions that seemed closer to people's demands.
13. Think Twice began its operations in 1998 and claims to have reached a total of 1,476 learners through all of their programmes.
14. Jubilee has been established in the context of the evangelical 'New Frontiers' movement. 'New Frontiers' originates from the UK and is, according to its self-description 'a group of apostolic leaders, partnering together on global mission' in order to establish the Kingdom of God by restoring the church, making disciples, training leaders and planting churches. See https://newfrontierstogether.org/about-newfrontiers/ (accessed 21 April 2022).
15. Xhosa for 'hands of hope'.
16. If collective prayers with participants were not possible as in the case of school-based interventions, FBO workers assembled in a separate corner before the course started and prayed for the success of their work.

Chapter 5

1. Momar was twenty-six years old, working as a carpenter in Dakar where he lived. All names in this chapter are pseudonyms.
2. Mbaye, forty years old, was from Thiès. He worked trading livestock.
3. A Mouride disciple I met in Touba who was from Rufisque. He owned a shop where he sold fruits and vegetables.
4. For example, in the cemetery, where a large tree rises known as *Guye Texe*, meaning baobab of felicity (see Ross 1995: 227). Mourides recounts the story of Bamba's vision of Touba as he sat shaded beneath a tree and was supposedly visited by the Angel Gabriel.
5. Coumba, thirty-two years old, was a stay-at-home mother to three children from Dakar.
6. Hamidou, fifty years old, was from Dakar. He worked as a port driver.
7. Schielke argues that to assume that all pious agents in their endeavours and rites are consistently coherent and that religion itself is practised in a manner that is free of discrepancies denies scholars the opportunity to understand the 'fragmented nature' of faith for believers who as a rule, rather than an exception, embrace 'double standards, fractures and shifts' in their spirituality, morality and religious realities (Schielke 2009: 38).
8. An order of the Mourides who follow Ibrahima Fall, one of Bamba's disciples.
9. A trader, forty years old, residing in Dakar.
10. Of course like in many African cities mobility in the form of migration is a cultural imperative also in Dakar, 'a coveted way of being and belonging, and a critical means of securing the future, especially for young men' (Melly 2017: 4).
11. Vasarhelyi (2013).
12. The date of the Grand Magal, as per the Islamic calendar.
13. See for example Leral, Friday 11 November 2016.
14. Senegal's principal telecommunications provider.
15. Base transceiver station.
16. In West Africa, amongst those who benefit are livestock producers; fruit, rice and vegetable farmers; telecommunication companies; construction firms; FMCG businesses; SMEs; banks; taxi companies; transportation firms as well as numerous others.
17. *Cheikh* Amadou Bamba's dream has been both fulfilled and forsaken, my translation.

Chapter 6

1. According to Guyer, evangelism, like monetarism, has separated actors from the near future, a temporality of 'thought and imagination, of planning and hoping, of tracing out mutual influences, of engaging in struggles for specific goals, in short, of the process of implicating oneself in the ongoing life of the social and material world'

---

17. Based on fieldwork in Zimbabwe, Bornstein (2002) argued that the specificities of FBO interventions (drilling wells, dispensing medicine) do not really matter to the scope of 'lifestyle evangelism' as it is mainly based on how employees understand their motivations.

(Guyer 2007: 409). For a critique of Guyer in African Pentecostal context see Van Dijk who argues that 'to be a Pentecostal is to be a time manager' (2012: 95).
2   See Delville (2018) for a study of rural land rights and land governance in Benin.
3   Most of the URHC parishes have now changed denominations, following internal schisms during the 2000s.
4   A return to the village can also be linked to retirement.
5   As explained before, it is not the fact of 'living' in the new house but 'building' the house that matters. This is different with regard to the family houses (the hut of the grandfather, the great grandfather, etc.): the family houses are often occupied by old women, especially widows, because it is important that somebody 'keeps the light on' and not to abandon ancestral house.

Chapter 7

1   Nsibidi Institute – The city that prays https://www.schoolandcollegelistings.com/NG/Lagos/215102638693408/Nsibidi-Institute (accessed 23 April 2022).
2   The church building committee did not respond to our request for an interview.

Chapter 8

1   In 2010, 38 per cent of Lusaka residents was born somewhere else in Zambia (IOM 2019: 46).
2   Some may just be allusions to a rumour that someone heard somewhere, others are brief reports in newspapers if accusations of involvement in Satanism have led to violence. The most extensive narratives about Satanism in Zambia can be found in testimonies which are given a platform in churches and on religious radio programmes.
3   This idea is prevalent in the whole 'modernity of witchcraft' approach; see Geschiere or Comaroff and Comaroff (1999). For an overview of this approach and the way it is still relevant to the study of witchcraft in Africa today, see Kroesbergen-Kamps (2020b).
4   See for example Comaroff and Comaroff (1999), who discuss a range of phenomena including witchcraft and Satanism under the label 'the occult'. This label has been taken up as an umbrella term for a wide range of phenomena linked to witchcraft and the potency of evil forces. For a critical discussion of the term see Kroesbergen-Kamps (2020b).
5   This clear distinction between rural witchcraft and urban Satanism may be a characteristically Zambian construction. Marian Burchardt (2017), for example, writes about witchcraft as a way of meaning-making in the urban environment of Cape Town, South Africa.
6   In traditional African thought, rivers are often regarded as points of entrance to the spirit world. One of the first African testimonies about Satanism, Emmanuel Eni's *Delivered from the Powers of Darkness* (1987), also mentions Satan's kingdom as a realm under the ocean. In other West African narratives the Mami Wata tradition that reveres an ocean goddess is also portrayed as a form of Satanism (Meyer 1995). In Naomi's testimony, rivers as entrances to the spirit world and a satanic kingdom under

the sea have come together: she enters a river and is transported under the ocean. The underworld of the Satanists is dry land, and in many respects similar to the 'normal world'.
7 For an overview of the changing role and view of chiefdom in the past 150 years see Kroesbergen-Kamps 2020a.
8 Note that Naomi uses the euro as her currency of choice here, rather than the Zambian kwacha. This again shows how the threat of satanism is related to the West – although I cannot explain why she chooses to speak about euros instead of dollars or pounds.

Chapter 9

1 We prefer the term 'religiously motivated organizations' over 'faith-based organizations' (FBOs). The former is more in line with emic perspectives: rather than faith and belief, our interlocutors privileged the performative power of religious practice that helps them confront the moral and socio-economic contingencies of urban life. As such, 'faith-based' is a much too narrow label for these institutions that are motivated by (religious) morality – and often political and market-driven agendas – but are not based on faith alone.
2 But even in the context of the so-called disabled state in Africa, in Tanzania some 80 per cent of educational provision remains in the hands of the government (Dilger 2017: 516n5), and in Nigeria the government is still regarded as the ultimate regulator or guarantor of education (de Sardan 2014: 401).
3 Drawing on philosopher MacIntyre's (1981) social theory, Thomas (2005: 238) argues that faith-based communities bond the virtues and practices of religious traditions with civic virtues as part of development. What is distinctive about this so-called virtue-ethics approach is the place it allows for religious organizations in building what theologian Hauerwas (1981) has called 'communities of character' as a part of aid policy.
4 Because of space, we cannot address the role of mainline churches and established Muslim organizations whose educational facilities have long-standing (colonial and post-colonial) histories in both countries. Similar to present-day religiously oriented schools and universities' mission to create moral citizens, colonial missionaries believed in the transformative power of education for it 'modernized' and 'civilized' students, equipping them for elite advancement and entry into the higher echelons of administration (e.g. Fumanti 2006; Simpson 1998).
5 Entrepreneurialism refers here both to proselytization and to the enmeshment of religious and business-oriented aspirations. This notion links with the educational marketplace where schools and universities compete for students and funding.
6 Throughout Africa, a trend of enclave style development has been established for elitist conspicuous consumption (Beall, Crankshaw and Parnell 2002), resource extraction (Ferguson 2006: 37) and development interventions (Sullivan 2011: 203).
7 Rather than the Africa Development Bank's economic definition of middle class, we employ a broader definition that includes social status, educational background, professionalism and moral behaviour, thereby affirming that middle class is 'a multi-dimensional concept that refers to a socio-economic category, a cultural world, and a political discourse' (Lentz 2016: 46).

8 Dr Rwakatare died in April 2020, at the time when the Covid-19 pandemic started to spread across the world.
9 In Tanzania, Kiswahili is the language of instruction at the primary level, and it is even used in most public secondary schools where the use of English is supposed to be mandatory.
10 The song *Tanzania Tanzania Nakupenda Kwa Moyo Wote* (Tanzania Tanzania I Love You with All My Heart) is sung in schools all over the country. Its exact history is unknown.
11 While the phenomenon of Muslim girls' possession exposed religious and ethnic differences in the school, the relations between Christian and Muslim students and teachers were not necessarily tense. For instance, there were explicit efforts to accommodate Muslim students' religious needs by creating separate spaces for prayer.
12 Interview conducted in Dar es Salaam on 16 April 2010.
13 AMA maintained close ties with some of these international Islamic educational centres, especially in Northeast, but also in East Africa (Zanzibar).
14 Data from a survey conducted by Dilger in 2009.
15 Interview conducted in Dar es Salaam on 7 October 2009.
16 Interview conducted in Dar es Salaam on 9 October 2009.
17 Interview conducted in Dar es Salaam on 22 October 2009.
18 The most severe punishment at Al-Farouq was caning, which is officially forbidden (or at least strongly restricted) in Tanzanian schools. While the practice was criticized by most students and teachers, others found it necessary to discipline students.
19 Group discussion with teachers in Dar es Salaam on 20 September 2009.
20 Informal conversation conducted in Dar es Salaam on 30 January 2009.
21 Interview conducted in Dar es Salaam on 6 October 2009.
22 Interview conducted in Lagos on 29 July 2010.
23 https://www.howwemadeitinafrica.com/nigerias-middle-class-how-we-live-and-what-we-want-from-life/12563/ (accessed 9 September 2019).
24 Interview conducted at RUN on 12 April 2017.
25 MTN and Glo are two competing telecommunication companies in Nigeria. Interview conducted in Lagos on 14 December 2011.
26 Interview conducted at FU on 11 April 2017.
27 Interview conducted at FU on 13 April 2017.
28 Interview conducted in Lagos on 17 March 2017.
29 Interview conducted at RUN on 12 April 2017.
30 Interview conducted in Lagos on 24 April 2017.
31 Janson was told during her field research that the first and most popular Pentecostal university, Covenant University (affiliated with Winners Chapel), went as far as introducing mandatory virginity tests for female students.
32 Interview conducted at RECSOM on 13 April 2017.
33 Focus group interviews conducted at RUN and FU on 11 and 12 April 2017.
34 Interview conducted at RUN on 12 April 2017.
35 In both Tanzania and Nigeria there are widespread rumors and media reports about sexual abuse in public schools and universities, where female students allegedly sleep with teachers in return for high marks. Drawing on Mbembe (1992), Nyamnjoh and Jua argue that low salaries and material hardship have contributed to African educational systems becoming part of the post-colonial 'phallocracy', where 'pride in possessing an active penis has to be dramatized' by male teachers seeking the 'unconditional subordination of women to the principle of male pleasure' (2002: 5).

Chapter 10

1. His aim was also to provide material recompense for years of neglect after Abuja, a newly built urban conurbation, had taken over from Lagos as the country's capital in 1991.
2. https://www.youtube.com/watch?v=eVPQJWBmPQA&ab_channel=QCPTV (accessed 25 April 2022).
3. For a form of popular culture that draws on some of the same visual tropes as Fashola's film – drawing images of functioning infrastructure into a celebration of secular urban life in Lagos – see the music videos produced by popular Nigerian-American musician Davido: https://www.youtube.com/watch?v=C2uyZVhWP8A&ab_channel=OlamideVEVO (accessed 25 April 2022).
4. https://www.nairaland.com/1324754/fashola-releases-fantasy-video-lagos (accessed 25 April 2022).
5. https://www.economist.com/middle-east-and-africa/2018/10/20/redemption-city-is-the-anti-lagos (accessed 25 April 2022).
6. For more discussion of urban sacrality in Ile-Ife see Olupona (2011).
7. Such encroachment may also involve deploying and discussing popular culture in class. An example of the latter mentioned by more than one professor was the video 'This is Nigeria' (https://www.youtube.com/watch?v=UW_xEqCWrm0&ab_channel=FalzVEVO, accessed 25 April 2022) by the Nigerian artist Falz, which is notable for its ribald imagery and satirical depiction of religion, as well as mention of infrastructure as index of the country's status.
8. 24 April 2018.
9. This chapter draws upon data collected as part of the Religious Urbanization and Infrastructural Lives in Africa Megacities Project (RUA) project, funded by the British Academy, https://rua-project.ac.uk (accessed 25 April 2022).
10. 19 June 2018.
11. Compare Dilger (2017).
12. David Oyedepo (born 1954), the founder of Winners' Chapel International, is now the Chancellor of both Covenant University and Landmark University. He studied architecture at the Kwara State Polytechnic Ilorin, before gaining a PhD in Human Development from Honolulu University.
13. 10 April 2018.
14. Nigerian slang for trouble.
15. 19 June 2018.
16. 25 July 2018.
17. 19 June 2018.
18. 10 April 2018.
19. Section 1.2.
20. Section 1.1.
21. See for example, https://ghanadmission.com/covenant-university-ota-cut-off-mark-2021-2022/ (accessed 25 April 2022).
22. https://www.webometrics.info/en/Africa/Nigeria (accessed 25 April 2022).
23. Indeed, CU was verified by the National Universities Commission (NUC) before it was allowed to operate.
24. https://covenantuniversity.edu.ng (25 April 2022).

25 Tuition costs for the 8,000 or so students are around 977, 500 Naira per session, or some 1,750 pounds sterling (based on figures for 2020-1– https://www.nairaland.com/6298546/covenant-university-2020-2021-school, accessed 25 April 2022). These prices are at the higher end of those charged by private institutions (with a few students being subsidized) but are not exceptional within this market. They are much cheaper than study in Europe or America, though they are considerably above those charged by federal universities.
26 18 July 2018.
27 19 June 2018.
28 19 June 2018.
29 18 July 2018.
30 24 April 2018.
31 19 June 2018
32 25 July 2018.
33 22 June 2018
34 25 April 2018.
35 22 June 2018.
36 24 April 2018.
37 The Handbook's term.
38 See Section EO.
39 25 July 2018.
40 25 July 2018.
41 Controlling access to technologies such as mobile phones has long been a point of contention between the state, phone companies, civil society and individual subscribers in Nigeria (Obadare 2006; see also Obadare 2018).
42 14 December 2018.
43 19 June 2018.
44 While Ogun State itself gathered the highest percentage of students, the latter figure was only 16.36 per cent, indicating a degree of national coverage achieved by the university.
45 25 July 2018.
46 25 May 2018.
47 10 April 2018.
48 25 July 2018.
49 19 July 2018.
50 25 July 2018.
51 https://www.unipage.net/en/universities?sort=rank_1 (accessed 25 April 2022).

Chapter 11

1 Burchardt (2021, personal communication).
2 Kirby, B. with Taru, J. and Chimbidzikai, T. (2020), https://theconversation.com/pentecostals-and-the-spiritual-war-against-coronavirus-in-africa-137424 (accessed February 2022).
3 Moyet, X. (2020), 'Pentecostalism, Public Health, and COVID-19 in Nigeria', *Religion in Public* (blog), 3 April. Available online: https://religioninpublic.leeds.ac.uk/2020/04/03/pentecostalism-public-health-and-covid-19-in-nigeria/.

4 Garbin, D. (2020), 'Reinventing Religious Urbanity in a (Post)Pandemic World? – A View from Africa', https://urbrel.hypotheses.org/996 (accessed February 2022).
5 Sturm, T. and Albrecht T. (2020).

Chapter 12: Afterword

1 https://www.thebritishacademy.ac.uk/programmes/cities-infrastructure/ (accessed April 2022).

REFERENCES

Abaza. M. (2004), 'Markets of Faith: Jakartan Da'wa and Islamic Gentrification', *Archipel*, 67: 172–302.
Adeboye. O. (2012), 'A Church in a Cinema Hall', *Journal of Religion in Africa*, 42 (1): 145–71.
Adeyeye, B., Ojih, S., Bello, D., Adesina, E., Yartey, D., Ben-Enukora, C. and Adeyee, Q. (2022), 'Online Learning Platforms and Covenant University Students' Academic Performance in Practical Related Courses during COVID-19 Pandemic', *Sustainability*, 14: 1–16.
Adichie (2005), 'Blinded by God's business', *Guardian*, 19 February.
Adogame. A. (2012), 'Dealing with Local Satanic Technology: Deliverance Rhetoric in the Mountain of Fire and Miracles Ministries', *Journal of World Christianity*, 5 (1): 75–101.
African Development Bank (2012), *Annual Development Effectiveness Review 2012. Growing African Economies Inclusively*, Tunis: African Development Bank.
Agamben, G. (2005), *The Time That Remains: A Commentary on the Letters to the Romans*. Stanford: Stanford University Press.
Agunbiade, E. M. and Olajide, O. A. (2016), 'Urban Governance and Turning African Cities Around: Lagos Case Study', Partnership for African Social and Governance Research Working Paper no. 19, Nairobi, Kenya.
Ahmed, C. (2009), 'Networks of Islamic NGOs in Sub-Saharan Africa: Bilal Muslim Mission, African Muslim Agency (Direct Aid), and al-Haramayn', *Journal of Eastern African Studies*, 3 (3): 426–37.
Ahmed, C. (2018), *Preaching Islamic Revival in East Africa*, Newcastle-upon-Tyne: Cambridge Scholars Publishing.
Ajadi. S. (2017), 'The "Gradient Forces" of Religion and Urbanism: The Gospel Town'. Available online: https://www.ifra-nigeria.org/publications/e-papers/ifra-e-papers (accessed 20 January 2021).
Alexander, J. C. and Smith, P. (2020), 'COVID-19 and Symbolic Action: Global Pandemic as Code, Narrative, and Cultural Performance', *American Journal of Cultural Sociology*. Available online: https://doi.org/10.1057/s41290-020-00123-w (accessed April 2022).
Allievi, S. and Nielsen, J., eds (2003), *Muslim Networks and Transnational Communities in and Across Europe*, Leiden: Brill.
AlSayyad, N. (2011), 'The Fundamentalist City?', in N. AlSayyad and M. Massoumi (eds), *The Fundamentalist City?: Religiosity and the Remaking of Urban Space*, 3–26, Abingdon: Routledge.
AlSayyad, N. and Ananya, R. (2006), 'Medieval Modernity: On Citizenship and Urbanism in a Global Era', *Space and Polity*, 10 (1): 1–20.
Althusser, L. (1971), 'Ideology and Ideological State Apparatuses', in *Lenin and Philosophy, and Other Essays*, trans. Ben Brewster, 127–88. London: New Left Books.
Amin, A. (2013), 'Telescopic Urbanism and the Poor', *City*, 17 (4): 476–92.
Amin, A. (2014), 'Lively Infrastructure', *Theory, Culture & Society*, 31 (7–8): 137–61.
Amin, A. and Thrift, N. (2002), *Cities: Reimagining the Urban*, Oxford: Polity Press.

Amin, A. and Thrift, N. (2017), *Seeing Like a City*, Cambridge: Polity Press.
Anderson, A. H. (2004), *An Introduction to Pentecostalism: Global Charismatic Christianity*, Cambridge: Cambridge University Press.
Anderson, B. (2006), *Imagined Communities: Reflections on the Origin and Spread of Nationalism*, London: Verso books.
Angelo, H. and Hentschel, C. (2015), 'Interactions with Infrastructures as Windows into Social Worlds: A Method for Critical Urban Studies: Introduction', *City*, 19 (2–3): 306–12.
Anugwom, E. (2002), 'Cogs in the Wheel: Academic Trade Unionism, Government, and the Crisis in Tertiary Education in Nigeria', *African Studies Review*, 45 (2): 141–55.
Anyansi-Archibong, C. (2015), 'Contemporary Issues Surrounding Ethical Research Methods and Practice', in F. Awajiusuk (ed.), *Prospects and Challenges of Teaching Religious Ethics in Nigerian Universities*, 306–23, Hershey, PA: IGI Global.
Anyanwu, O. (2011), *The Politics of Access: University Education and Nation-Building in Nigeria, 1948–2000*, Calgary: University of Calgary Press.
Appadurai, A. (2004), 'The Capacity to Aspire: Culture and the Terms of Recognition', in V. Rao and M. Walton (eds), *Culture and Public Action*, 59–84, Stanford: Stanford University Press.
Appadurai, A. (2013), *The Future as Cultural Fact: Essays on the Global Condition*, London: Verso Books.
Archambault, J. S. (2018), '"One Beer, One Block": Concrete Aspiration and the Stuff of Transformation in a Mozambican Suburb', *Journal of the Royal Anthropological Institute*, 24 (4): 692–708.
Asad, T. (1993), *Genealogies of Religion: Discipline and Reasons of Power in Christianity and Islam*, Baltimore, MD: Johns Hopkins University Press.
Asamoah-Gyadu, Kwabena J. (2019), 'God is Big in Africa: Pentecostal Mega Churches and a Changing Religious Landscape', *Material Religion*, 15 (3): 390–2. DOI: 10.1080/17432200.2019.1590012.
Ashforth, A. (2005), *Witchcraft, Violence, and Democracy in South Africa*, Chicago: University of Chicago Press.
Atkinson, R. (2007), 'Ecology of Sound: The Sonic Order of Urban Space', *Urban Studies*, 44 (10): 1905–17.
Awoleye, O., Siyanbola, W. and Oladipo, F. (2008), 'Adoption Assessment of Internet Usage Amongst Undergraduates in Nigerian Universities – A Case Study Approach', *Journal of Technology Management & Innovation*, 3 (1): 84–9.
Babere, N. J. (2013), 'Struggle for Space: Appropriation and Regulation of Prime Locations in Sustaining Informal Livelihoods in Dar es Salaam City, Tanzania', PhD diss., Newcastle University.
Bahendwa, F. (2013), 'Urban Form through Residents' Practices: The Unconventional Transformation Processes in Suburban Areas in Dar es Salaam, Tanzania', PhD diss., Oslo School of Architecture and Design.
Baker, C. (2015), 'Preface', in Y. Narayanan (ed.), *Religion and Urbanism, Reconceptualising Sustainable Cities for South Asia*, London: Routledge.
Bakhtin, M. (1968), *Rabelais and His World*, Cambridge, MA: MIT Press.
Banégas, R. (2003), *La démocratie à pas de caméléon: transition et imaginaires politiques au Bénin*, Paris: Karthala.
Baudrillard, J. (1981), *Simulacra and Simulation*, Ann Arbor: University of Michigan Press.

Bava, S. (2003), 'De la baraka aux affaires: ethos économico-religieux et transnationalité chez les migrants sénégalais mourides', *Revue Européenne des Migrations internationales*, 19 (2): 69–84.
Bayart, J. (1993), *The State in Africa: The Politics of the Belly*, London: Longman.
Bayart, J. (2005), *The Illusion of Cultural Identity*, London: Hurst & Co.
Beall, J., Crankshaw, O. and Parnell, S. (2002), *Uniting a Divided City: Governance and Social Exclusion in Johannesburg*, London: Routledge.
Beaumont, J. (2008a), 'Introduction: Faith-Based Organisations and Urban Social Issues', *Urban Studies*, 45 (10): 2011–17.
Beaumont, J. (2008b), 'Faith Action on Urban Social Issues', *Urban Studies*, 45 (101): 2019–34.
Beaumont, J., and Cloke, P., eds (2012), *Faith-Based Organisations and Exclusion in European Cities*, Bristol: Policy Press.
Becci, I., Burchardt, M. and Giorda, M. (2017), 'Religious Super-Diversity and Spatial Strategies in Two European Cities', *Current Sociology*, 65 (1): 73–91.
Becker, F. (2008), *Becoming Muslim in Mainland Tanzania, 1890–2000*, Oxford: Oxford University Press.
Becker, F. (2016), 'Fashioning Selves and Fashioning Styles: Negotiating the Personal and the Rhetorical in the Experiences of African Recipients of ARV Treatment', in R. van Dijk, H. Dilger, M. Burchardt and T. Rasing (eds), *Religion and AIDS Treatment in Africa: Saving Souls, Prolonging Lives*, 27–48, Farnham: Ashgate.
Becker, F. (2018), 'The History of Islam in East Africa', *The Oxford Research Encyclopedia of African History*. Available online: https://oxfordre.com/africanhistory/view/10.1093/acrefore/9780190277734.001.0001/acrefore-9780190277734-e-151 (accessed 16 August 2021).
Becker, F. and Cabrita, J. (2017), 'Introduction: Religion, Media, and Marginality in Modern Africa', in F. Becker, J. Cabrita, and M. Rodet (eds), *Religion, Media, and Marginality in Modern Africa*, 1–37, Athens: Ohio University Press.
Becker, J., Klingan, K. and Lanz, S. (2013), *Global Prayers: Contemporary Manifestations of the Religious in the City*, Zürich: Lars Müller Publishers.
Bennett, J. (2010), *Vibrant Matter: A Political Ecology of Things*, Durham, NC: Duke University Press.
Besteman, C. (2008), *Transforming Cape Town*, vol. 19, Berkeley: University of California Press.
Bhardwaj S. M. (1994), 'The Concept of Sacred Cities in Asia with Special Reference to India', in A. K. Dutt, F. J. Costa, S. Aggarwal and A. G. Noble (eds), *The Asian City: Processes of Development, Characteristics and Planning*, 17–80, New York: Springer.
Bierschenk, T. and Olivier de Sardan, J. P., eds (1998), *Les pouvoirs au village: le Bénin rural entre démocratisation et décentralisation*, Paris: Karthala.
Bjarnesen, J. (2015), 'The Ambivalence of Neighbourhood in Urban Burkina Faso', *Anthropology Southern Africa*, 38 (3–4): 331–43.
Bloch, M. and Parry, J. (1982), *Death and the Regeneration of Life*, Cambridge: Cambridge University Press.
Boccagni, P. (2020), 'So Many Houses, as Many Homes? Transnational Housing, Migration, and Development', in T. Bastia and R. Skeldon (eds), *The Routledge Handbook of Migration and Development*, 251–60, London: Routledge.
Bompani, B. (2006), 'Mandela Mania: Mainline Christianity in Post-Apartheid South Africa', *Third World Quarterly*, 27 (6): 1137–49.

Bonhomme, J. (2012), 'The Dangers of Anonymity: Witchcraft, Rumour, and Modernity in Africa', *HAU: Journal of Ethnographic Theory*, 2 (2): 205–33.
Bornstein, E. (2002), 'Developing Faith: Theologies of Economic Development in Zimbabwe', *Journal of Religion in Africa*, 32 (1): 4–31.
Bornstein, E. (2005), *The Spirit of Development: Protestant NGOs, Morality, and Economics in Zimbabwe*, Palo Alto: Stanford University Press.
Bouma, G. and Hughes, P. (2000), 'Religious Residential Concentrations in Australia', *People and Place*, 8 (1): 18–27.
Bourdieu, P. ([1984] 2006), *Distinction: A Social Critique of the Judgement of Taste*, New York: Routledge.
Brenner. N. and Schmid, C. (2015), 'Towards a New Epistemology of the Urban?', *City*, 19 (2–3): 151–82.
Brenner, N. (2019), *New Urban Spaces: Urban Theory and the Scale Question*, Oxford: Oxford University Press.
Brenner, N., Madden, D. and Wachsmuth, D. (2011), 'Assemblage Urbanism and the Challenges of Critical Urban Theory', *City*, 15: 225–40.
Brown, A. and Lyons M. (2010), 'Seen but Not Heard: Urban Voice and Citizenship for Street Traders', in I. Lindell (ed.), *Africa's Informal Workers: Collective Agency, Affiliations and Transnational Organizing in Urban Africa*, 33–45, London: Zed Books.
Bruce, S. (2002), *God Is Dead: Secularization in the West*, Oxford: Blackwell.
Buggenhagen, B. A. (2012), *Muslim Families in Global Senegal: Money Takes Care of Shame*, Bloomington: Indiana University Press.
Burchardt, M. (2011), 'Challenging Pentecostal Moralism: Erotic Geographies, Religion and Sexual Practices Among Township Youth in Cape Town', *Culture, Health and Sexuality*, 13 (6): 669–83.
Burchardt, M. (2013), 'Belonging and Success: Religious Vitality and the Politics of Urban Space in Cape Town', in I. Becci, M. Burchardt and J. Casanova (eds), *Topographies of Faith*, 167–87, Leiden: Brill.
Burchardt, M. (2015), *Faith in the Time of AIDS: Religion, Biopolitics and Modernity in South Africa*, Basingstoke: Palgrave Macmillan.
Burchardt, M. (2017), 'Pentecostal Productions of Locality: Urban Risks and Spiritual Protection in Cape Town', in D. Garbin and A. Strhan (eds), *Religion and the Global City*, 78–95, London: Bloomsbury.
Burchardt, M. and Becci, I. (2013), 'Introduction: Religion Takes Place: Producing Urban Locality', in Irene Becci, Marian Burchardt and J. Casanova (eds), *Topographies of Faith: Religion in Urban Spaces*, 1–21, Leiden: Brill.
Burchardt, M. and Westendorp, M. (2018), 'The Im-materiality of Urban Religion: Towards an Ethnography of Urban Religious Aspirations', *Culture and Religion*, 19 (2): 160–76.
Burchardt, M. (2020), 'From Mission Station to Tent Revival: Material Forms and Spatial Formats in Africa's Missionary Encounter', in P. Clart and A. Jones (eds), *Transnational Religious Spaces*, 35–50, Berlin: De Gruyter.
Burton, A. (2005), *African Underclass: Urbanisation, Crime & Colonial Order in Dar es Salaam*, Oxford: James Currey.
Butticci, A. (2013), 'Crazy World, Crazy Faith! Prayer, Power and Transformation in a Nigerian Prayer City', *Annual Review of the Sociology of Religion*, 243–61. DOI: https://doi.org/10.1163/9789004260498.

Butticci, A. (2016), *African Pentecostals in Catholic Europe, the Politics of Presence in the Twenty-First Century*, Cambridge, MA: Harvard University Press.

Caldeira, T. P. (2017), 'Peripheral Urbanization: Auto-Construction, Transversal Logics, and Politics in Cities of the Global South', *Environment and Planning D: Society and Space*, 35 (1): 3–20.

Campbell, H. A., ed. (2013), *Digital Religion: Understanding Religious Practice in New Media Worlds*, London: Routledge.

Carrier, N. (2016), *Little Mogadishu: Eastleigh, Nairobi's Global Somali Hub*, London: Hurst & Company.

Çavdar, A. (2016), 'Building, Marketing and Living in an Islamic Gated Community: Novel Configurations of Class and Religion in Istanbul', *International Journal of Urban and Regional Research*, 40 (3): 507–23.

Central Statistical Office (2015), *Zambia Demographical and Health Survey 2013–13*, Rockville: CSO, Ministry of Health and ICF International.

Chabal, P. and Daloz, J. (1999), *Africa Works: Disorder as Political Instrument*, Oxford: James Currey.

Chidester, D. (2006), 'Religion Education and the Transformational State in South Africa', *Social Analysis*, 50 (3): 61–83.

Chiluwa, I. (2012), 'Online Religion in Nigeria: The Internet Church and Cyber Miracles', *Journal of Asian and African Studies*, 47 (6): 734–49.

Choplin, A. (2019a), 'Produire la ville en Afrique de l'Ouest: le corridor urbain de Accra à Lagos', *L'Information géographique*, 83 (2): 85–103.

Choplin, A. (2019b), 'Cementing Africa: Cement Flows and City-Making along the West African Corridor (Accra, Lomé, Cotonou, Lagos)', *Urban Studies*, 57 (9): 1977–93.

Choudry, A. and Kapoor, D. (2013), *NGOization: Complicity, Contradictions and Prospects*, London: Zed Books.

Chu, J. (2014), 'When Infrastructures Attack: The Workings of Disrepair in China', *American Ethnologist*, 41 (2): 351–67.

CIA World Factbook (2021), 'Zambia'. Available online: https://www.cia.gov/the-world-factbook/countries/zambia/ (accessed 22 February 2021).

Cimino, R. (2013), 'Filling Niches and Pews in Williamsburg and Greenpoint: The Religious Ecology of Gentrification', in R. P. Cimino, N. A. Mian and W. Huang (eds), *Ecologies of Faith in New York City: The Evolution of Religious Institutions*, 55–80, Bloomington: Indiana University Press.

Clarke, G. and Jennings, M. (2008), 'Introduction', in G. Clarke and M. Jennings (eds), *Development, Civil Society and Faith-Based Organizations: Bridging the Sacred and the Secular*, 1–16, Basingstoke: Palgrave Macmillan.

Cobbinah, P. B., Erdiaw-Kwasie, M. and Adams, E. A. (2020), 'COVID-19: Can It Transform Urban Planning in Africa?' *Cities & Health*, 1–4. DOI: 10.1080/23748834.2020.1812329.

Cochrane, J. (2011), 'A Model of Integral Development: Assessing and Working with Religious Health Assets', in G. Haar (ed.), *Religion and Development: Ways of Transforming the World*, 231–52, London: C. Hurst & Co Press.

Coleman, S. (2004), 'The Charismatic Gift', *Journal of the Royal Anthropological Institute*, 10 (2): 421–42.

Coleman, S. (2011), 'Prosperity Unbound? Debating the "Sacrificial Economy"', in Lionel Obadia and Donald Wood (eds), *The Economics of Religion: Anthropological Approaches*, 23–45, Bingley: Emerald.

Coleman, S. and Chattoo, S. (2019), 'Megachurches and Popular Culture: On Enclaving and Encroaching', in S. J. Hunt (ed.), *Handbook of Megachurches*, 84–102, Leiden: Brill.

Coleman, S. and Elsner, J. (1995), *Pilgrimage: Past and Present in the World Religions*, Cambridge, MA: Harvard University Press.

Coleman, S. and Maier, K. (2013), 'Redeeming the City: Creating and Traversing "London-Lagos"', *Religion*, 43: 353–64.

Coleman, S. and Vásquez, M. (2017), 'On the Road: Pentecostal Pathways through the Mega-City', in D. Garbin and A. Strhan (eds), *Religion and the Global City*, 27–47, London: Bloomsbury.

Collins, J. (2009), 'Social Reproduction in Classrooms and Schools', *Annual Review of Anthropology*, 38: 33–48.

Comaroff, J. (2009), 'The Politics of Conviction: Faith on the Neo-Liberal Frontier', *Social Analysis*, 53 (1): 17–38.

Comaroff, J. (2012), 'Pentecostalism, Populism and the New Politics of Affect', in D. Freeman (ed.), *Pentecostalism and Development*, 41–66, Basingstoke: Palgrave Macmillan.

Comaroff, J. and Comaroff, J. L., eds (1993), *Modernity and Its Malcontents. Ritual and Power in Postcolonial Africa*, Chicago: University of Chicago Press.

Comaroff, J. and Comaroff, J. L. (1997), *Of Revelation and Revolution. The Dialectics of Modernity on a South African Frontier Vol. II*, Chicago: University of Chicago Press.

Comaroff, J. and Comaroff, J. L., eds (1999), 'Occult Economies and the Violence of Abstraction. Notes from the South African Postcolony', *American Ethnologist*, 26 (2): 279–303.

Comaroff, J. and Comaroff, J. L., eds (2001), *Millennial Capitalism and the Culture of Neoliberalism*, Durham, NC: Duke University Press.

Comaroff, J. and Comaroff, J. L. (2012), *Theory from the South: Or, How Euro-America Is Evolving toward Africa*, London: Paradigm.

Cooper, E. and Pratten, D., eds (2014), *Ethnographies of Uncertainty in Africa*, London: Palgrave Macmillan.

Copjec, J. and Sorkin, M., eds (1999), *Giving Ground: The Politics of Propinquity*, London: Verso.

Coulon, C. (1999), 'The Grand Magal in Touba: A Religious Festival of the Mouride Order of Senegal', *African Affairs*, 98 (391): 195–210.

Covenant University Academic Handbook (Undergraduate) (2018), Ogun State: College of Leadership Development Studies.

Crang, M. (2005), 'Time: Space', in P. Cloke and R. Johnston (eds), *Spaces of Geographical Thought: Deconstructing Human Geography's Binaries*, 199–220, London: Sage.

Cruise O'Brien, D. B. (1971), *The Mourides of Senegal: The Political and Economic Organization of an Islamic Order*, Oxford: Clarendon Press.

Cruise O'Brien, D. B. (2003), *Symbolic Confrontations, Muslims Imagining the State in Africa*, London: Hurst.

Day, K. (2014), *Faith on the Avenue: Religion on a City Street*, Oxford: Oxford University Press.

De Blij, H. J. (1963), *Dar es Salaam: A Study in Urban Geography*, Evanston, IL: Northwestern University.

De Boeck, F. and Plissart, M.-Fr. (2004), *Kinshasa: Tales of the Invisible City*, Ghent: Ludion.

De Boeck, F. (2011), 'Spectral Kinshasa: Building the City through an Architecture of Words', in Tim Edensor and Mark Jayne (eds), *Urban Theory Beyond the West: A World of Cities*, 309–26, London: Routledge.

De Boeck, F. (2012), 'Infrastructure: Commentary from Filip de Boeck', curated collections, *Cultural Anthropology Online*. Available online: https://journal.culanth.org/index.php/ca/infrastructure-filip-de-boeck (accessed 16 August 2021).

De Boeck, F. (2013), 'The Sacred and the City: Modernity, Religion, and the Urban Form in Central Africa', in M. Lambek, and J. Boddy (eds), *A Companion to the Anthropology of Religion*, 528–48, London: Wiley.

De Boeck, F. and Baloji, S. (2016), *Suturing the City: Living Together in Congo's Urban Worlds*, London: Autograph ABP.

De Bruijn, M. and van Dijk R. (2012a), 'Connecting and Change in African Societies: Examples of "Ethnographies of Linking" in Anthropology', *Anthropologica*, 54 (1): 45–59.

De Bruijn, M. and van Dijk R. (2012b), 'Connectivity and the Postglobal Moment: (Dis)connections and Social Change in Africa', in M. de Bruijn and R. van Dijk (eds), *The Social Life of Connectivity in Africa*, 1–20, London: Palgrave Macmillan.

De Bruijn, M. and van Dijk, R., eds (2012c), *The Social Life of Connectivity in Africa*, New York: Palgrave Macmillan.

Deeb, L. (2015), 'Thinking Piety and the Everyday Together: A Response to Fadil and Fernando', *HAU: Journal of Ethnographic Theory*, 5 (2): 93–6.

Della Dora, V. (2016) 'Infrasecular Geographies: Making, Unmaking and Remaking Sacred Space', *Progress in Human Geography*, 42 (1): 44–71.

Delville, P. L. (2018) 'Les marchés ruraux fonciers au Bénin', *Les Cahiers du Pôle Foncier*, 19: 1–53.

Demart, S. (2017), *Les territoires de la délivrance Le réveil congolais en situation postcoloniale (RDC et diaspora)*, Paris: Karthala.

Deneulin, S. (2009), *Religion in Development: Rewriting the Secular Script*, London: Zed Books.

De Vries, H. (2001), 'In Media Res: Global Religion, Public Spheres, and the Task of Contemporary Comparative Religious Studies', in H. deVries and S. Weber (eds), *Religion and Media*, 3–43, Stanford: Stanford University Press.

De Waal, A. (2003), 'A Disaster with No Name: The HIV/AIDS Pandemic and the Limits of Governance', in G. Ellison, M. Parker and C. Campbell (eds), *Learning from HIV and AIDS*, 238–68, Cambridge: Cambridge University Press.

De Witte, M. (2008), 'Accra's Sounds and Sacred Spaces', *International Journal of Urban and Regional Research*, 32 (2): 690–709.

De Witte, M. (2010), 'Religious Media, Mobile Spirits: Publicity and Secrecy in African Pentecostalism and Traditional Religion', in G. Hüwelmeier and K. Krause (eds), *Travelling Spirits: Migrants, Markets, and Mobilities*, 83–10, London: Routledge.

De Witte, M. (2012), 'Neo-Traditional Religions', in E. K. Bongmba (ed.), *The Wiley-Blackwell Companion to African Religions*, 173–83, Chichester: John Wiley & Sons.

Dilger, H. (2013), 'Religion and the Formation of an Urban Educational Market: Transnational Reform Processes and Social Inequalities in Christian and Muslim Schooling in Dar es Salaam, Tanzania', *Journal of Religion in Africa*, 43 (4): 451–79.

Dilger, H. (2017), 'Embodying Values and Socio-Religious Difference: New Markets of Moral Learning in Christian and Muslim Schools in Urban Tanzania', *Africa: Journal of the International African Institute*, 87 (3): 513–36.

Dilger, H. (2020), 'Governing Religious Multiplicity: The Ambivalence of Christian-Muslim Public Presences in Postcolonial Tanzania', *Social Analysis*, 64 (1): 125–32.

Dilger, H. (2022), *Learning Morality, Inequalities, and Faith: Christian and Muslim Schools in Tanzania*, Cambridge: Cambridge University Press/International African Institute.

Dilger, H. and Schulz, D. (2013), 'Politics of Religious Schooling: Christian and Muslim Engagements with Education in Africa', *Journal of Religion in Africa*, 43 (4): 365–78.

Dilger, H., Burchardt, M. and van Dijk, R. (2010), 'Introduction – The Redemptive Moment: HIV Treatments and the Production of New Religious Spaces', *African Journal of AIDS Research*, 9 (4): 373–83.

Dilger, H., Bochow, A., Burchardt, M. and Wilhelm-Solomon, M., eds (2020a), *Affective Trajectories: Religion and Emotion in African Cityscapes*, Durham, NC: Duke University Press.

Dilger, H., Bochow, A., Burchardt M. and Wilhelm-Solomon, M. (2020b), 'Introduction: Affective Trajectories in Religious African Cityscapes', in H. Dilger, A. Bochow, M. Burchardt and M. Wilhelm-Solomon (eds), *Affective Trajectories: Religion and Emotion in African Cityscapes*, 1–26, Durham, NC: Duke University Press.

Diop, M. C. (1981), 'Les affaires mourides à Dakar', *Politique africaine*, 1 (4): 90–100.

Dulin, J. (2020), ' "My Fast Is Better Than Your Fast": Concealing Interreligious Evaluations and Discerning Respectful Others in Gondar, Ethiopia', *Ethnos*, DOI: 10.1080/00141844.2020.1725093.

Durizzo, K., Asiedu, E., Van der Merwe, A., Van Niekerk, A. and Günther, I. (2021), 'Managing the COVID-19 Pandemic in Poor Urban Neighborhoods: The Case of Accra and Johannesburg', *World Development*, 137: 105–75.

Dussel, E. (2002), 'World Religions and Secularization from a Postcolonial and Anti-Eurocentric Perspective', in D. Peterson and D. Walhof (eds), *The Invention of Religion: Rethinking Belief in Politics and History*, 179–89, New Brunswick, NJ: Rutgers University Press.

Eade, J. (2012), 'Religion, Home-Making and Migration across a Globalising City', *Culture and Religion*, 13 (4): 469–83.

Eade, J. and Sallnow, M. J. (1991), *Contesting the Sacred: The Anthropology of Christian Pilgrimage*, London: Routledge.

Echtler, M. and Ukah, A. (2016), 'Introduction: Exploring the Dynamics of Religious Fields in Africa', in Magnus Echtler and Asonzeh Ukah (eds), *Bourdieu in Africa: Exploring the Dynamics of Religious Fields*, 1–32, Leiden: Brill.

Eiesland, N. L. (2000), *A Particular Place: Urban Restructuring and Religious Ecology in a Southern Exurb*, New Brunswick, NJ: Rutgers University Press.

Eisenstadt, S. N. (2000), 'Multiple Modernities', *Daedalus*, 129 (1): 1–29.

Eliade, M. (1959), *The Sacred and the Profane: The Nature of Religion*, 1st American edn, New York: Harcourt, Brace.

Ellis, S. (2011), *Het regenseizoen: Afrika in de wereld*, Amsterdam: Bert Bakker.

Engelke, M. (2007), *A Problem of Presence. Beyond Scripture in an African Church*, Berkeley: University of California Press.

Engelke, M. (2010), 'Past Pentecostalism: Notes on Rupture, Realignment, and Everyday Life in Pentecostal and African Independent Churches', *Africa*, 80 (2): 177–99.

Engelke, M. (2013), *God's Agents: Biblical Publicity in Contemporary England*, Berkeley: University of California Press.

Engelke, M. (2020), 'Number and the Imagination of Global Christianity; Or, Mediation and Immediacy in the Work of Alain Badiou', *South Atlantic Quarterly*, 109 (4): 811–29.

Eni, E. A. ([1987] 1996), *Delivered from the Powers of Darkness*, St-Germain-de-Calberte: Editions Parole de Vie.

Elyachar, J. (2010), 'Phatic Labor, Infrastructure, and the Question of Empowerment in Cairo', *American Ethnologist*, 37 (3): 452–64.
Elyachar J. (2011), 'The Political Economy of Movement and Gesture in Cairo', *Journal of the Royal Anthropological Institute*, 17 (1): 82–99.
Farías, I. (2011), 'The Politics of Urban Assemblages', *City*, 15 (3–4): 365–74.
Fawaz. M. (2009), 'Hezbollah as Urban Planner: Questions to and from Planning Theory', *Planning Theory*, 8 (4): 323–34.
Feed the Future, Senegal FY2011–2015, US Government Report.
Ferguson, J. (1990), *The Anti-Politics Machine: 'Development', Depoliticization and Bureaucratic Power in Lesotho*, Cambridge: Cambridge University Press.
Ferguson, J. (1999), *Expectations of Modernity: Myths and Meanings of Urban Life on the Zambian Copperbelt*, Berkeley: University of California Press.
Ferguson, J. (2006), *Global Shadows: Africa in the Neoliberal World Order*, Durham, NC: Duke University Press.
Ferguson, J. (2015), *Give a Man a Fish: Reflections on the New Politics of Distribution*, Durham, NC: Duke University Press.
Fichtner, S. (2012), *The NGOisation of Education: Case Studies from Benin*, Cologne: Köppe.
Fischer, E. F. (2014), *The Good Life: Aspiration, Dignity, and the Anthropology of Wellbeing*, Stanford: Stanford University Press.
Foley, E. E. and Babou, C. A. (2010), 'Diaspora, Faith, and Science: Building a Mouride Hospital in Senegal', *African Affairs*, 110 (438): 75–95.
Förster, T. and Ammann, C. (2018), *African Cities and the Development Conundrum*, Leiden: Brill.
Förster, T. and Siegenthaler, F. (2018), 'Introduction: Re-Imagining Cities in Africa', *Social Dynamics*, 44 (3): 395–404.
Foucault, M. (1983), 'The Subject and Power', in Hubert L. Dreyfus and Paul Rabinow (eds), *Michel Foucault: Beyond Structuralism and Hermeneutics*, 208–26, Chicago: University of Chicago Press.
Fourchard, L. (2021), *Classify, Exclude, Police: Urban Lives in South Africa and Nigeria*, Oxford: Wiley.
Fredericks, R. (2018), *Garbage Citizenship: Vital Infrastructures of Labor in Dakar, Senegal*, Durham, NC: Duke University Press.
Freeman, D. (2012), 'The Pentecostal Ethic and the Spirit of Development', in D. Freeman (ed.), *Pentecostalism and Development: Churches, NGOs and Social Change in Africa*, Basingstoke: Palgrave Macmillan.
Fumanti, M. (2006), 'Nation Building and the Battle for Consciousness: Discourses on Education in Post-Apartheid Namibia', *Social Analysis: The International Journal of Anthropology*, 50 (3): 84–108.
Gandy, M. (2005), 'Learning from Lagos', *New Left Review*, 33: 36–52.
Gandy, M. (2006), 'Planning, Anti-Planning and the Infrastructure Crisis Facing Metropolitan Lagos', *Urban Studies*, 43: 2.
Garbin, D. (2012), 'Marching for God in the Global City: Public Space, Religion and Diasporic Identities in a Transnational African Church', *Culture and Religion*, 13 (4): 425–47.
Garbin, D. (2013), 'The Visibility and Invisibility of Migrant Faith in the City: Diaspora Religion and the Politics of Emplacement of Afro-Christian Churches', *Journal of Ethnic and Migration Studies*, 39 (5): 677–96.

Garbin, D. (2014), 'Regrounding the Sacred: Transnational Religion, Place Making and the Politics of Diaspora among the Congolese in London and Atlanta', *Global Networks*, 14: 363–82.
Garbin, D. (2018), 'Sacred Remittances: Money, Migration and the Moral Economy of Development in a Transnational African Church', *Journal of Ethnic and Migration Studies*, 45: 11.
Garbin, D. (2020), 'Building New Jerusalem(s) in Africa: Religious Urbanisation and the Divine City Yet to Come', colloquium paper, Max Weber Centre for Advanced Studies, Erfurt, Germany.
Garbin, D. and Strhan, A., eds (2017a), *Religion and the Global City*, London: Bloomsbury.
Garbin, D. and Strhan, A. (2017b), 'Introduction: Locating Religion and the Global City', in David Garbin and Anna Strhan (eds), *Religion and the Global City*, 1–24, London: Bloomsbury.
Geschiere, P. (1997), *The Modernity of Witchcraft. Politics and the Occult in Postcolonial Africa*, Charlottesville: University of Virginia Press.
Geschiere, P. and Gugler, J. (1998), 'Introduction: The Urban–Rural Connection: Changing Issues of Belonging and Identification', *Africa: Journal of the International African Institute*, 68 (3): 309–19.
Geschiere, P. and Socpa, A. (2016), 'Changing Mobilities, Shifting Futures', in B. Goldstone and J. Obarrio (eds), *African Futures: Essays on Crisis, Emergence, and Possibility*, 167–80, Chicago: University of Chicago Press.
Geyer, H. S. and Mohammed, F. (2016), 'Hyper-Segregation and Class-Based Segregation Processes in Cape Town 2001–2011', *Urban Forum*, 27 (1): 35–58.
Gez, Y., Droz, Y., Rey, J. and Soares, E. (2021), *Butinage: The Art of Religious Mobility*, Toronto: Toronto University Press.
Ghertner, D. A. (2015), 'Why Gentrification Theory Fails in "Much of the World"', *City*, 19 (4): 552–63.
Gilbert, J. (2018), '"They're My Contacts, Not My Friends": Reconfiguring Affect and Aspirations through Mobile Communication in Nigeria', *Ethnos*, 83 (2): 237–54.
Gilsenan, M. (1982), *Recognizing Islam: Religion and Society in the Modern Arab World*, New York: Pantheon Books.
Girard, P. and Chapoto, A. (2017), 'Zambia: Internal Migration at the Core of Territorial Dynamics', in Sara Mercandalli and Bruno Losch (eds), *Rural Africa in Motion. Dynamics and Drivers of Migration South of the Sahara*, 34–5, Rome: FAO-CIRAD.
Glassman, J. (1995), *Feasts and Riot: Revelry, Rebellion, & Popular Consciousness on the Swahili Coast, 1856–1888*, Portsmouth: Heinemann.
Goffman, E. (1959), *The Presentation of Self in Everyday Life*, London: Penguin.
Gooding, P. (2017), 'Lake Tanganyika: Commercial Frontier in the Era of Long-Distance Caravan Commerce, East and Central Africa, c.1830–1890', PhD diss., SOAS, University of London.
Goonewardena, K. (2018), 'Planetary Urbanization and Totality', *Environment and Planning D: Society and Space*, 36 (3): 456–73.
Gotham, K. F. (2002), 'Beyond Invasion and Succession: School Segregation, Real Estate Blockbusting, and the Political Economy of Neighborhood Racial Transition', *City & Community*, 1 (1): 83–111.
Graham, S. and Marvin, S. (2001), *Splintering Urbanism: Networked Infrastructures, Technological Mobilities, and the Urban Condition*, London: Routledge.

Graham, S. and McFarlane, C. (2015), 'Introduction', in S. Graham and C. McFarlane (eds), *Infrastructural Lives: Urban Infrastructure in Context*, 1–14, Abingdon: Routledge.
Graham, S. and McFarlane, C., eds (2015), *Infrastructural Lives: Urban Infrastructure in Context*, New York: Routledge.
Green, M. and Mesaki, S. (2005), 'The Birth of the "Salon": Poverty, "Modernization", and Dealing with Witchcraft in Southern Tanzania', *American Ethnologist*, 32 (3): 371–88.
Green-Simms, L. B. (2017), *Postcolonial Automobility: Car Culture in West Africa*, Minneapolis: University of Minnesota Press.
Gregory, D. (1994), *Geographical Imaginations*, Oxford: Blackwell.
Guèye, C. (2002), *Touba: La capitale des Mourides*, Paris: Karthala.
Guma, P. (2020), 'Incompleteness of Urban Infrastructures in Transition: Scenarios from the Mobile Age in Nairobi', *Social Studies of Science*, 50 (5): 728–50.
Gupta, A. (2018), 'The Future in Ruins: Thoughts on the Temporality of Infrastructure', in H. Appel, N. Anand and A. Gupta (eds), *The Promise of Infrastructure*, 62–79, Durham, NC: Duke University Press.
Guyer, J. (2007), 'Prophecy and the Near Future: Thoughts on Macroeconomic, Evangelical, and Punctuated Time', *American Ethnologist*, 34 (3): 409–21.
Guyève, L. (2017), 'Magal Touba: étude des impacts économiques 2016–2017'. Available online: https://www.leral.net/Magal-Touba-etude-des-impacts-economiques-2016-2017-Par-Professeur-Lamine-Gueye_a236186.html (accessed 26 April 2022).
Hackett, R. and Soares, B. (2015), 'Introduction: New Media and Religious Transformations in Africa', in R. Hackett and B. Soares (eds), *New Media and Religious Transformations in Africa*, 1–18, Bloomington: Indiana University Press.
Hackworth, J. and Gullikson E. (2013), 'Giving New Meaning to Religious Conversion: Churches, Redevelopment, and Secularization in Toronto', *The Canadian Geographer/Le Géographe canadien*, 57 (1): 72–89.
Hage, G. (2009), 'Waiting Out the Crisis: On Stuckedness and Governmentality', in G. Hage (ed.), *Waiting*, 97–106, Carlton: Melbourne University Press.
Hancock, M. and Srinivas, S. (2008), 'Spaces of Modernity: Religion and the Urban in Asia and Africa', *International Journal of Urban and Regional Research*, 32 (3): 617–30.
Hansen, K. T. (1999), 'Second-Hand Clothing Encounters in Zambia: Global Discourses, Western Commodities and Local Histories', in R. Fardon, W. van Binsbergen and R. van Dijk (eds), *Modernity on a Shoestring: Dimensions of Globalization, Consumption and Development in Africa and Beyond*, 207–26, Leiden: EIDOS.
Hansen, T. B. and Verkaaik, O. (2009), 'Introduction – Urban Charisma: On Everyday Mythologies in the City', *Critique of Anthropology*, 29 (1): 5–26.
Harvey, D. (2001a), 'Globalization and the "Spatial Fix"', *Geographische Revue*, 2: 23–30.
Harvey, D. (2001b), *Spaces of Capital: Towards a Critical Geography*, Edinburgh: Edinburgh University Press
Harvey, D. (2012), *Rebel Cities: From the Right to the City to the Urban Revolution*, New York: Verso.
Hastrup, K. (1992), 'Introduction', in K. Hastrup (ed.), *Other Histories*, London: Routledge.
Hauerwas, S. (1981), *A Community of Character: Toward a Constructive Christian Social Ethic*, Notre Dame: University of Notre Dame Press.
Hendriks, J. and Erasmus, J. (2005), 'Religion in South Africa. The 2001 Population Census Data', *Journal of Theology for Southern Africa*, 121: 88–111.
Highmore, B. (2002), *Everyday Life and Cultural Theory an Introduction*, London: Routledge.

Hirschkind, C. (2006), *The Ethical Soundscape: Cassette Sermons and Islamic Counterpublics*, New York: Columbia University Press.

Hobsbawm, E. J. and Ranger, T. O. (1983), *The Invention of Tradition*, Cambridge: Cambridge University Press.

Holston, J. (1991), 'Auto-Construction in Working-Class Brazil', *Cultural Anthropology*, 6 (4): 447–65.

Houtman, D. and Meyer, B., eds (2012), *Things: Religion and the Question of Materiality*, New York: Fordham University Press.

Hull. M. (2012), *Government of Paper: The Materiality of Bureaucracy in Urban Pakistan*, Berkeley: University of California Press.

Hunt, S. (1998), 'Managing the Demonic: Some Aspects of the Neo-Pentecostal Deliverance Ministry', *Journal of Contemporary Religion*, 13 (2): 215–30.

Ilo, S. C., ed. (2018), *Wealth, Health, and Hope in African Christian Religion: The Search for Abundant Life*, Lanham, MD: Lexington Books.

Ilubala-Ziwa, J., Mwale, N., Banja, M. and Milingo, T. C. (2020), 'Religion and Migration in Zambia: Experiences of Christian Household Hosts of Migrant Youths in Lusaka's Urban Context', *Multidisciplinary Journal of Language and Social Sciences Education*, 3 (1): 1–23.

IOM (2019), *Migration in Zambia: A Country Profile 2019*, Lusaka: IOM.

Isetti, G., Innerhofer, E., Pechlaner, H. and de Rachewiltz, M., eds (2021), *Religion in the Age of Digitalization: From New Media to Spiritual Machines*, New York: Routledge.

Ivaska, A. M. (2007), 'In the "Age of Minis": Women, Work and Masculinity', in J. R. Brennan, A. Burton and Y. Lawi (eds), *Dar es Salaam: Histories from an Emerging African Metropolis*, 213–31, Dar es Salaam: Mkuki na Nyota.

Janeja, M. K. and Bandak, A., eds (2018), *Ethnographies of Waiting: Doubt, Hope and Uncertainty*, London: Bloomsbury.

Jansen, S. (2014), 'On Not Moving Well Enough: Temporal Reasoning in Sarajevo Yearnings for "Normal Lives"', *Current Anthropology*, 55 (S9): S74–84.

Janson, M. (2016), 'Unity through Diversity: A Case Study of Chrislam in Lagos', *Africa*, 86 (4): 646–72.

Janson, M. (2021), *Crossing Religious Boundaries: Islam, Christianity, and 'Yoruba Religion' in Lagos, Nigeria*, Cambridge: Cambridge University Press.

Janson, M. (2020), 'Crossing Borders: The Case of NASFAT or "Pentecostal Islam" in Southwest Nigeria', *Social Anthropology*, 28 (2): 418–33. DOI: 10.1111/1469-8676.12769.

Janson, M. and Akinleye, A. (2015), 'The Spiritual Highway: Religious World Making in Megacity Lagos (Nigeria)', *Material Religion*, 11 (4): 550–62.

Janson, M. and Meyer, B. (2016), 'Introduction: Towards a Framework for the Study of Christian–Muslim Encounters in Africa', *Africa*, 86 (4): 615–19.

Jensen, C. B. and Morita, A. (2017), 'Introduction: Infrastructures as Ontological Experiments', *Ethnos*, 82 (4): 615–26.

Jones, B. and Petersen, M. J. (2011), 'Instrumental, Narrow, Normative? Reviewing Recent Work on Religion and Development', *Third World Quarterly*, 32 (7): 1291–306.

Jones, B. (2012), 'Pentecostalism, Development NGOs and Meaning in Eastern Uganda', in D. Freeman (ed.), *Pentecostalism and Development: Churches, NGOs and Social Change in Africa*, 181–202, Basingstoke: Palgrave Macmillan.

Kamps, J. (2018), 'Speaking of Satan in Zambia: The Persuasiveness of Contemporary Narratives about Satanism', PhD diss., Utrecht University, Utrecht. Available online: http://dspace.library.uu.nl/handle/1874/359194 (accessed 25 June 2021).

Karaman, O., Sawyer, L., Schmid, C. and Wong, K. P. (2020), 'Plot by Plot: Plotting Urbanism as an Ordinary Process of Urbanisation', *Antipode*, 52 (4): 1122–51.
Kaspin, D. (1993), 'Chewa Visions and Revisions of Power. Transformations of the Nyau Dance in Central Malawi', in J. Comaroff and J. L. Comaroff (eds), *Modernity and Its Malcontents. Ritual and Power in Postcolonial Africa*, 34–57, Chicago: University of Chicago Press.
Katsaura, O. (2019), 'Pentecosmopolis: On the Pentecostal Cosmopolitanism of Lagos', *Religion*, 50 (4): 504–28.
Keane, W. (2021), 'Religion and Moral Economy', *Oxford Research Encyclopedia of Anthropology*, Oxford: Oxford University Press.
Kihato, C. W., and Landau, L. B. (2020), 'Coercion or the Social Contract? COVID 19 and Spatial (in) Justice in African Cities; *City & Society*, 32 (1): 1–11.
Kingsbury, K. (2014), 'New Mouride Movements in Dakar and the Diaspora', PhD diss., University of Oxford.
Kingsbury, K. (2018), 'Modern Mouride Marabouts and Their Young Disciples in Dakar', *Anthropologica*, 60 (2): 467–79.
Kirby, B. (2017a), 'Muslim Mobilisation, Urban Informality, and the Politics of Development in Tanzania: An Ethnography of the Kariakoo Market District', PhD diss., University of Leeds, Leeds.
Kirby, B. (2017b), 'Occupying the Global City: Spatial Politics and Spiritual Warfare among African Pentecostals in Hong Kong', in D. Garbin and A. Strhan (eds), *Religion and the Global City*, 62–77, London: Bloomsbury Academic.
Kirby, B (2019), 'Pentecostalism, Economics, Capitalism: Putting the Protestant Ethic to Work', *Religion*, 49 (4): 571–91.
Kirby, B. (2020), 'Flags and Shields: Muslim Socialities and Informal Livelihoods in Dar es Salaam', *City and Society*, 32 (3): 556–78.
Kirby, B., Sibanda, F. and Charway F. (2021), 'Disarming the Xenophobic Everyday: Muslim Migrants and the Horizons of Urban Mutuality in Durban', *Africa*, 91 (2): 296–316.
Kirby, B. and Hölzchen, Y. (forthcoming), 'Introduction: Conceptualising Religious Infrastructure', *Religion*.
Knibbe, K. (2009), '"We Did Not Come Here as Tenants, but as Landlords": Nigerian Pentecostals and the Power of Maps', *African Diaspora*, 2 (2): 133–58.
Knott, K. (2005), *The Location of Religion: A Spatial Analysis*, London: Routledge.
Knott, K. (2008), 'Spatial Theory and the Study of Religion', *Religion Compass*, 2 (6): 1102–16.
Knott, K. (2012), 'Spatial Theory and Method for the Study of Religion', *Temenos – Nordic Journal of Comparative Religion*, 41 (2): 153–84.
Kong, L. (2010), 'Global Shifts, Theoretical Shifts: Changing Geographies of Religion', *Progress in Human Geography*, 34 (6): 755–76.
Koch, R. and Latham, A. (2013), 'On the Hard Work of Domesticating a Public Space', *Urban* Studies, 50 (1): 6–21.
Krause, K. (2008), 'Spiritual Places in Post-Industrial Spaces: Transnational Churches in North East London', in M. P. Smith and J. Eade (eds), *Transnational Ties: Cities, Migrations, and Identities*, 109–30, New Brunswick, NJ: Transaction Publishers.
Kresse, K. (2018), *Swahili Muslim Publics and Postcolonial Experience*, Bloomington: Indiana University Press.
Kroesbergen, H. (2020), *The Language of Faith in Southern Africa: Spirit World, Power, Community, Holism*, Cape Town: AOSIS.

Kroesbergen-Kamps, J. (2020a), 'The Usual Suspects: Accusations of Satanism against Politicians in Zambia', in M. Hinfelaar and C. Kaunda (eds), *Competing for Caesar: Religion and Politics in Post-Colonial Zambia*, 173–93, Minneapolis, MN: Fortress Press.

Kroesbergen-Kamps, J. (2020b), 'Witchcraft after Modernity: Old and New Directions in the Study of Witchcraft in Africa', *HAU: Journal of Ethnographic Theory*, 10 (3): 860–73.

Kroesbergen-Kamps, J. (2020c), 'Horizontal and Vertical Dimensions in Zambian Sermons about the COVID-19 Pandemic', *Journal of Religion in Africa*, 49 (1): 73–99.

Kuppinger, P. (2014), 'Mosques and Minarets: Conflict, Participation, and Visibility in German Cities', *Anthropological Quarterly*, 87 (3): 793–818.

La Fontaine, J. (2016). *Witches and Demons: A Comparative Perspective on Witchcraft and Satanism*, Oxford: Berghahn Books.

Lagos State Government (2013), *Lagos State Mainland Central Model City Plan (2012–2030)*.

Lagos State Government (2014), *Summary of Space Standards for Planning Approval*, Handbook of the Lagos State Physical Planning Permit Authority.

Lagos State Urban Renewal Agency (2010), *Iwaya North Urban Regeneration Draft Plan –2010*.

Lamb, G. (2020), 'Fear and Policing in the Time of Covid-19' *News 24*, 3 April 2020. Available online: https://www.news24.com/Columnists/GuestColumn/opinion-fear-and-policing-in-the-time-of-covid-19-20200403 (accessed 29 May 2020).

Lanz, S. (2013), 'Assembling Global Prayers in the City: An Attempt to Repopulate Urban Theory with Religion', in J. Becker, K. Klingan, S. Lanz and K. Wildner (eds), *Global Prayers: Contemporary Manifestations of the Religious in the City*, 17–43. Zürich: Lars Müller.

Lanz, S. (2016), 'The Born-Again Favela: The Urban Informality of Pentecostalism in Rio de Janeiro', *International Journal of Urban and Regional Research*, 40 (3): 541–58.

Lanz, S. and Oosterbaan, M. (2016), 'Entrepreneurial Religion in the Age of Neoliberal Urbanism', *International Journal of Urban and Regional Research*, 40 (3): 487–506.

Larkin, B. (2008), *Signal and Noise: Media, Infrastructure, and Urban Culture in Nigeria*, Durham, NC: Duke University Press.

Larkin, B. (2013), 'The Politics and Poetics of Infrastructure', *Annual Review of Anthropology*, 42: 327–43.

Larkin, B. (2016), 'Entangled Religions: Response to J. D. Y. Peel', *Africa*, 86 (4): 633–39.

Larkin, B. (2018), 'Promising Forms: The Political Aesthetics of Infrastructure', in N. Anand, A. Gupta and H. Appel (eds), *The Promise of Infrastructure*, Durham, NC: Duke University Press.

Lauterbach, K. (2016), 'Religious Entrepreneurs in Ghana', in Ute Röschenthaler and Dorothea Schulz (eds), *Cultural Entrepreneurship in Africa*, 19–36, London: Routledge.

Lefebvre, H. (1996), *Writings on Cities*, Oxford: Blackwell.

Lefebvre, H. (2000), *Everyday Life in the Modern World*, London: Routledge.

Lefebvre, H. (2003), *The Urban Revolution*, Minneapolis: University of Minnesota Press.

Lefebvre, H. (2014), 'Dissolving City, Planetary Metamorphosis', *Environment and Planning D: Society and Space*, 32 (2): 203–5.

Lemanski, C. (2019), 'Infrastructural Citizenship: Spaces of Living in Cape Town, South Africa', in C. Lemanski (ed.), *Citizenship and Infrastructure: Practices and Identities of Citizens and the State*, London: Routledge.

Lemanski, C. (2020), 'Infrastructural Citizenship: (De)Constructing State–Society Relations', *International Development Planning Review*, 42 (2): 115–25.

Lentz, C. (2016), 'African Middle Classes: Lessons from Transnational Studies and a Research Agenda', in H. Melber (ed.), *The Rise of Africa's Middle Class*, 17–53, London: Zed Books.

Leutloff-Grandits, C., Peleikis, A. and Thelen, T. (2009), *Social Security in Religious Networks: Anthropological Perspectives on New Risks and Ambivalences*, Oxford: Berghahn Books.

Levine, S. and Ross, F. (2002), 'Perceptions of and Attitudes to HIV/AIDS among Young Adults in Cape Town', *Social Dynamics*, 28 (1): 89–108.

Levitt, P. and Merry S. (2009), 'Vernacularization on the Ground: Local Uses of Global Women's Rights in Peru, China, India and the United States', *Global Networks*, 9 (4): 441–61.

Ley, D. and Martin, R. B. (1993), 'Gentrification as Secularization: The Status of Religious Belief in the Post-Industrial City', *Social Compass*, 40 (2): 217–32.

Livsey, T. (2017), *Nigeria's University Age: Reframing Decolonisation and Development*, London: Palgrave Macmillan.

Loimeier, R. (2007), 'Perceptions of Marginalization: Muslims in Contemporary Tanzania', in Benjamin F. Soares and René Otayek (eds), *Islam and Muslim Politics in Africa*, 137–56. New York: Palgrave Macmillan.

Lupala, J. M. (2002), 'Urban Types in Rapidly Urbanising Cities: Analysis of Formal and Informal Settlements in Dar es Salaam', PhD diss., KTH Royal Institute of Technology.

Lupala, J. and Bhayo S. A. (2014), 'Building Densification as a Strategy for Urban Spatial Sustainability: Analysis of Inner-City Neighbourhoods of Dar es Salaam, Tanzania', *Global Journal of Human–Social Science*: B, 14 (8): 29–44.

Mabin, A., Butcher, S. and Bloch R. (2013), 'Peripheries, Suburbanisms, and Change in Sub-Saharan Africa', *Social Dynamics*, 39 (2): 167–90.

MacIntyre, A. ([1981] 2007), *After Virtue: A Study in Moral Theory*, Notre Dame: University of Notre Dame Press.

Magina, F. B. (2016), 'Housing Market in Redeveloping Inner-City Areas in Dar es Salaam: Supply Dynamics and Their Effects on the Urban Fabric', PhD diss., Technische Universität Dortmund.

Mahmood, S. (2011), *Politics of Piety: The Islamic Revival and the Feminist Subject*, Princeton, NJ: Princeton University Press.

Malefakis, A. (2019), *Tanzania's Informal Economy: The Micro-Politics of Street Vending*, London: Zed.

Manglos, N. D. (2010), 'Born Again in Balaka: Pentecostal Versus Catholic Narratives of Religious Transformation in Rural Malawi', *Sociology of Religion*, 71 (4): 409–31.

Marsden, M. and Retsikas, K. (2013), 'Introduction', in M. Marsden and K. Retsikas (eds), *Articulating Islam: Anthropological Approaches to Muslim Worlds*, 1–32, New York: Springer.

Marshall. R. (1991), 'Power in the Name of Jesus', *Review of African Political Economy*, 18 (52): 21–37.

Marshall, R. (2009), *Political Spiritualities. The Pentecostal Revolution in Nigeria*, Chicago: University of Chicago Press.

Marshall-Fratani, R. (1998), 'Mediating the Global and Local in Nigerian Pentecostalism', *Journal of Religion in Africa*, 28 (3): 278–315.

Marshall, R. (2014), '"Dealing with the Prince over Lagos": Pentecostal Arts of Citizenship', in M. Diouf and R. Fredericks (eds), *The Arts of Citizenship in African Cities: Africa Connects*, New York: Palgrave Macmillan.

Martin, D. (2002), *Pentecostalism: The World Their Parish*, Oxford: Blackwell.

Massey, D. (1992), 'Politics and Space/Time', *New Left Review*, 196: 65–84.

Mauss, M. ([1934] 1973), 'Techniques of the Body', *Economy and Society*, 2 (12): 70–88.

Maxwell, D. (2006), *African Gifts of the Spirit. Pentecostalism and the Rise of a Zimbabwean Transnational Religious Movement*, Oxford: James Currey.

Mbembe, A. (1992), 'Provisional Notes on the Postcolony', *Africa*, 62 (1): 3–37.

McAdams, D. (2006), *The Redemptive Self. Stories Americans Live By*, Oxford: Oxford University Press.

McDow, T. F. (2018), *Buying Time: Debt and Mobility in the Western Indian Ocean*, Athens: Ohio University Press.

McFarlane, C. (2018), 'Fragment Urbanism: Politics at the Margins of the City', *Environment and Planning D: Society and Space*, 36 (6): 1007–25.

McGuire, J. (2008), *Lived Religion: Faith and Practice in Everyday Life*, Oxford: Oxford University Press.

McLeod, H. (1996), *Piety and Poverty: Working-Class Religion in Berlin, London and New York 870–1914*, New York: Holmes and Meier.

Meiers, B. (2013), *Le Dieu de Maman Olangi. Ethnographie d'un combat spirituel transnational*, Louvain-la-Neuve: Academia-Bruylant.

Mekking, A. J. J. (2009), *The Global Built Environment as a Representation of Realities*, Leiden: Leiden University Press.

Merleau-Ponty, M. (2002), *Phenomenology of Perception*, London: Routledge.

Melly, C. (2010), 'Inside–Out Houses: Urban Belonging and Imagined Futures in Dakar, Senegal', *Comparative Studies in Society and History*, 52 (1): 37–65.

Melly, C. (2017), *Bottleneck: Moving, Building, and Belonging in an African City*, Chicago: University of Chicago Press.

Metzinger, T. (2003), *Being No One: The Self-Model Theory of Subjectivity*, Cambridge, MA: MIT Press.

Meyer, B. (1995), '"Delivered from the Powers of Darkness." Confessions of Satanic Riches in Christian Ghana', *Africa*, 65 (2): 236–55.

Meyer, B. (1998), 'Make a Complete Break with the Past: Memory and Postcolonial Modernity in Ghanaian Pentecostalist Discourse', *Journal of Religion in Africa*, 28 (3): 316–49.

Meyer, B. (1999), *Translating the Devil: Religion and Modernity among the Ewe in Ghana*, vol. 21, Edinburgh: Edinburgh University Press.

Meyer, B. (2002), 'Pentecostalism, Prosperity and Popular Cinema in Ghana', *Culture and Religion*, 3 (1): 67–87.

Meyer, B. (2004), '"Praise the Lord": Popular Cinema and Pentecostalite Style in Ghana's New Public Sphere', *American Ethnologist*, 31 (1): 92–110.

Meyer, B. (2010), 'Aesthetics of Persuasion: Global Christianity and Pentecostalism's Sensational Forms', *South Atlantic Quarterly*, 109 (4): 741–63.

Meyer, B. (2012), 'There is a Spirit in That Image: Mass-Produced Jesus Pictures and Protestant-Pentecostal Animation in Ghana', in D. Houtman and B. Meyer (eds), *Things: Religion and the Question of Materiality*, 296–320, New York: Fordham University Press.

Meyer, B. (2013), 'Lessons from "Global Prayers": How Religion Takes Place in the City', in J. Becker, K. Klingan, S. Lanz and K. Wildner (eds), *Global Prayers: Contemporary Manifestations of the Religious in the City*, 590–9, Zürich: Lars Müller.

Meyer, B. and Sounaye, A. (2017), 'Introduction: Sermon in the City: Christian and Islamic Preaching in West Africa', *Journal of Religion in Africa*, 47 (1): 1–8.

Mian, N. (2008), 'Prophets-for-Profits: Redevelopment and the Altering Urban Religious Landscape', *Urban Studies*, 45 (10): 2143–61.

Millington, G. (2016), 'The Cosmopolitan Contradictions of Planetary Urbanization', *British Journal of Sociology*, 67 (3): 476–96.

Miyazaki, H. (2006), *The Method of Hope: Anthropology, Philosophy, and Fijian Knowledge*, Stanford, CA: Stanford University Press.

Mokoko-Gampiot, A. (2017), *Kimbanguism, An African Understanding of the Bible*, University Park: Pennsylvania State University Press.

Moshi, E. Z. M. (2009), 'Urban Transformation: Changing Building Types in Kariakoo, Dar es Salaam, Tanzania', PhD diss., Oslo School of Art and Design.

Msoka, C. T. and Ackson, T. (2017), 'The Politics and Regulation of Street Trading in Dar es Salaam', in A. Brown (ed.), *Rebel Streets and the Informal Economy: Street Trade and the Law*, 183–204, Abingdon: Routledge.

Ndaluka, T. (2012), *Religious Discourse, Social Cohesion and Conflict: Muslim–Christian Relations in Tanzania*, Münster: LIT.

Nielsen, M., Sumich, J. and Bertelsen, B. E. (2021), 'Enclaving: Spatial Detachment as an Aesthetics of Imagination in an Urban Sub-Saharan African Context', *Urban Studies*, 58 (5): 881–902.

Noret, J. (2004), 'De la conversion au basculement de la place des morts', *Politique africaine*, 93 (1): 143–55.

Nuttall, S. and Mbembe, A., eds (2008), *Johannesburg: The Elusive Metropolis*, Durham, NC: Duke University Press.

Nyamnjoh, F. B. and Jua. N. B. (2002), 'African Universities in Crisis and the Promotion of a Democratic Culture: The Political Economy of Violence in African Educational Systems', *African Studies Review*, 45 (2): 1–26.

Obadare, E. (2006), 'Playing Politics with the Mobile Phone in Nigeria: Civil Society, Big Business and the State', *Review of African Political Economy*, 33 (107): 93–111.

Obadare. E. (2018), *Pentecostal Republic: Religion and the Struggle for State Power in Nigeria*, London: Zed Books.

Obono, O and Obono, K. (2012), 'Ajala Travel: Mobility and Connections as Forms of Social Capital in Nigerian Society', in M. de Bruijn, and R. van Dijk (eds), *The Social Life of Connectivity in Africa*, 227–41, New York: Palgrave Macmillan.

Ogbu, O. (2014), 'Is Nigeria a Secular State? Law, Human Rights and Religion in Context', *The Transnational Human Rights Review*, 1: 135–78.

Ogungbile, D. O. (2011), 'Tradition and Response: Islam and Muslim Societies in a Nigerian City', in Tugrul Keskin (ed.), *The Sociology of Islam: Secularism, Economy and Politics*, 319–41, Reading: Ithaca Press.

Ojo, M. S. (2007), 'Pentecostal Movements, Islam and the Contest for Public Space in Northern Nigeria', *Islam and Christian – Muslim Relations*, 18 (2): 175–88.

Okeowo, A. (2013), 'A Safer Waterfront in Lagos, If You Can Afford It', *The New Yorker*. Available online: http://www.newyorker.com/business/currency/a-safer-waterfront-in-lagos-if-youcan-afford-it (accessed April 2022).

Olenmark, E. and Westerberg, U. (1973), *Tanzania: Kariakoo, a Residential Area in Dar es Salaam*, Lund: University of Lund Department of Architecture.

Olivier de Sardan, J. P. (2014), 'The Delivery State in Africa: Interface Bureaucrats, Professional Cultures and the Bureaucratic Mode of Governance', in Thomas Bierschenk and Jean-Pierre Olivier de Sardan (eds), *States at Work: Dynamics of African Bureaucracies*, 399–429, Leiden: Brill.

Olivier de Sardan, J. P. (2014), *States at Work: Dynamics of African Bureaucracies*, Leiden: Brill.

Olukoya. D. (2003), *Dominion Prosperity*, Lagos, Nigeria: Battle Cry Books.

Olupona, J. (2011), *City of 201 Gods: Ilé-Ifè in Time, Space, and the Imagination*, Berkeley: University of California Press.

Ong, A. (2006), *Neoliberalism as Exception: Mutations in Citizenship and Sovereignty*, Durham, NC: Duke University Press.

Onyinah, O. (2004), 'Contemporary "Witchdemonology" in Africa', *International Review of Mission*, 93 (370/371): 330–45.

Orsi, R. (1999), 'Introduction: Crossing the City Line', in R. Orsi (ed.), *Gods of the City*, 1–78, Bloomington: Indiana University Press.

Osella, F. and Soares, B. (2020), 'Religiosity and Its Others: Lived Islam in West Africa and South India', *Social Anthropology*, 28 (2): 466–81.

Osinulu, A. (2014), 'The Road to Redemption: Performing Pentecostal Citizenship in Lagos', in *The Arts of Citizenship in African Cities: Infrastructures and Spaces of Belonging*, 115–32, New York: Palgrave Macmillan.

Park, R., Burgess, E., McKenzie, R. and Wirth, L. (1925), 'The City', University of Chicago Studies in Urban Sociology, Chicago: University of Chicago Press.

Parnell, S. and Robinson, J. (2012), '(Re)theorizing Cities from the Global South: Looking Beyond Neoliberalism', *Urban Geography*, 33 (4): 593–617.

Peck, J., Theodore, N. and Brenner, N. (2013), 'Neoliberal Urbanism Redux?', *International Journal of Urban and Regional Research*, 37 (3): 1091–9.

Peña, E. A. (2011), *Performing Piety Making Space Sacred with the Virgin of Guadalupe*, Berkeley: University of California Press.

Perrazone, S. (2019), ' "Shouldn't You Be Teaching Me?" State Mimicry in the Congo', *International Political Sociology*, 13 (2): 161–80.

Pieterse, E. (2008), *City Futures: Confronting the Crisis of Urban Development*, London: Zed Books.

Pieterse, E. (2011), 'Grasping the Unknowable: Coming to Grips with African Urbanisms', *Social Dynamics*, 37 (1): 5–23.

Piot, C. (2010), *'Nostalgia for the Future: West Africa after the Cold War'*, Chicago: University of Chicago Press.

Popoola, S., Atayero, A., Badejo, J., Odukoya, J., Omole, D. and Ajayi P. (2018), 'Datasets on Demographic Trends in Enrollment into Undergraduate Engineering Programs at Covenant University, Nigeria', *Data in Brief*, 18: 47–59.

Premawardhana, D. (2018), *Faith in Flux: Pentecostalism and Mobility in Rural Mozambique*, Philadelphia: University of Pennsylvania Press.

Pype, K. (2010), 'Of Fools and False Pastors. Tricksters in Kinshasa's TV Fiction', *Visual Anthropology*, 23 (2): 115–35.

Pype, K. (2012), *The Making of the Pentecostal Melodrama: Religion, Media, and Gender in Kinshasa*, Oxford: Berghahn Books.

Pype, K. (2015), 'Geographies of the Occult and the Divine', in C. Währisch-Oblau and H. Wrogemann (eds), *Witchcraft, Demons and Deliverance. A Global Conversation on Intercultural Challenge*, 69–92, Zürich: LIT.

Pype, K. (2016), '(Not) Talking like a Motorola: Practices of Masking and Unmasking in Kinshasa's Mobile Phone Culture', *Journal of the Royal Anthropological Institute*, 22 (3): 633–53.
Pype, K. (2017), 'Branhamist Kindoki: Ethnographic Notes on Connectivity, Technology, and Urban Witchcraft in Contemporary Kinshasa', in K. Rio, et al. (eds), *Pentecostalism and Witchcraft Spiritual Warfare in Africa and Melanesia*, London: Palgrave Macmillan.
Rasing, T. (1999), 'Globalization and the Making of Consumers. Zambian Kitchen Parties', in R. Fardon, W. van Binsbergen and R. van Dijk (eds), *Modernity on a Shoestring: Dimensions of Globalization, Consumption and Development in Africa and Beyond*, 227–46, Leiden: EIDOS.
Reichmuth, S. (1996), 'Education and the Growth of Religious Associations among Yoruba Muslims: The Ansar-Ud-Deen Society of Nigeria', *Journal of Religion in Africa*, 26 (4): 365–405.
Reinhardt, B. (2018), 'Waiting for God in Ghana: The Chronotopes of a Prayer Mountain', in M. K. Janeja and A. Bandak (eds), *Ethnographies of Waiting: Doubt, Hope and Uncertainty*, 113–37, London: Bloomsbury.
Reno, W. (2006), 'Congo: From State Collapse to "Absolutism", to State Failure', *Third World Quarterly*, 27 (1): 43–56.
Rey, J. (2015), 'Missing Prosperity: Economies of Blessing in Ghana and the Diaspora', in A. Heuser (ed.), *Pastures of Plenty: Tracing Religio-Scapes of Prosperity Gospel in Africa and Beyond*, 339–53, Frankfurt am Main: Peter Lang.
Rey, T. (2007), *Bourdieu on Religion: Imposing Faith and Legitimacy*. London: Routledge.
Rey, T. and Stepick, A. (2015), *Crossing the Water and Keeping the Faith: Haitan Religion in Miami*, New York: New York University Press.
Riccio, B. (2003), 'L'urbanisation mouride et les migrations transnationales sénégalaises' *Islam et villes en Afrique au sud du Sahara: Entre soufisme et fondamentalisme*, 359–75, Paris: Karthala.
Rich, J. (2019), *An African Jerusalem Found and Lost: Ecumenical Churches, Foreign Aid, and the Kimbanguist Church in the Democratic Republic of Congo, 1965–1974*, presentation at the Greater New York Area African History Workshop, Princeton University.
Richey, L. A. (2012), 'Counselling Citizens and Producing Patronage: AIDS Treatment in South African and Ugandan Clinics', *Development and Change*, 43 (4): 823–45.
Robbins, J. (2004), 'The Globalization of Pentecostal and Charismatic Christianity', *Annual Review of Anthropology*, 33: 117–43.
Robbins, J. (2007), 'Continuity Thinking and the Problem of Christian Culture: Belief, Time, and the Anthropology of Christianity', *Current Anthropology*, 48 (1): 5–38.
Robbins, J. (2010), 'Anthropology, Pentecostalism, and the New Paul: Conversion, Event, and Social Transformation', *South Atlantic Quarterly*, 109 (4): 633–52.
Robbins, J. (2014), 'The Anthropology of Christianity: Unity, Diversity, New Directions: An Introduction to Supplement 10', *Current anthropology: A World Journal of the Sciences of Man*, 10: 157–71.
Robbins, J. (2019), 'Pentecostalism and Forms of Individualism', in A. Eriksen, R. L. Blanes and M. MacCarthy (eds), *Going to Pentecost: An Experimental Approach to Studies in Pentecostalism*, 187–92, New York: Berghahn.
Robins, S. (2014), 'Poo Wars as Matter Out of Place: "Toilets for Africa" in Cape Town', *Anthropology Today*, 30 (1): 1–3.
Robinson, D. (1999), 'The Murids: Surveillance and Collaboration', *Journal of African History*, 40 (2): 193–213.

Robinson, J. (2006), *Ordinary Cities: Between Modernity and Development*, London: Routledge.

Robinson, J. (2016), 'Thinking Cities through Elsewhere: Comparative Tactics for a More Global Urban Studies', *Progress in Human Geography*, 40 (1): 3–29.

Ross, E. (1995), 'Touba: A Spiritual Metropolis in the Modern World', *Canadian Journal of African Studies*, 29 (2): 222–59.

Ross, A. A. G. (2014), *Mixed Emotions: Beyond Fear and Hatred in International Conflict*, Chicago: University of Chicago Press.

Roy, A. (2005), 'Urban Informality: Toward an Epistemology of Planning', *Journal of the American Planning Association*, 71 (2): 147–58.

Rüpke, J. (2020), *Urban Religion: A Historical Approach to Urban Growth and Religious Change*, Berlin: de Gruyter.

Sarró, R. (2015), 'Hope, Margin, Example: The Kimbanguist Diaspora in Lisbon', in J. Garnett and S. L. Hausner (eds), *Religion in Diaspora. Migration, Diasporas and Citizenship*, 226–44, London: Palgrave Macmillan.

Sassen, S. (2007), *Sociology of Globalization*, New York: W. W. Norton.

Savage, M., Warde, A. and Ward, K. (2003), *Urban Sociology, Capitalism and Modernity*, Basingstoke: Palgrave Macmillan.

Sawyer, L. (2014), 'Piecemeal Urbanisation at the Peripheries of Lagos', *African Studies*, 73 (2): 271–89.

Schieffelin, E. L. (1985), 'Performance and the Cultural Construction of Reality', *American Ethnologist*, 12 (4): 707–24.

Schieffelin, Edward L. (2013), 'Construction of Reality', *The Anthropology of Performance: A Reader*, Oxford: Wiley-Blackwell, 107–23.

Schielke, S. (2009), 'Being Good in Ramadan: Ambivalence, Fragmentation, and the Moral Self in the Lives of Young Egyptians', *Journal of the Royal Anthropological Institute*, 15: S24–S40.

Schielke, S. (2015), *Egypt in the Future Tense: Hope, Frustration, and Ambivalence before and after 2011*, Bloomington: Indiana University Press.

Schielke, S. (2018), 'Islam', in F. Stein, S. Lazar, M. Candea, H. Diemberger, J. Robbins, A. Sanchez and R. Stasch (eds), *The Cambridge Encyclopedia of Anthropology*. Available online: http://doi.org/10.29164/18islam (accessed 16 August 2021).

Scott, J. C. (1976), *The Moral Economy of the Peasant: Rebellion and Subsistence in Southeast Asia*, New Haven, CT: Yale University Press.

Shmaryahu-Yeshurun, Y. and Ben-Porat, G. (2021), 'For the Benefit of All? State-Led Gentrification in a Contested City', *Urban Studies*, 58 (13): 2605–22.

Simone, A. (2001), 'On the Worlding of African Cities', *African Studies Review*, 44 (2): 15–41.

Simone, A. (2004), *For the City Yet to Come: Changing African Life in Four Cities*, Durham, NC: Duke University Press.

Simone, A. (2007), 'Sacral Spaces in Two West African Cities', in P. Ahluwahlia, L. Bethlehem and R. Ginio (eds), *Violence and Non-Violence in Africa*, 63–83, London: Routledge.

Simone, A. (2010), *City Life from Jakarta to Dakar: Movements at the Crossroads*, Abingdon: Routledge.

Simone, A. (2011), 'The Politics of Urban Intersection: Materials, Affect, Bodies', in G. Bridge and S. Watson (eds), *The New Blackwell Companion to the City*, 357–66, Oxford: Wiley Blackwell.

Simone, A. (2013), 'Religiously Urban and Faith in the City: Reflections on the Movements of the Youth in Central Africa and Southeast Asia', in J. Becker, K. Klingan, S. Lanz and K. Wildner (eds), *Global Prayers: Contemporary Manifestations of the Religious in the City*, 156–63, Zürich: Lars Müller.
Simone, A. (2014), '"We Are Here Alone": The Ironic Potentials and Vulnerabilities of Mixed (Up) Districts in Central Jakarta', *International Journal of Urban and Regional Research*, 38 (4): 1509–24.
Simone, A. (2018), *Improvised Lives: Rhythms of Endurance in an Urban South*, Cambridge: Polity Press.
Simone, A. and Pieterse, E. (2017), *New Urban Worlds: Inhabiting Dissonant Times*, Cambridge: Polity Press.
Simone, A. and Rao V. (2021), 'Counting the Uncountable: Revisiting Urban Majorities', *Public Culture*, 33 (2): 151–60.
Simpson, A. (1998), 'Memory and Becoming Chosen Other: Fundamentalist Elite-Making in a Zambian Catholic Mission School', in Richard Werbner (ed.), *Memory and the Postcolony: African Anthropology and the Critique of Power*, 209–28, London: Zed Books.
Sivan, E. (1995), 'The Enclave Culture', in Martin E. Marty and R. Scott Appleby (eds.), *Fundamentalisms Comprehended* 5, 11–68, Chicago: University of Chicago Press.
Smit, W. (2020), 'The Challenge of COVID-19 in African Cities: An Urgent Call for Informal Settlement Upgrading, *Cities & Health*, 1–3. Available online: https://doi.org/10.1080/23748834.2020.1816757.
Smith, D. J. (2003), 'Patronage, per diems and "the Workshop Mentality"', *World Development*, 31 (4): 703–15.
Smith, N. (1987), 'Gentrification and the Rent Gap', *Annals of the Association of American Geographers*, 77 (3): 462–5.
Sow, D., Oumar, S. and Gomis, J. (2020), 'Dynamiques spatiales et problématique de gouvernance urbaine du modèle de Touba (Sénégal)', *Environmental and Water Sciences, Public Health and Territorial Intelligence*, 4 (1): 345–54.
Stambach, A. (2006), 'Revising a Four-Square Model of a Complicated Whole: On the Cultural Politics of Religion and Education', *Social Analysis*, 50 (3): 1–18.
Stambach, A. (2010a), 'Education, Religion, and Anthropology in Africa', *Annual Review of Anthropology*, 39: 361–79.
Stambach, A. (2010b), *Faith in Schools: Religion, Education and American Evangelicals in East Africa*, Stanford, CA: Stanford University Press.
Steiler, I. (2018), "What's in a Word? The Conceptual Politics of 'Informal' Street Trade in Dar es Salaam", Articulo, *Journal of Urban Research* [Online], vols. 17–18. DOI: https://doi.org/10.4000/articulo.3376
Steinforth, Arne S. (2009), *Troubled Minds: On the Cultural Construction of Mental Disorder and Normality in Southern Malawi*, Frankfurt am Main: Peter Lang.
Stevenson, D., Dunn, K., Possamai A. and Piracha A. (2010), 'Religious Belief across "Post-Secular" Sydney: The Multiple Trends in (De) Secularisation', *Australian Geographer*, 41 (3): 323–50.
Stockmans, J. and Büscher, K. (2017), 'A Spatial Reading of Urban Political-Religious Conflict: Contested Urban Landscapes in Addis Ababa, Ethiopia', *Journal of Modern African Studies*, 55 (1): 79–104.
Stoler, A. L. (2008), 'Imperial Debris', *Cultural Anthropology*, 23 (2): 191–219.

Streule, M., Karaman, O., Sawyer, L. and Schmid C. (2020), 'Popular Urbanization: Conceptualizing Urbanization Processes Beyond Informality', *International Journal of Urban and Regional Research*, 44 (4): 652-72.

Sturm, T. and Albrecht T. (2020) 'Constituent Covid-19 Apocalypses: Contagious Conspiracism, 5G, and Viral Vaccinations', *Anthropology and Medicine*, 28 (1): 122-39. DOI: 10.1080/13648470.2020.1833684.

Sullivan, N. (2011), 'Mediating Abundance and Scarcity: Implementing an HIV/AIDS-Targeted Project within a Government Hospital in Tanzania', *Medical Anthropology* 30 (2): 202-21.

Swidler, A. and Watkins, S. C. (2009), '"Teach a Man to Fish": The Sustainability Doctrine and Its Social Consequences', *World Development*, 37 (7): 1182-96.

Tall, S. M. (1998), 'Un instrument financier pour les commerçants et émigrés mourides de l'axe Dakar-New-York: Kara International Foreign Money Exchange', in L. Harding, L. Marfaing and M. Sow (eds), *Les opérateurs économiques au Sénégal*, 73-90, Hamburg: LIT Verlag.

Taussig M. (2004), *My Cocaine Museum*, London: University of Chicago Press.

ter Haar, G. and Ellis S. (2006), 'The Role of Religion in Development: Towards a New Relationship Between the European Union and Africa', *European Journal of Development Research*, 18 (3): 351-67.

ter Haar, G. (2009), *How God Became African: African Spirituality and Western Secular Thought*, Philadelphia: University of Pennsylvania Press.

ter Haar, G. (2011), 'Religion and Development: Introducing a New Debate', in G. ter Haar and J. D. Wolfensohn (eds), *Religion and Development: Ways of Transforming the World*, London: Hurst.

Thomas, S. M. (2005), *The Global Resurgence of Religion and the Transformation of International Relations: The Struggle for the Soul of the Twenty-First Century*, New York: Palgrave Macmillan.

Thompson, E. P. (1971), 'The Moral Economy of the English Crowd in the Eighteenth Century', *Past and Present*, 50: 76-136.

Till, K. E. (2012), 'Wounded Cities: Memory-Work and a Place-Based Ethics of Care', *Political Geography*, 31 (1): 3-14.

Titeca, K., De Herdt, T. and Wagemakers, I. (2013), 'God and Caesar in the Democratic Republic of Congo: Negotiating Church–State Relations through the Management of School Fees in Kinshasa's Catholic Schools', *Review of African Political Economy*, 40 (135): 116-31.

Tonkiss, F. (2013), *Cities by Design: The Social Life of Urban Forms*, Cambridge: Polity Press.

Trefon, T. (2009), 'Hinges and Fringes: Conceptualizing the Periurban in Central Africa', in F. Locatelli and P. Nugent (eds), *Competing Claims on Urban Spaces*, 15-36, Leiden: Brill.

Trefon, T. (2011), *Congo Masquerade: The Political Culture of Aid Inefficiency and Reform Failure*, London: Zed.

Trovolla, U. (2015), 'Competing Prayers: The Making of a Nigerian Urban Landscape', *Anthropology Southern Africa*, 38 (3-4): 302-13.

Uberoi, J. P. S. (2002), *The European Modernity: Science, Truth and Method*, Delhi: Oxford University Press.

Ukah, A. (2004), 'The Redeemed Christian Church of God (RCCG), Nigeria: Local Identities and Global Processes in African Pentecostalism', PhD diss., University of Bayreuth.

Ukah, A. (2011), 'God Unlimited: Economic Transformations of Contemporary Nigerian Pentecostalism', in L. Obadia and D. C. Wood (eds), *Economics of Religion: Anthropological Approaches*, 187–216, London: Emerald.

Ukah, A (2012), 'Religion and Globalization', in Elias Kifon Bongmba (ed.), *The Wiley-Blackwell Companion to Africa Religions*, 503–14, New York: Blackwell.

Ukah, A (2013a), 'Prosperity Theology", in A. Butticci (ed.), *Na God. Aesthetics of African Charismatic Power*, 77–9, Padova: Grafiche Turato Edizioni.

Ukah, A. (2013b), 'Redeeming Urban Spaces: The Ambivalences of Building a Pentecostal City in Lagos, Nigeria', in J. Becker, K. Klingan, S. Lanz and K. Wildner (eds), *Global Prayers: Contemporary Manifestations of the Religious in the City*, 178–97, Zürich: Lars Müller.

Ukah, A. (2016a), 'Building God's City: The Political Economy of Prayer Camps in Nigeria', *International Journal of Urban and Regional Research*, 40 (3): 524–40.

Ukah, A. (2016b), 'Re-Imagining the Religious Fields: The Rhetoric of Nigerian Pentecostal Pastors in South Africa', in Magnus Echtler and Asonzeh Ukah (eds), *Bourdieu in Africa: Exploring the Dynamics of Religious Fields*, 70–95, Leiden: Brill.

Urciuoli, E. and Rüpke, J. (2018), 'Urban Religion in Mediterranean Antiquity: Relocating Religious Change', *Mythos*, 12: 117–35.

UNFPA (2009), *Guidelines for Engaging Faith-Based Organizations (FBOs) as Agents of Change*, New York: The United Nations Population Fund.

UN Habitat (2007), *Zambia: Lusaka Urban Profile*, Nairobi: UNON.

Van Binsbergen, W. (1981), *Religious Change in Zambia. Exploratory Studies*, London: Kegan Paul International.

Van Binsbergen, W. (1999), 'Mary's Room: A Case Study on Becoming a Consumer in Francistown, Botswana', in R. Fardon, W. van Binsbergen and R. van Dijk (eds), *Modernity on a Shoestring. Dimensions of Globalization, Consumption and Development in Africa and Beyond*, 179–206, Leiden: EIDOS.

Vandermeulen, R., Patterson, A. and Burchardt, M. (2013), 'HIV Activism, Framing and Identity Formation in Mozambique's *Equipas de Vida*', *Canadian Journal of African Studies*, 47 (2): 249–72.

Van der Veer, P., ed. (1996), *Conversion to Modernity: The Globalization of Christianity*, London: Routledge.

Van der Veer, P. (2001), *Imperial Encounters: Religion and Modernity in India and Great Britain*, Princeton, NJ: Princeton University Press.

Van der Veer, P. (2013), 'Urban Aspirations in Mumbai and Singapore', in I. Becci, M. Burchardt and J. Casanova (eds), *Topographies of Faith*, 61–71, Leiden: Brill.

Van der Veer, P. (2015), 'Introduction: Urban Theory, Asia, and Religion', in P. Van der Veer (ed.), *Handbook of Religion and the AsianCity: Aspiration and Urbanization in the Twenty-First Century*, 1–17, Oakland: University of California Press.

Van Dijk, R. (2001), 'Time and Transcultural Practices of the Self in the Ghanian Pentecostal Diaspora', in A. Corten and R. Marshall-Fratini (eds), *Between Babel and Pentecost: Transnational Pentecostalism in Africa and Latin America*, 216–34, Bloomington: Indiana University Press.

Van Dijk, R. (2002), 'Religion, Reciprocity and Restructuring Family Responsibility in the Ghanaian Pentecostal Diaspora', in D. Bryceson and U. Vuorela (eds), *The Transnational Family: New European Frontiers and Global Network*, 173–96, London: Bloomsbury.

Van Dijk, R. (2010), 'Social Catapulting and the Spirit of Entrepreneurialism', in G. Hüwelmeier and K. Krause (eds), *Traveling Spirits: Migrants, Markets and Mobilities*, 101–17, New York: Routledge.

Van Dijk, R. (2012), 'Pentecostalism and Post-Development: Exploring Religion as a Developmental Ideology in Ghanaian Migrant Communities', in D. Freeman (ed.), *Pentecostalism and Development: Churches, NGOs and Social Change in Africa*, 87–108, London: Palgrave Macmillan.

Vasarhelyi, E. C. (2013), 'Touba', documentary, produced by Little monster Films1hour 23minutes.

Vásquez, M. A. (2009), 'The Global Portability of Pneumatic Christianity: Comparing African and Latin American Pentecostalisms', *African Studies*, 68 (2): 273–86.

Vásquez, M. A. and Garbin, D. (2016), 'Globalization', in M. Stausberg and S. Engler (eds), *The Oxford Handbook of the Study of Religion*, 684–701, Abingdon, Oxfordshire: Oxford University Press.

Vásquez, M. A. and Marquardt M. F. (2003), *Globalizing the Sacred: Religion Across the Americas*, New Brunswick, NJ: Rutgers University Press.

Velthuis, K. and Spennemann, D. H. R. (2007), 'The Future of Defunct Religious Buildings: Dutch Approaches to Their Adaptive Reuse', *Cultural Trends*, 16 (1): 43–66.

Verschaffel, B. (2012), '(Sacred) Places Are Made of Time: Observations on the Persistence of the Sacred in Categorizing Space in Modernity', in Thomas Coomans (ed.), *Loci Sacri: Understanding Sacred Places*, Leuven: Leuven University Press.

Vokes, R. and Pype K. (2018), 'Chronotopes of Media in Sub-Saharan Africa', *Ethnos* 83 (2): 207–17.

Von Schnitzler, A. (2008), 'Citizenship Prepaid: Water, Calculability, and Techno-Politics in South Africa', *Journal of Southern African Studies*, 34 (4): 899–917.

Vukonic, B. (1998), 'Religious Tourism: Economic Value or an Empty Box?' *Zagreb International Review of Economics and Business*, 1 (1): 83–94.

Wachsmuth, D. (2014), 'City as Ideology: Reconciling the Explosion of the City Form with the Tenacity of the City Concept', *Environment and Planning D: Society and Space*, 32 (1): 75–90.

Wacquant, L. (2016), 'Revisiting Territories of Relegation: Class, Ethnicity and State in the Making of Advanced Marginality', *Urban Studies*, 53 (6): 1077–88.

Warf, B. (2003), 'Splintering Urbanism: Networked Infrastructures, Technological Mobilities, and the Urban Condition', *Annals of the Association of American Geographers*, 93 (1): 246–7.

Warikobo, N. (2014), *The Charismatic City and the Public Resurgence of Religion: A Pentecostal Social Ethics of Cosmopolitan Urban Life*, New York: Palgrave Macmillan.

Weng, H. W. (2017), 'Consumer Space as Political Space: Liquid Islamism in Malaysia and Indonesia', in E. Hansson and M. L. Weiss (eds), *Political Participation in Asia: Defining and Deploying Political Space*, 112–30, London: Routledge.

Werbner, P. (1996), 'Fun Spaces: On Identity and Social Empowerment Among British Pakistanis', *Theory, Culture and Society*, 13 (4): 53–79.

Werbner, P. (2002), *Imagined Diasporas among Manchester Muslims*, Santa Fe: School of American Research Press.

White, L. (2000), *Speaking with Vampires. Rumor and History in Colonial Africa*, Berkeley: University of California Press.

Wiig, A. and Silver, J. (2019), 'Turbulent Presents, Precarious Futures: Urbanization and the Deployment of Global Infrastructure', *Regional Studies*, 53 (6): 912–23.

Williams, O. and Fagite, K. (2017), 'Life in a Religious Space: The Case of Gospel Town, Ibadan', IFRA-Nigeria. Available online: http://www.ifra-nigeria.org/publications/e-papers/227-williams-oluwaseun-fagite-kayode-2017-life-in-a-religious-space-the-case-of-gospel-town-ibadan (accessed 5 January 2021).

Wodon, Q. (2015), *The Economics of Faith-Based Service Delivery: Education and Health in Sub-Saharan Africa*, London: Palgrave Macmillan.

Zambian Watchdog (2011), 'Southern Province Minister Confesses to Practising Satanism', 13 December 2011. Available online: https://www.zambiawatchdog.com/southern-province-minister-confesses-to-practising-satanism/ (accessed 25 June 2021).

Žižek, S. (1994), *Mapping Ideology,* London: Verso.

Zukin, S. (1995), *The Cultures of Cities*, Oxford: Blackwell.

Other Sources: (from chapter 9)

https://fuo.edu.ng/ (accessed April 2021).

https://www.howwemadeitinafrica.com/nigerias-middle-class-how-we-live-and-what-we-want-from-life/12563/ (accessed April 2021).

https://run.edu.ng (accessed April 2021).

St. Mary's Mirror, A Quarterly Magazine for St. Mary's International Schools (2002–3). *Quality Education in Tanzania, a Vision Come True. Issue No. 001, Academic Year 2002–03*, Dar es Salaam: Professional Publications.

INDEX

ancestors, ancestrality 11, 38, 40, 44, 51, 52, 95, 97, 99, 100, 132, 139, 150
assemblage(s) 9, 14, 31, 37, 41, 54, 62, 70, 186

body, embodiment 12, 19, 24, 28, 32–3, 41, 42, 44, 53, 77, 84, 124, 137, 139, 141, 145, 147, 150, 153, 158, 162, 168, 175, 179, 180, 185–6
Bourdieu, Pierre 38, 40, 162

capital *see* money
capitalism *see* neoliberalism
Catholicism, Catholic Church 4, 6, 36–40, 42, 44, 46, 48, 39, 47–8, 55, 114, 178, 185
'Chrislam' (in Nigeria) 179, 181
Coleman, Simon 9, 41, 45, 83, 91, 100, 104, 110, 144, 166, 185
colonization, colonial (including missionary) 4, 22, 31, 38, 45, 46, 48, 55, 57, 80, 83–4, 100, 110, 145, 167, 196 n.4

De Boeck, Filip 4, 10, 21, 36, 46, 52, 53, 132, 192 n.8
Deeper Life Church 1, 2, 3, 4, 10, 93, 94, 178
development 2, 3, 4, 6, 10–13, 15, 16, 23, 32, 36, 37, 38, 40–4, 46–8, 49, 51, 53, 56–7, 61, 62, 64, 67–8, 69–70, 71, 91–2, 93, 94, 97–99, 100, 105, 108, 138, 140–2, 143, 144, 147, 148, 151, 160, 165
diaspora 14, 35, 36, 39, 46, 47, 50–1, 52, 75, 77, 86, 98, 110
donations and tithes *see* money

Eliade, Mircea 76, 85
enclave, enclaving 2, 3, 4, 7, 15, 16, 20, 21, 40–1, 45–6, 52, 53, 54, 107–8, 110–11, 113, 114, 118, 120, 125, 126, 144, 145–8, 153, 154, 159–62, 165–6, 168, 169, 173, 174, 179, 180–1, 188, 196 n.6
Engelke, Matthew 6, 43, 52, 67, 100, 171
everyday *see* present

Fashola, Babatunde 1, 2, 164, 180, 181, 198 n.3
FBO (Faith-based organization) and 'FBO-ization' 8, 13, 55–7, 60–70, 108, 114, 184, 193 nn.2, 3, 12, 16
finance, financial *see* money

Garbin, David 5, 36, 51, 71, 111, 115, 124, 160, 161, 185, 186
gender 61, 64, 138–9, 148, 151–3, 179, 180
and education 145, 150–2, 158–9, 179
gender mainstreaming 193 n.9
masculinity 23–5
women's roles 102–4
women's NGO 148
gentrification 15, 108, 110, 111–13, 125, 126

Harvey, D. 7, 111, 185
hierophany 52, *see also* Eliade
HIV/AIDS 11, 13, 55, 56, 57, 59–65, 69, 152, 184, 193 nn.10, 11, 12
holy *see* sacred

informal, informality, informalization 6, 14, 36, 46, 54, 57, 58, 89, 109, 113–14, 130, 183, 186
infrastructure, infrastructural 2, 6, 8–10, 12, 13, 14, 15, 16, 19–20, 21, 28, 29, 31, 33, 36–7, 45–6, 47, 49, 51, 52, 53–4, 57–8, 62, 71, 75, 82, 84, 107, 108, 109, 114, 121, 130, 138, 144, 152, 156, 161, 163, 168, 172–3, 184, 188
Islam, Muslim
  dress 22, 25–7, 29, 158
  and education 151–3, 158–62
  gender 151–3
  Islamophobia 28–9
  Mosque 4, 12, 21, 22, 25, 27–31, 32, 75, 76, 77, 79, 81–3, 118, 152, 159, 168
  rituals 21, 24, 26, 28, 30–1, 83, 84, 85–8, 152–3, 158–9
  Umma 146, 152, 153
  visibility 24–6

Kimbanguism, Kimbanguist
  bodily regime 50

colonization/colonial repression 48, 51
conflict 50
development 48–50, 51–3
and health 48–51
prophetism 35, 36, 37, 44, 51–3
relation with state 48–9, 50, 54
sacred space 51–2, 54, *see also* Nkamba
values 35, 49, 51
and witchcraft 35, 40, 50, 52

Lanz, Stephan, 5, 7, 8, 19, 10, 21, 22, 36, 37, 109, 111, 118, 146, 161, 165
Larkin, Brian 10, 19, 20, 21, 28, 107, 121
Lefebvre, Henri 5, 8, 10

mapping 6, 13, 14, 15, 36, 37, 47, 51, 56, 109, 115, 140, 185
Marshall, Ruth 38, 54, 56, 59, 60, 91, 104, 109, 110, 116, 133, 185
media (including digital media) 19, 30, 37, 41, 48, 60, 75, 87, 113, 134, 139, 140, 143, 158, 166–9, 172, 174, 176–7, 181, 185–6
Meyer, Birgit 2, 20, 21, 24, 27, 43, 56, 68, 77, 92, 100, 107, 125, 132, 140, 181, 195 n.6
modern, modernity 1, 3, 4, 5, 6, 8, 11, 12, 14, 15, 16, 23, 28, 32, 37, 41, 47, 51, 55, 76–7, 83, 91, 98–9, 100, 105, 108, 129–31, 138–42, 148, 154, 163, 165, 167, 172, 174, 180, 181, 186
money 4, 14, 15, 22, 25, 30, 32, 35–6, 41, 46–7, 49, 50–2, 61, 64, 77–80, 86–8, 94, 100, 103, 104, 188, 198, 111, 113, 131, 137, 140, 155, 156, 161, 185
moral economies 10–12, 13, 57, 71, 188
Mountain of Fire and Miracles Ministries (MFM) 10, 14–15, 40, 41, 45, 108, 109, 110, 111, 113–26, 143
Mouride, Mouridism
  Bamba, Amadou 75, 78, 79, 80, 83, 85, 85, 87, 88, 194 nn.4, 8, 17
  baraka 78, 79, 82, 85, 88
  and colonization 80, 83–4
  diaspora 75, 77, 86
  La Grande Mosquée 76, 77, 79, 81, 82–3, 84, 86, 87, 88
  Le Grand Magal pilgrimage 14, 75–7, 80, 81, 82, 83, 84, 85–8, 194 n.12
  Marabout-Talibé relations 78–9, 80
  marabout politics 79–82
  media 75, 87

money/donations 77, 78, 79–80, 81, 86–7, 88, *see also* money
  relation with Senegalese state 76, 78, 81, 84–5, 87
  Touba 13–14, 54, 75–82, 84, 85–9, 186, 194 nn.1, 4

neoliberal, neoliberalism 3, 7, 8, 9, 11, 20, 21, 33, 44, 57, 107, 110, 111, 125, 126, 146, 163, 181–2
Nkamba 13, 35, 36, 37, 48, 50, 51–3, 186

Olangi Church (Ministère du Combat Spirituel) 36, 37, 39, 40–3, 45
Orsi, R. 6, 77, 142

Pentecostalism, Pentecostal
  aspiration and ambition 11, 56, 57–60, 71, 167–9, 170, 171, 174, 182, 188
  born again 2, 4, 38, 41, 43, 44, 66, 67, 69, 100, 110, 115, 135, 180, *see also* conversion
  citizen, citizenship 10, 15, 38, 40–3, 44, 56–8, 68, 70–1, 110, 121, 147, 160–2, 166, 174, 182, 184
  conversion 2, 3, 13, 45, 66, 68–70, 105, 135, 144, 179
  cosmopolitanism 168, 180, 182
  development (and progress) 10–11, 12, 13, 15, 36, 40–1, 44, 47, 68, 92, 97–8, 131–2, 143, 144, 147, 148, 165
  discipline 4, 15, 43, 145, 152, 158, 160, 165, 171, 174–9, 180
  and education 10, 37, 40–3, 45, 55, 56, 60–1, 118, 144–5, 148–51, 153, 154–62, 165–82
  enclave and enclaving (moral/spatial) 2, 3, 4, 15, 16, 20, 40–1, 45–6, 52, 53, 54, 107–8, 110–11, 113, 114, 118, 120, 125, 126, 144, 145–8, 153, 154, 159–62, 165–6, 168, 169, 173, 174, 179, 180–1, 188
  gender 61, 64, 102–4, 138–139, 148, 179, 180
  and health 10, 40, 45, 56–7, 62–5, 68–9, 183–6, *see also* HIV/Aids
  as holistic 11, 41, 44, 45
  and infrastructure 2, 6, 8–10, 37, 45–6, 54, 57–8, 62, 71, 75, 82, 84, 107, 108, 109, 114, 121, 161, 164, 168, 172–3, 184, 188, *see also* infrastructure
  materiality 8, 41, 44, 59, 62, 71, 92, 93–4, 97–100, 101, 104–6, 107, 111, 120, 124, 131, 141–4, 163, 164, 166, 173
  mission 3, 38, 43, 53, 56, 68, 96, 147, 154, 155–6, 168, 179, 180

and modernity, modern 12, 15, 16, 37, 41, 55, 92, 98–9, 100, 105, 108, 111, 129–31, 138–42, 154, 165, 167, 172, 174, 180, 181, 186, *see also* modern
and moral mapping/regeneration 12, 13–14, 15, 37, 44–5, 47, 56, 59, 107, 110, 115–16, 120, 130, 132–3, 136–8, 185
and neoliberalism 44, 57, 107, 110, 111, 125, 126, 146, 163, 181–2
spiritual warfare 12, 14, 39, 44, 110, 124, 131–3, 134, 136, 142, 184
and temporality 83, 92–4, 97–8, 99, 100, *see also* time
pilgrimage 14, 35–6, 51, 52, 75–6, 186, *see also Le Grand Magal* under Mouride, Mouridism
police, policing 29–30, 31, 32, 33, 84, 87, 176
public space 2, 4, 6, 7, 24–6, 28, 30, 32, 38–9, 41, 86, 88, 105, 112, 117, 124, 125, 147, 172, 173, 176–7, 179
Pype, Katrien 4, 37, 38, 39, 41, 47, 137, 185, 191 n.9, 192 nn.2, 7

Redeemed Christian Church of God (RCCG) 5, 10, 40, 45, 54, 107, 108, 109, 110, 111, 125, 154
RUA (Religious Urbanization in Africa) project 36, 37, 40, 198 n.9

sacred space, sacred city 3, 14, 35, 45, 52, 54, 75–7, 78, 79, 82–5, 88, 110, 186, 198 n.6
secular, secularisation 3, 4, 5, 6, 12, 36, 41, 54, 58, 61. 76, 77, 92, 112, 165, 180, 182, 198 n.3
secular education 145, 147, 157, 159, 166, 172–6, 180
Simone, AbdouMaliq 12, 20–1, 23, 24, 28, 31, 33, 58, 184, 191 n.3 (ch.2)

time, temporality
abstract time 77
future 5, 8, 14, 33, 36, 47, 51–2, 59, 83, 92–4, 97–8, 99, 100, 104–6, 130, 131, 138, 150, 170
hope 51, 52–3, 54, 92, 93, 103, 104, 133, 134, 140, 184
memory 29, 48, 77, 81, 89

past 5, 13, 15, 51, 68, 69, 83, 84, 92–3, 97, 100, 183, *see also* ancestors
present 13, 38, 51, 52, 54, 83, 93, 98, 99, 104, 105, 170
rhythms 10, 14, 28, 46, 52, 85, 99, 109, 121, 123, 186
sacred time 14, 37, 52, 76–7, 85–6, 87, 89, 92, 103–4, 131
waiting 14, 52, 93, 131, 100–5, 106
transnational, transnationalism 22, 31, 32, 33, 36, 39, 45, 52, 71, 76, 92, 98, 181, 188

urbanization/urban
density, densification 8, 22, 23, 28, 32, 45, 71, 58, 160, 186
gentrification *see* gentrification
mega-urbanization/megacity 1, 2–3, 7, 13, 14, 36, 45, 46, 53, 54, 76, 91, 160, 163, 181
'ordinary city' 13, 71–2
peri-urbanization 37, 45–6, 49, 57, 98, 100, 130, 146, 164, 166, 169, 181, 202
pioneering/frontier urbanization 13, 33, 37, 43–8, 68, 93, 96, 100
planetary urbanization 4, 5, 7, 10
planning 4, 14, 15, 19, 23, 31, 107–20, 123, 124–5, 172, 183, 188
'popular urbanization' 12, 15, 19, 33, 108, 111–13, 118, 122, 123, 126
poverty 23, 42, 49, 56–8, 60, 62, 64, 68, 129, 130, 161, 163, 169, 182, 183
and rurality 3, 5, 7, 14, 23, 25, 46, 49, 68, 76, 91–7, 129, 139, *see also* village
'rurbanization' 3, 14, 91–2, 99
scales 2, 8, 10, 16, 31, 33, 36, 40, 46, 53, 107, 110–11, 168
as 'spatial fix' 7, 14, 52, 79, 87, 88, 111, 185
suburbanization, suburb *see* peri-urbanization
theory 5–6, 7–9, 19–20, 112, 125, 165, 169, 181

village 7, 48, 76, 80, 92, 94–8, 100, 105, 130, 133, 136, 138, 139, 140, 141

Weber, Max 40, 193 n.11

Yoruba 165

www.ingramcontent.com/pod-product-compliance
Lightning Source LLC
Chambersburg PA
CBHW062215300426
44115CB00012BA/2076